Palgrave Executive Essentials

AF497422

Today's complex and changing business environment brings with it a number of pressing challenges. To be successful, business professionals are increasingly required to leverage and spot future trends, be masters of strategy, all while leading responsibly, inspiring others, mastering financial techniques and driving innovation.

Palgrave Executive Essentials empowers you to take your skills to the next level. Offering a suite of resources to support you on your executive journey and written by renowned experts from top business schools, the series is designed to support professionals as they embark on executive education courses, but it is equally applicable to practicing leaders and managers. Each book brings you in-depth case studies, accompanying video resources, reflective questions, practical tools and core concepts that can be easily applied to your organization, all written in an engaging, easy to read style.

Design Thinking with Artificial Intelligence

Practical Tools for Business Innovation

Daniel Graff • Mark A. Clark • Dan Li • Lei Xia

palgrave
macmillan

Daniel Graff
Tongji University
Shanghai, China

Mark A. Clark
American University
Washington, DC, USA

Dan Li
Tongji University
Shanghai, China

Lei Xia
Tongji University
Shanghai, China

ISSN 2731-5614   ISSN 2731-5622   (electronic)
Palgrave Executive Essentials
ISBN 978-3-032-10542-4   ISBN 978-3-032-10543-1   (eBook)
https://doi.org/10.1007/978-3-032-10543-1

© The Editor(s) (if applicable) and The Author(s), under exclusive license to Springer Nature Switzerland AG 2026

This work is subject to copyright. All rights are solely and exclusively licensed by the Publisher, whether the whole or part of the material is concerned, specifically the rights of translation, reprinting, reuse of illustrations, recitation, broadcasting, reproduction on microfilms or in any other physical way, and transmission or information storage and retrieval, electronic adaptation, computer software, or by similar or dissimilar methodology now known or hereafter developed.

The use of general descriptive names, registered names, trademarks, service marks, etc. in this publication does not imply, even in the absence of a specific statement, that such names are exempt from the relevant protective laws and regulations and therefore free for general use.
The publisher, the authors and the editors are safe to assume that the advice and information in this book are believed to be true and accurate at the date of publication. Neither the publisher nor the authors or the editors give a warranty, expressed or implied, with respect to the material contained herein or for any errors or omissions that may have been made. The publisher remains neutral with regard to jurisdictional claims in published maps and institutional affiliations.

"AI generated image created with Ideogram, Inc., Ideogram.ai, 3.0, 2025." The rights team confirmed that the use of the images aligns with our AI policy.

This Palgrave Macmillan imprint is published by the registered company Springer Nature Switzerland AG
The registered company address is: Gewerbestrasse 11, 6330 Cham, Switzerland

If disposing of this product, please recycle the paper.

Daniel
To all the members of the stinky socks and the flying underpants. You fill my heart with joy each and every day. I love you.

Mark
To my wife Cindy, who is my muse, my rock, and the joy in my life.

Dan
To the students and professors, with whom I explore AI. To my husband and parents, with whom I explore life.

Lei
To my wife Macy, who is my greatest adventure and my quietest harbor.

Praise for Design Thinking
with Artificial Intelligence

"We live in a world where technology is not just a tool, but a partner. In a new era of AI, the conversation is shifting from whether machines can be creative to what happens when we collaborate with them. It's a fundamental change in how we innovate and solve problems, moving beyond the "man vs. machine" debate and into a powerful new synergy. In this groundbreaking guide, authors Graff and his team demonstrate that AI doesn't diminish human ingenuity; it augments it. Drawing on real-world experiments, they reveal how the future of creative work lies in a dynamic dialogue between human intuition and computational power. This book is a manifesto for the next great leap in innovation—a practical framework for unlocking human-AI collaboration and building a future where imagination and computation work hand-in-hand."

— Anna Phan, *UX Lead, Monetization, Google*

"Most people think of design as a way to make things look better. This book asks a deeper question: what happens when design itself starts to think? In *Design Thinking with Artificial Intelligence*, Graff and his team show how AI doesn't replace creativity—it reorganizes it. Their experiments with students, businesses, and algorithms reveal something quietly revolutionary: the future of innovation isn't man or machine, but the conversation between them. It's a manual for the next creative leap—when intuition meets computation, and imagination learns to collaborate."

— Ling Fan, *Founder, Tezign & Atypica.AI*

"*Design Thinking with Artificial Intelligence* explores how designers and AI systems can work together to enhance creativity and problem-solving. Graff, Clark, Li, and Xia examine the intersection of emerging AI tools and established design methods, emphasizing practical workflows and human-centered judgment. The authors offer a pragmatic playbook of workflows, prompts, and use-cases that explore how teams can ideate faster, prototype smarter, and make decisions with greater insight."

— Prateek Kukreja, *Head of Product and Design, Workhelix*

"*Design Thinking with Artificial Intelligence* bridges the essential gap between human creativity and machine intelligence. This timely and practical book offers a structured roadmap for design scholars and practitioners to meaningfully integrate AI into the design process, fostering more collaborative and connected innovation."
— Sheng-Hung Lee, *Assistant Professor of Urban Technology, University of Michigan; Founder, d-mix Lab*

"This comprehensive, thoughtful book masterfully lays out the foundations of Design Thinking and the immense potential of integrating AI to accelerate and improve any design process. Packed with practical, 'how-to' examples, the authors demonstrate how to seamlessly weave AI into your existing workflow, equipping you with powerful new tools and techniques for every step of the design process. Most importantly, the book proves how AI can augment—not replace—human innovation and creativity, providing the knowledge to effectively upskill talented designers. By putting design and human creativity firmly at its core, this is a foundational, essential resource for anyone looking to enhance their creative edge in the age of AI."
— John O'Hara, *Design and Technology Leader*

"*Design Thinking with Artificial Intelligence* is an essential guide for navigating the future of innovation. This book provides a relevant framework for professionals and students to deploy effective human-AI collaborations to solve complex problems and drive meaningful innovation."
— Prof. Yongqi LOU, *Honorary Doctor, Royal College of Art, President, Shanghai University of Engineering Science, Chaired Professor, Tongji University*

Preface

Welcome to our book! If you are reading this, you are probably thinking about how artificial intelligence (AI) will influence the design of your work, your life, and your future. Design is about creating a desired future state, and design thinking offers a process to achieve that future across a wide variety of professions and activities. AI can be a tool, a partner, or even a competitor in this process. We believe that innovators and business organizations are best served by welcoming AI as a partner, and preparing themselves for collaboration.

Whether you are a business manager, design professional, or student, you likely suspect that AI will change the way organizations accomplish their goals and how your own role may change. As scholars and consultants in the USA, Europe, and China, we have encountered important questions about the issues and practices associated with AI in design, business, and education. In the following pages, we address several important questions about the integration of AI into the design processes which produce innovation for people and organizations.

- What design processes produce innovation, and how can AI augment our capabilities?
- What skills are needed to leverage the opportunities offered by AI, and how should we prepare to use AI?
- What examples of process tools can we offer that enhance design innovation with AI, and how might these be applied to real-world problems?
- How can we bring together human vision and AI capabilities to meet the innovation needs of individuals and societies?

Fundamentally, these questions concern our relationship with technology, the value added of human talent, and how best to deploy human-AI collaborations to address design innovation. Make no mistake—AI is a disruptive technology, and we follow the thinking of leading experts who expect that some changes will be uncomfortable for people and organizations. However, this discomfort is not worth decrying new technology, like the proverbial buggy-whip manufacturers protesting the advent of the automobile. Nor is it prudent to deny progress, whether inevitable or merely promising, that can become a competitive advantage if we know how to use it. Thus, our approach is to emphasize the complementary roles that humans and AI can play, in pursuit of evolving effective partnerships and organizational structures that support current and future innovation.

Our approach is flavored by the composition of our author team, as a collaboration among scholars from multiple backgrounds, including contribution from our design students (many of whom have professional design experience). One author is a design professor with extensive experience in design thinking, another is a business management professor with expertise in collaborative processes, and two authors are designers with AI expertise currently working on their doctorate degrees. We deployed teams of design students to develop and test early versions of the design tools in this book, under our careful supervision, as a way of ensuring that they are accessible and impactful. The students then applied their AI design thinking tools in use cases based on real business organizations and design challenges.

For our readers, we hope to offer practical insights toward using AI in design thinking across a variety of business areas to create products, services, and concepts to meet the needs of society. We do this by providing basic background of design thinking and AI, giving examples of how AI can enhance traditional design thinking tools, and outlining practical use cases to help the reader contextualize their own design needs.

We also offer readers insights that go beyond short-term applications to rethink how design thinking should leverage advances in technology and human process abilities, including ethics and workforce impact. In short, we examine:

1. **how AI supports the process of innovation** in an efficient, effective manner, perhaps finally resolving the conundrum of attempting to work faster (more information and theme processing), better (higher quality, more innovation), and cheaper (minimizing time and human effort).
2. **how to improve existing design thinking processes and tools through leveraging AI**, adapting the design thinking process and its associated

tools, incorporating the many aspects of AI, and moving from human-created to AI-human collaboration.
3. **increasing workforce readiness to utilize AI**, including skills and preparation strategies for innovators and organizations.

We are all designers. We seek to shape our own futures, whether for ourselves, our students, our professions, or our organizations. Some may choose to embrace new technology to optimize innovation potential, while others simply seek to minimize the disruption to their work. In either case, understanding our relationship with emerging AI technology and how we can apply it to innovation processes is crucial to success.

Acknowledgments

This book would have not been possible without the support of many people. First, and foremost, we would like to thank the students from Tongji University, College of Design & Innovation who took part in the Design Method course in 2024. They worked very hard and smart to produce a first draft of the AID tools and use cases of this book. We very much appreciate your contribution to this book and have, therefore, listed you all as contributors in here. We wish you all the best for your future collaborating with AI, creating lovely innovations.

Ling Fan, Professor of Design at Tongji University and Co-Founder and CEO of Tezign Shanghai Information Technology Co Ltd, for supporting the involvement of authors Dan Li and Lei Xia, who work as doctoral students in his Design A.I. Lab.

In addition, we would like to thank people who were involved in our 2024 research project in which we interviewed several designers and design managers in Europe and USA. Some findings of this work can be found in Clark, M. & Graff, D. (in press 2026). AI & Design Collaboration: Not a Full Member (Yet). In S. Paletz & S. S. Dubrow, Research on Managing Groups and Teams: AI in Teams. Emerald Publishing. Here, in this book, we summarize the more practical observations and implications. We would like to thank all our interviewees for their open and honest discussions we had. We hope all of you will be successful transforming to AI as a collaborator.

Special thanks to Mohammed Umais Javed, research assistant and MBA student at the Kogod School of Business, American University in Washington DC, for his editing expertise and insights.

Contents

List of Figures

List of Tables

About the Authors

Daniel Graff D.Sc., is Distinguished Research Fellow at the College of Design & Innovation, Tongji University and Research Director at the Design A.I. Lab in Shanghai, China. Building on over 20 years of experience in design innovation, his current research explores designing in different contexts, such as how designing is influenced by culture and how designers and design teams collaborate with AI. His research is published in highly ranked international academic journals in design (e.g., Design Studies, Journal of Engineering Design). At Tongji, Daniel teaches Design Thinking, Design Methods, and Business Model Innovation. Previously, he taught new product development, and multidisciplinary teamwork to various audiences around the world (e.g., Aalto University in Finland, Loughborough University in the UK, ESADE in Spain, American University in the USA). Through his teaching, he worked with about 100 organizations (e.g., KESKO in Finland, VW in Germany, Panasonic in China) helping to develop new products and services.

Mark A. Clark Ph.D., is Professor, Department Chair, and Fellow of the Institute for Applied Artificial Intelligence at the Kogod School of Business, American University, in Washington, DC. He has expertise in high performing teams, leadership, culture, and strategic human capital, gained in over 30 years of experience in research, teaching, and consulting. His research includes work on the integration of artificial intelligence in design, leadership paths, team knowledge networks, and stigmatized occupations. In these projects he engages a variety of organizations, including design, medical, sports, and high-tech companies, as well as entrepreneurial startups. His work has appeared in top academic outlets, including the *Academy of Management Journal, Journal of Applied Psychology*, and *Design Studies*, and has been presented at conferences and workshops around the world. In 2021, he published a co-authored book, *Six Paths to Leadership: Lessons from Successful Executives, Politicians, Entrepreneurs, and More.* Dr. Clark teaches business management courses such as high performing teams, organizational change, learning from failure, network analysis, and leadership. Before earning his Ph.D. from Arizona State University, Professor Clark gained a variety of experiences in public and private sector management, as a consultant, program director, trainer, treatment specialist, and board member. His clients have included some of the largest—and some of the smallest—companies in the world.

Dan Li is a Ph.D. candidate at the Design A.I. Lab, Tongji University, focusing on the integration of art, design, and computation. She is currently exploring how LLMs and diffusion models restructure design applications, and addressing the transformation of design roles in the AI era. At MIT, she worked with the Learning Engineering and Practice (LEAP) Group developing augmented reality applications for engineering education and conducting user experience research. Her collaborative work with the LEAP team on educational technology was recognized with two Best Paper Awards from the American Society for Engineering Education (2021). She also served as an Educational Associate for the MITx MicroMasters Program in Principles of Manufacturing. Her work with MIT's Architecture Computation Group focused on computational applications in the built environment, producing Design Heritage VR/AR projects and demonstration materials for design computation classes. Professionally, Dan has worked at Tezign Technology on AI-driven design research projects and founded CCC Design Studio. She holds a Master of Architecture from the Massachusetts Institute of Technology and a Bachelor of Architecture from the China Central Academy of Fine Arts, Beijing.

Lei Xia is a Ph.D. candidate at the College of Design and Innovation at Tongji University, specializing in product design, user experience, and enterprise systems. With an interdisciplinary background spanning design, business, and technology, his work focuses on user-centered innovation and the role of design in shaping complex socio-technical systems. His current research explores the intersection of technology, human experience, and product ecosystems, with the goal of enhancing user engagement and system performance. Lei also serve as a Research Affiliate with the Tangible Media Group at the MIT Media Lab and has collaborated with industry partners on a range of applied design projects. He actively contributes to academic conferences and research publications and is driven by a commitment to developing innovative, high-impact design solutions that meet real-world challenges. Lei holds an M.S. in Integrated Design and Management from the Massachusetts Institute of Technology and a B.S. in Finance and Management Information Systems from the University of Minnesota—Twin Cities. His interdisciplinary training enables him to approach design challenges with both strategic rigor and creative depth.

About the Contributors

The design students, listed below, initially drafted AID tools based on traditional design tools, then applied the tools in teams to real-world challenges as part of a Design Method course in Autumn 2024, taught by Professor Graff together with Lei Xia & Dan Li. The authors then adapted the work of several students to produce the tools and use cases included in this book. While not all student submissions were included in this book, all students contributed to the development of AID tools and use cases.

Anastasya Fidelia Communication Design. She is a design student from Indonesia. Her curiosity about how visuals can communicate complex ideas led her to pursue design. She often relies on AI programs like ChatGPT, Midjourney, Figma, and Canva to experiment with design concepts. Outside of her studies, Fidelia enjoys playing basketball, watching movies, and listening to music.

Dong Chen Product Design. Chen Dong comes from an industrial design background and his research interest lies between human-computer interaction, AI and MR technologies. He likes to play badminton and board games in his free time.

Hongyu Chen Communication Design. Chen is a student from Chengdu. She is studying design because she thinks that turning wild imagination into reality is a very cool endeavor. Her most commonly used AI program is ChatGPT, which she often uses to organize information during research activities or to help brainstorm ideas. In her spare time, she enjoys reading comics and going for a walk.

Jiajie Chen Communication Design. Chen is a student from Zhejiang. He is studying design because he hopes to convey innovative ideas and inclusivity to more people. His favorite AI program is Midjourney, assisting idea visualization. He is passionate about new ideas in the design field. Outside of his studies, he enjoys watching films and volunteering at museums.

Yichen Cheng Design strategy management. She is very interested in cross-disciplinary research and currently focuses on human-computer interaction and cutting-edge applications based on AI. As generative AI technology is advancing rapidly, design also needs to expand its own domain of ontological knowledge. She hopes that she can integrate design thinking into the latest technological applications to create new value.

Qingyuan Gao Industrial Design. Gao is a student from Beijing, who has a keen interest in exploring AI programs and using them to spark new ideas, yet she believes that human designers possess irreplaceable qualities that AI cannot replicate. In her free time, she enjoys playing Go and reading. She is also the fur parent of a 7-year-old German Shepherd.

Ruoyan Gao Industrial design. Gao Ruoyan comes from Changchun, a beautiful city in the northeastern part of China. She likes to watch movies in her free time. The AI programs she frequently uses include ChatGPT and DeepSeek. These AI programs helped her organize the research direction in the early stage of the investigation and provide new ideas and refine details during the design process.

Aimee Hadikrisno Environmental Design. Aimee is a student from Indonesia. She is studying design because she wishes to bring stories to life. Her most used/favorite AI programs are ChatGPT, Ideogram, and Adobe Firefly. She often uses them for generating text, visuals, and sparking inspiration. In her free time, she enjoys exploring new food spots with friends and volunteers dabbling in stage lighting.

Zixuan Han Communication Design. Han is a student from Beijing. She is studying design because she aspires to create beautiful and meaningful things that she admires, rather than merely appreciating and evaluating them. Her most frequently used AI programs are ChatGPT, Perplexity, and Clipdrop, which she uses for brainstorming to generate concept prototypes and for image processing. She is excited about the prospect of using AI as a powerful tool and even a team partner in future design fields. In her spare time, she is a photography enthusiast.

Chenpu Li Communication Design and AI. Li Chenpu is a student from Zhe-Jiang. He is studying for a double degree because he thinks design and AI both make the world greater. In his free time, he explores how AI can enhance the design workflow, using programs like ChatGPT to brainstorm ideas, Cursor for code-assisted design, and Midjourney for creating unique visual assets. His goal is to inspire others to see AI as a collaborative partner in the creative process, making technology more accessible and meaningful in everyday life.

Seul Lee Communication Design. Lee Seul is a design student from Seoul. She's in design school because everything else seemed like a bad reality show. Her trusty therapist (AI program) is ChatGPT, has a sexy voice that makes therapy feel like a spa day! When she's not designing, she's busy dancing like no one's watching and drumming like she's in a music video!

Soun Y. Siv Communication Design. Siv Y. is a student from Cambodia. She's in design school because she grew up drawing her emotions in her diary instead of writing them. Her favorite AI program has to be ChatGPT. She used it as her daily emotional support assistant to navigate school and life. In her spare time, she enjoys playing guitar, scrolling TikTok, and exploring interesting cafés.

Xinyue Liu Communication Design. Liu is a student from Fengxian. She is studying design because she wishes to create something novel. Her favorite AI programs are ChatGPT, Otter.ai, and Jasper AI. She used them for helping carry out group cooperation. She is excited about her collection and collation of opinions in the design field. In her spare time, she plays with schoolmate and volunteers for some design exhibitions and lectures.

Artem Muradyan Communication Design. Artem is a student from Armenia. He is studying design because he wants to blend art and technology in innovative ways. His most used/favorite AI programs are ChatGPT and Adobe Firefly. He often uses them for visualizing abstract ideas, making mockups, and analyzing data. In his spare time, he likes reading books, writing poems, and making art.

Yijin Pan Industrial Design. Pan Yijin is a student from Jiangsu. She is studying industrial design because she wishes to help more people in their daily lives. Her most used AI programs are ChatGPT, Ernie Bot, and Microsoft copilot. She used them to organize the information and generate creative images. In her spare time, she likes to go outside and find the beauty of life.

Siqi Peng Communication Design. Peng is a student from Guangdong province. She is studying design because she wishes to create innovation in hospitals. Her favorite AI programs are ChatGPT, Tiangong AI, and Kimi. She used them for network data collection and inspiration. She is excited about her future career and creations in the design field.

Haolu Qi Product Design. Qi Haolu is a student from Ordos. He is studying Product design because he wishes to make more interesting things. His favorite AI programs are Tongyiqianwen, ChatGPT, and Midjourney. He used them for user research. In his spare time, he plays computer games and take a walk.

Tian Qi Communication Design and AI. Qi Tian is a student from Qingpy. He is studying for a double degree because he thinks integrating design and AI must be interesting. His most used/favorite AI programs are ChatGPT, Stable Diffusion, and Midjourney. He used them for daily work and creation. He is excited about his every trial in the design field. In his spare time, he plays with classmates and volunteers for some college activities.

Yaxin Ren Industrial Design. Ren is a student from Shanxi province, passionate about creating innovations for the future. She uses AI programs like ChatGPT, Perplexity, and Flowith to enhance her design concepts. In her free time, she enjoys watching a variety of movies.

Nan Shen Communication Design. Shen is a student from Chengdu. She is studying design because she enjoys the feeling of coming up with new ideas and yearns for creating something brand new. Her most used AI programs is ChatGPT. She used it to assist her in the research part of the design process when she was assigned with some design projects. In her spare time, she enjoys music and video games.

Yaqing Shen Industrial Design. Shen is a student from Pudong. She is studying design because she wishes to create innovation in society. Her most used AI programs are ChatGPT and Midjourney. He used them for advices and resources. In her spare time, she plays video games and makes some visual arts.

Ruihong Shi Industrial Design. Shi is a student from Harbin. She is studying design because she is interested in it and wants to learn new things. Her favorite AI program is Midjourney. She used it to quickly visualize her ideas. In her spare time, she just wants to be alone and rest.

Leiying Su Communication Design and AI. Su is a student from Sanya. She actually has a double degree in Communication Design and AI because her academic pursuits are deeply intertwined with her love for AI, as she envisions a future where AI and design seamlessly blend to create groundbreaking innovations.

Yiram Wan Communication Design. Wan is a student from Jiangxi. She is studying design with the aim of using design methods to explore more possibilities. Her most used AI programs are ChatGPT, Midjourney, and Perplexity. She used them for greater efficiency and more creativity. She is excited about innovation in the design world and the cross-border integration of design. She also likes to walk around the city and observing life.

Xuan Wang Industrial Design. Wang Xuan is an industrial design student from Haikou. She studies design to create a better future. Her commonly used AI programs include ChatGPT and Midjourney, primarily for design prototyping and user research. She is excited about the future of the design field and enjoys watching movies and taking walks in her spare time.

Yuyu Wang Communication Design. Wang is a student from Xi'an, Shaanxi. She is studying design because she has a passion for exploring beautiful sensory effects, as well as innovative media communication methods. Her most used/ favorite AI programs are ERNIE Bot, Tiangong AI, and Vega AI. She used them to collect and summarize information, translate and refine articles, obtain inspiration and plans, generate conceptual or fancy images. In her spare time, she loves watching movies, stage performances, and exhibitions.

Zhaoji Wang Industrial Design. Wang is a student from Pudong. He is studying design because he wishes to create innovation in hospitals. His most used/ favorite AI programs are GPT and Midjourney. He used them for prototyping, visual design, and idea generation. He is excited about designing logos and visual identities. In his spare time, he plays with graphic design apps and volunteers for local design communities.

Dohan Xia Environmental Design. Xia is a student from Zhejiang Province. She is studying design because she hopes to create better connections between people and space. She frequently uses ChatGPT for inspiration, knowledge, and organizing ideas. She feels excited about her research work in the field of design. In her spare time, she enjoys relaxing in nature.

Jiarui Xu Communication Design. Xu is a student from Gansu. He is studying design because he wants to be more creative and articulate. He uses AI programs like ChatGPT and DALL·E to analyze data, visualize concepts, and enhance research. He seeks more software to improve his expression. In his spare time, he enjoys reading or sleeping.

Luyao Xu Design Strategy & Management. Xu is a student from Hebei. Her research focuses on AI product management, and feminist-oriented technology governance. In her free time, she likes to bend time and space into shapes of rhythm—which is dance, of course.

Lei Yang Communication Design. Yang is a student from Hebei. She is studying design because she loves communication design. Her most used/favorite AI program is ChatGPT. She used it for inspiration and sometimes for recreation. She is excited about her potential in the design field. In her spare time, she finds the possibility of combining design with happy daily things.

Yaqi Yang Communication Design and AI. Yang is a student from SongJiang. She actually has a double degree in Communication Design and AI because she believes AI-assisted design will become mainstream. Her most use and favorite AI programs are GPT-4o and TianGong AI. She used them for coding homework. She is excited about her further developing AI that is more suitable for design in the design field.

Yunling Zang Industrial Design. Zang is a student from Shenzhen studying design to play with future possibilities. Her most used AI programs are ChatGPT, Perplexity, and Midjourney, which she uses to validate concepts and showcase ideas in the early design stages. She's also a detective fiction fan and a Shanghai street wanderer.

Ouqi Zhang Communication Design. Zhang is a student from Beijing. She is studying design with the aim of using design methods to explore more possibilities. Her most used AI programs are ChatGPT, Midjourney, and Runway. She used them to broaden horizons and increase creativity. She is excited about Brand design and the cross-border integration of design. She also likes exploring the mind and body, as well as cross-media experimental illustration.

Yuxuan Zhong Communication Design. Zhong is a student from Fujian. She is studying design because she wants to convey her observations, thoughts, and feelings to others through her work and enhance user experiences with design. Her favorite AI programs are ChatGPT and Midjourney, which she uses to assist her in creating and to improve the efficiency of handling tasks. In her free time, she loves singing and dancing, enjoys hiking and photography, and immerses herself in the world around her.

Zhou Quin Communication Design. Qian Zhou is a student from Shanghai. She is studying design because she wishes to create different experience. Her favorite AI program is 635 method. She used it for creating new ideas. In his spare time, he plays video games and listens to electronic music.

Section I
Overview of AI in Design Thinking

1

Design Thinking

Design thinking, as a process of innovating solutions through understanding human needs and developing viable ideas, has been popular and effective for many years, helping organizations to develop desirable and functional human-centered products and services. The emergence of AI is an opportunity for organizations to augment the most demanding aspects of the design process. Before we detail AI's means of leveraging the design thinking approach, it is important to outline the basics of design thinking itself. In the following sections, we introduce its roots in the field and practice of design, then discuss design thinking processes—including activities, which are sometimes called stages and phases—attributes, methods, associated cognitions, and outcomes. Finally, we detail the specific design thinking activities used throughout this book, laying the foundation for understanding and enacting the potential of AI for improving design thinking processes and tools.

Design

The origin of design thinking lies in the perspective offered by the broader field of design. Nobel laureate and business guru Herbert Simon wrote in 1986 that he saw design as the creation of blueprint for a desired future, which reflected the presence of design across a wide variety of disciplines and activities, including art, architecture, healthcare, biochemistry, engineering, and business product innovation. While this characterization is inspirational, it is also focused more on the design outcome, whether as a physical artifact or idea, without including the process of achieving the design. Therefore we

© The Author(s), under exclusive license to Springer Nature Switzerland AG 2026

D. Graff et al., *Design Thinking with Artificial Intelligence*, Palgrave Executive Essentials,
https://doi.org/10.1007/978-3-032-10543-1_1

prefer to use a more practical definition, based within design scholarship by Jones in 1970 but augmented through our own experience: "*the activities of a human or machine in creating or contributing to the creation of physical or conceptual things.*" Importantly, in these definitions there is no restriction on who does the design work, which means a designer could be a human, an AI agent, or other entity.

Design Thinking Journey

Design thinking may be thought of as the journey from a design problem to a desired outcome. In its early incarnation, it was closely linked to the design perspective and methods initiated the 1950s, as Cross noted in 1993. Before design thinking processes were established, designers often worked intuitively and experimentally, without many guidelines.

Scholars argued whether design should be its own discipline, and in their efforts expounded on what was unique, and what was held in common, about designers' methods (i.e., how designers work) and their cognition (i.e., how designers think). In 1970, a book by Jones suggested that further understanding of methods and cognition could advance support for designers in their work, paving the way for development of relatively standard design thinking processes. Interestingly, we may be at a similar threshold for the use of AI in design thinking, which is currently also experimental and intuitive. To help cross this threshold, in this book we offer specific examples integrating AI to update the effectiveness of design thinking processes and tools.

To enhance understanding of the design value for non-design audiences, the practice of design thinking was simplified by IDEO, a global design consulting firm, and the d.school (a common term for the Hasso Plattner Institute of Design at Stanford University) in the late 1990s to early 2000s. One aim was to market more design thinking services, such as consultancies and educational workshops, to interested individuals and organizations. While this simplified design thinking framework enhanced communication and understanding of the value of design, it also took the role of a prescriptive process to improve innovation across multiple disciplines. Since then, many organizations (e.g., Procter & Gamble, a global consumer goods corporation) have incorporated the simplified and standardized design-thinking framework into their new product and service development. Beyond the utility of design thinking in practice, researchers across disciplines also began to incorporate it into their research. Books about design thinking became very popular and well-received (e.g., Tom Kelly, *Creative Confidence*; Roger Martin, *The Design of Business*; Tim Brown, *Change by Design*) and the concept of design thinking took off.

It is important to note that a split occurred around this time. Design thinking remained an important academic aspect of the design discipline, but it also became popular in academia and practice outside of traditional design fields, initially in innovation management, where it was linked to design innovation. While the resulting two concepts are both called design thinking, they are quite different due to the simplification introduced by IDEO and d.school and by the independent progress of these two frameworks within their respective fields. This has led to some confusion and even frustration within the design discipline; perhaps because the simplified version of design thinking gave the impression that design is a relatively simple activity that anyone with a bit of reading and training could do. More recently, within the discipline of design, the concept was separated into designerly thinking (based on the original academic work in the design discipline) and design thinking (based on the simplifications made by IDEO and d.school work), according to Johansson-Sköldberg and his colleagues in their 2013 paper. We adopt this distinction in this book.

Since then, the simplified and standardized design thinking concept has become widely recognized as a human-centered, creative problem-solving approach that can be applied not only to innovation, but also to virtually any problem and context. Consequently, design thinking is applied to services, as Stickdorn in 2014 described in "*This is Service Design Thinking,*" to politics as von Aaron and colleagues in 2023 discussed in *Policy-Making as Designing: The Added Value of Design Thinking for Public Administration and Public Policy*, to the military, as Jackson in 2024 analyzed in *Military Design Thinking: An Historical and Paradigmatic Analysis*, to social innovation as Manzini in 2015 introduced in *Design, When Everybody Designs: An Introduction to Design for Social Innovation*, and even to life itself, as Burnett and Evans in 2016 proposed in *Designing your Life*. It seems there is no problem in the world that design thinking cannot solve.

Many companies have since implemented design thinking in their new product development as it allows organizations to balance their need for planning and control with that of freedom and experimentation required to develop novel and creative products and services. Additionally, many colleges outside of the design discipline have implemented design thinking in their curriculum. Specifically, business and engineering schools have often incorporated a design thinking course, partly to counter the otherwise analytically focused syllabi but also to teach relevant skills and knowledge for their graduates. Even some design colleges have implemented the simplified version of design thinking as it is a concept that is easier to teach, especially in larger classes. This is not widely acknowledged within design as it is still a contentious topic for many. The designerly way of designing is more likely taught in smaller studio classes where the teacher takes the role of a mentor and guides the students throughout the design process.

In the next section, we will introduce concepts to allow the reader to get a deeper insight into how designers work. It will also allow a look beyond design thinking and further advance their own knowledge about designing with AI. To enhance the readers' understanding, we will highlight the differences between designerly and design thinking within each section below.

Designers and Innovators

Some, such as Cross in 2011, claim that everyone is a designer because most people, at some stage, create a physical artifact or develop a concept. This expression has value in highlighting the importance of design thinking and its accessibility as a process. At the same time, it also contributes to identity issues within the design discipline. If everyone designs, then who qualifies as a designer? Is "designer" a specialized professional label, or a more generic description of those who intend to innovate, or those who follow a set of process steps such as those in design thinking? Other professions face similar dilemma; those who act cheerful when they are feeling down don't call themselves "actors," nor do those who regulate interactions with their coworkers claim the title of "manager."

We suggest that while those engaging in design thinking processes may consider themselves designers, they may often be more specifically described as "innovators" to better align with their intention and, often, their organizational purpose. This further distinguishes designers as those working in a traditional design discipline e.g., industrial design, UX software, generally holding a deeper understanding of design approaches in terms of cognition and methods. For designers, a variety of challenging design problems need not be approached with preset steps or tools, but instead represent endless creative opportunities. What we term "innovators," by contrast, are those who follow more explicit design thinking methods to achieve specific goals, without necessarily being immersed in design cognition and theory. For instance, many projects in the military and business follow design thinking process steps without the involvement of designers or concern for design theory beyond their immediate goals.

The context in which a designer works may make designing easier in some cases, and more complex in others. Designers who work on their own enjoy maximum freedom in how to approach their design projects, which may make it less likely for them to follow pre-defined design thinking process steps. Even when working with other professional designers, while the need to coordinate may increase, there is less likelihood of using a standard approach. This is one reason that a truly open design process—a designerly approach—is not often employed in large organizations.

Designers and innovators often work together, capitalizing on their complementary reservoirs of content and process knowledge toward specific ends. In some projects, they may share a context with a broader team of individuals from many different professional backgrounds. For example, a multidisciplinary team aimed at new product development may include specialists in operations, finance, and marketing working alongside designers and innovators. With the increased number of stakeholders trained in different perspectives, it becomes difficult to allow a freewheeling approach in line with preferences of a creative designer. Instead, designers and innovators are more likely to succeed through the use of standard processes and tools such as design thinking. The orderly sequence of design activities, based on design principles, becomes not only an advantage, but sometimes a necessity. Such a series of steps simplifies the innovation process while retaining the essence of design theory, resulting in a design thinking approach.

Design Problem

Design problems are often described as different from other problems because they are wicked, as mentioned by Cross in 1982. Wicked problems are impossible to solve because they have several causes and no specific solutions; e.g., global warming, inequality, pollution, and drug addiction. The conceptualization of wicked problems was originally introduced in city planning by Rittel and Webber in 1973, but since then has spread to many other disciplines, including design. The design discipline was an eager and early adopter of the wicked problem concept, to the point that some regard all design problems as wicked problems. As such, wicked problems have become commonplace in design, providing a conceptual justification for designerly thinking as a prime problem-solving approach. This led to an overreliance on designerly thinking approaches to the neglect of other potentially more analytical design approaches that are more efficient but less creative. Similarly, as wicked problems became more popular outside the design field, design thinking grew in prominence, often viewed as a way of finding solutions to these unsolvable problems, rather than relying on the traditional analytical approaches.

These days, design thinking may be applied to any problem within and outside of the design field. The reasoning for using design thinking is twofold. First, a creative and or human-centered solution is preferred over an analytical one. Second, the problem expresses some kind of wickedness, indicating that the analytical approach would not lead to a good solution. Under those circumstances, design thinking is often employed.

There is also a difference between designerly thinking and design thinking in how each approach views the design problem. The simplification of design thinking led to an overemphasis of the problem. In design thinking, it is often viewed that a designer's aim is to identify the hidden, underlying problem that the human user is facing and to design a solution based on this finding. Problem identification is always the starting point in design thinking, but this is not as clearly the case for designerly thinking. Yes, the problem identification can be a guide in the design process, but designers can also focus on the solution instead on the problem. Here, designers idealize a potential solution, moving away from existing problems.

Design Process

In the designerly thinking framework, the work of designers proceeds in many ways, depending on individual factors such as their knowledge, skills, and goal, as well as contextual factors such as whether they design alone or within a team, what resources are available, and other external aspects, as discussed by Dorst and Dijkhuis in 1995. Design processes within designerly thinking are broadly separate into the rational approach and the reflective process.

The rational approach is largely based on the work of Herbert Simon in 1969 and is closer to an analytical and linear solution process, embedded in positivist philosophy. Most popular design thinking processes build on this logic. Here, we can clearly separate the different components of the design process which often include phases similar to the following: (1) Empathize, (2) Define, (3) Ideate, (4) Prototype, (5) Test, and (6) Implement. While the design thinking process is often described in phases that are iterative, it is often executed in linear stages, particularly in less experienced innovators. To align more closely with the designerly thinking approach, in this book we primarily use the term "activities" to reflect that they do not necessarily operate in a particular sequence.

Other variations of the design thinking process have been popularized as well, based on similar building blocks. For example, the Design Council introduced the Double Diamond process in the early 2000s. This process consists of separate phases of (1) Discover, (2) Define, (3) Develop, and (4) Deliver. It is similar to other design thinking processes in that they start with research into the design problem to identify the main challenge, then imagine some kind of solution to be developed and tested before implementation. While the authors of these design thinking processes highlight that they are not instruction manuals but guidelines, in practice we have seen over the years that specifically design novices are using them in a prescriptive, orderly manner.

While traditional design thinking processes do promote the use of iterations among phases, in organizational practice it often proceeds in linear fashion, reified by official demarcation of movement to each successive phase, sometimes accompanied by a change in personnel to operate the subsequent activities. Iterations occur mostly within the individual stages (e.g., various iterations of prototypes) rather than among the stages (e.g., learning from the prototyping leads to an alteration of the problem identified earlier), especially among design novices. The reason for this might be that design novices use it in a very prescribed and linear manner, because they lack the confidence gained through design experience.

A relatively lockstep, linear design thinking process is often preferred and implemented within organizations because it is easier to manage, with stricter and more efficient control of resources such as personnel, time, and materials. The process can also be simpler to manage because a team can orient themselves to their place within the process, helping them to understand next steps. Such a process can be also controlled via potential phase gates (e.g., yes/no decisions on taking the projects forward). Finally, the phases provide a guide for planning that is essential for management. As such, the design thinking process straddles a zone between the analytical process of management and the more artistic process of designerly thinking. This makes it easier for organizations to implement design thinking within their new product or service developments. Similarly, design thinking processes are also often implemented within other fields such as education. The planning possible in a linear sequence lends itself to the need to clearly communicate and teach, and the discrete phases are often easier for students to comprehend.

The reflective designerly thinking approach is more iterative in nature, such as reflected in the work of Schön in 1983, as it is embedded in the constructivist philosophical perspective, as explained by Dorst and

Dijkhuis in 1995. While there are different activities that align with the phases in the design thinking process, they do not necessarily occur one after the other in designerly thinking process. It all depends on the designers. For example, designers can start with identifying the problem as in a sequential design thinking process, but they may instead start with an ideal, preferred solution and work toward it. Furthermore, iterations occur commonly within the individual phases, as well as between the design problem and solution. This is often described in the interaction of the problem and solution space, both of which are constantly moving until an optimized or preferred solution is found, according to Dorst and Cross in 2001.

The designerly thinking process is unconsciously used by many professional designers when working alone. Within design education, especially when based in art schools, design thinking process may only be used to introduce students to the different design activities. The students then advance to using a designerly thinking framework, such as in studio work based more on tacit knowledge and less guidance.

Recently, we have observed more flexible design thinking processes proposed by organizations whose principal work is not design, which seems to reflect a changing environment of designing with AI. One example of this is the Stingray model which was designed for using AI in innovation, discussed by Gibbins in 2025. This model has three stages: (1) Train, (2) Develop, and (3) Iterate. Within the train stage, the team sets goals and collects data used to teach an AI model (e.g., AI agent). This allows the team to identify a clear direction and gain a better understanding of the problem and solution space. This is followed by the Develop stage. Here, the team generates both hypotheses as well as a wide range of potential solutions. This stage aligns with the generate idea phase within the design thinking process. However, the company suggest an AI idea-led ideation activity that also uses AI not only to generate ideas but also to select promising solutions. The outcome is a set of promising solutions which are then refined in the next stage, iteration. Iteration is the stage or set of activities in which the team takes the most promising ideas to test and refine them.

Like many current ideas about the future of the design thinking process, this model is based on a somewhat simplified understanding of the design field, subsuming art for a more engineering-like focus on incremental progress and goal fulfilment. We will explore this further in Chapter 3. Regardless of the specific design process or approach, it is important to recognize that design thinking is likely to change with the influence of AI, which we will discuss at the end of this chapter.

Design Method

Designers and innovators will use various design methods throughout the design thinking process to solve the identified or given problem. Design methods emerged during the 1970s when designers did not have much guidance on how to design as highlighted by Jones in 1970). Currently, design methods can refer to or include individual tools, such as brainstorming, or an overarching idea such as human-centered design that is applied throughout the design process.

There are not many differences between design thinking and designerly thinking methods in terms of what tools are used; the difference is often more subtle and reflect how tools are used and applied to the world. While innovators in design thinking tend to follow the pre-described methods step by step, designers individualize and adapt their preferred tools to the given situation. In this section, we focus on broad design perspectives within design methods. Some have made their way into design thinking, such as the most prevalent notions of being human-centered and multi-disciplinary. However, there are many more ideas, including some that have not found their way into design thinking. The choice of which overarching idea to use will be determined by designers facing specific problems, as well as by the preferred solution and working style of those who design.

Here are some of the most influential overarching ideas.

Design thinking is often regarded as *human-centered*, which keeps the human in focus throughout the entire design process. It may be surprising for some to learn that that the origin of human-centered design lies in fields such as ergonomics, computer science, and artificial intelligence, by Giacomin in 2014. Originally human-centered design focused solely on functional aspects; however, it has since evolved to understand also what humans perceive and experience, and what meanings they create, as Giacomin noted in 2014. Design thinking tends to be more focused on functional aspects as it is pulled by the requirements of potential users. By contrast, designerly thinking encourages designers to push the organizations vision toward new meaning and language for their products, as Verganti mentioned in 2008. While functional aspects of products or services can be relatively easily tested, this is much harder for generating new meanings.

In more recent times, the design discipline has in some part begun to move away from human-centered design, trending toward more holistic and systemic approaches. This stems from a belief, articulated by Borthwick and colleagues in 2022, that while human-centered design fulfils human needs and desires, it can come with some negative consequences for the ecosystem. It is often further weakened by unintended consequences for human groups that the design did not consider. The broader approaches suggested include a humanity-focused lens championed by Norman in 2024, life-centered focus based on Thackara's 2006 work, Abram's 1997 more than human-centered mode, and systemic design promoted by Jones and Kijima in 2019. These approaches often add sustainable aspects into human-centered design or combine it with other approaches, such as design practice and system thinking into systemic design. It is not clear if one of these relatively new approaches might replace the human-centered approach, but it seems that other sustainable aspects taken a more prominent role in designerly thinking. These new approaches have not yet had a large influence design thinking, particularly not in commercial settings.

Design thinking is also seen as a *creative* practice, and is sometimes defined as a creative problem-solving approach. Here, creativity is not embedded in one method (e.g., brainstorming) but occurs throughout the design process in several ways. First, several design tools are developed to generate novel and valuable solutions, through a variety of approaches including brainstorming, analogical thinking, re-framing, visualization techniques, and prototyping by, as demonstrated in the work of Graff and Clark's 2019 work. Next, enhancing creativity requires shaping the mindset of the designer, adopting an open mindset and risk-taking attitude that allows exploration of novel and unconventional ideas. Relatedly, design thinkers wishing to enhance their creativity must manage their own uncertainty avoidance. This refers to the idea that designers need to accept fuzzy conceptualizations of their design problem and solutions, embrace risk, and put off decisions about the specifications of their design goals to later stages of the project.

Furthermore, design thinking is supposed to be *iterative*. This iteration can refer to the individual phases of the process, to individual design methods and, or between the design problem and solution. As stated before, the design process is iterative, meaning that designers often go back in the design process to restart it because something did not work in the way they wanted. This is in close relationship to the iteration between the design problem and the solution. Often, designers or innovators propose a solution and after testing they learn about a new problem and re-adjust the problem and solution in an iterative manner until a solution is found. But it also refers to the individual tools used. It requires designers and innovators to be open to make changes and adjustments to the design method, allow for failures, and listen to the stakeholder's feedback.

Design thinking can also be *co-designed*. Co-design involves other stakeholders in the design process. Involving other stakeholders in the design process allows the outcome to better fulfil needs of the users and enhances the products or service useability. Stakeholders co-design can be employees, end users, and or customers. Some authors include co-design as an aspect of human-centered design. There are many different variations, such as participatory, contextual, and emphatic design, that are distinct by the designer's research orientation (designing for the present or future) and the level of involvement of the stakeholders in the design process by Steen in 2011.

Design thinking can be *collaborative*. While designers can work alone, they often work on complex design tasks that require the input of many other disciplines. For example, when they work in *multi-disciplinary design teams* to develop a new product, service, or system. While collaboration helps to find solutions on more complex problems, it also complicates the work of designers and innovators. This is one fundamental aspect of design thinking and is often shown in the three circles of design innovation. Here, design is seen as bringing in the perspective of the user and the products desirability. The engineering perspective ensures that the design is feasible, and the business perspective allows for viability of the solution.

In a multi-disciplinary team, designers and innovators are often more limited in their design process and tools as they often need to justify their design choices. Furthermore, these teams will be more likely to follow the design thinking process as it helps to communicate and coordinate within the team. Designerly thinking approaches seem not to be applicable as it's iterative, intuitive work, and un-predictable process makes teamwork very difficult. Professional designers might take a facilitator role as they are more knowledgeable about the design process. Many design tools (e.g. visualization and analogical communication) can be used in such teams to enhance understanding according to Graff & Clark in 2019.

These overarching design perspectives will lead professional designers to prefer certain design tools when designing. Some designers believe that the users do know what they want and so incorporate more user focused design tools and co-design together. Others might believe that the users do not know what they want and work independently and more creatively on their designs. Both can be successful, depending on the design problem, preferred design solution and context in which the designers' designs. However, there is a tendency that involving the user will often lead to marginal but also safer innovations in terms of commercial success.

Supporting these overarching ideas are a variety of tools to advance the design process. Developed across many academic disciplines and through organizational practice, these include various research methods (e.g., interviews, ethnography, focus groups), creative techniques (e.g., brainstorming, analogical thinking), and prototyping tools (e.g., simple sketches, physical prototypes). The book will introduce many of the most popular tools in Section II, augmenting them with AI.

Design Cognition

Design cognition refers to the designers' mental processes and representations during designing. According to Hassi and Laakso (2011), the most common dimensions discussed are: abductive reasoning, reflective reframing, holistic view, and integrative thinking.

As Dorst communicated in his 2011 paper, the heart of design thinking is *abductive reasoning*. Abductive reasoning is based on logic and aims to find the simplest most likely solution without verifying them with empirical data. It is forming a hypothesis about a design problem non-systematically; that is, without relying either on deductive (moving from general principles to a logical conclusion) or inductive (starting with observations to forming a general rule) processes. Abductive reasoning is often used in defining design thinking problems by experienced professional designers who use intuition to identify potential solution spaces. Later in this book we will demonstrate a design thinking tool that employs abductive thinking, "*How might we,*" which can be used early in the process as part of research or ideation activities, as outlined by Forshaw in 2024.

Abductive reasoning is specifically useful when innovators do not have complete information. This lack of information is often deemed to result from the complexity of novel design problems, as explained by Forshaw in 2024. Abductive reasoning allows professional designers to manage the uncertainty involved in solving complex problems. Novice designers may struggle to proceed through abductive reasoning due to the increased risk that the outcome of such a cognitive process is not guaranteed to be true. Hence, design thinking tools often incorporate abductive reasoning processes to enhance their use.

While abductive reasoning is a key pattern of design thinking, this does not mean designers and innovators do not use more conventional problem-solving repertoire such as induction and deduction as well, depending on the design thinkers' aim and context. Deduction, using interference based on facts, is for example used in prototyping when designers test their solution with users. Induction, using interference based on observation, is used in design when analyzing qualitative datasets from interviews to identify themes and patterns as per Forshaw in 2024.

Another, and related design cognition is *reflected reframing*. Reflected reframing refers to the designers' ability to look at the design problem in new ways as noted by Paton and Dorst in 2011. Designers intrinsically questioning the design problem representation, framing and reframing it throughout the design process. This is also shown by the iteration, or co-evolution of the problem and solution space by Dorst and Cross in 2001. This reframing can lead to more surprising, and, hence, more creative perceived outcomes of design projects.

Furthermore, designers and innovators take often a *holistic perspective* in the design project. This holistic perspective starts with the design problem and finishes with the design outcome. The design problem's environment is widely scanned to allow all requirements for the solutions to be identified, but also to identify potential reframing opportunities. We will later discuss this in the design outcomes, but briefly, designers consider not only functional and aesthetics aspects, but also social and cultural to generate valuable meanings for the user or consumer. *System design thinking* is similar in that it takes a broader approach and focuses on the visualization of a problem as a system of structures, patterns, and events, highlighting the interrelationships of individual components on the system as mentioned by Jones & Kijima in 2019.

Finally, design thinking is also based on *integrative thinking*. It is most likely one of the most recognized aspects of design thinking. It refers to two main aspects. The first is that designers often combine ideas rather than choosing one or the other, this integration makes the outcomes better. Second, design thinking is of collaborative, specifically within multi-disciplinary teams. This aspect is often shown in graphs incorporating business (i.e., valuable), technical (i.e. feasible) and human (i.e. desirable) aspects throughout the process.

The above cognitive patterns are often linked to design thinking and designerly thinking. In addition, some authors state specific mindsets of designers and innovators as being important when designing. Hassi and Laakkso in 2011 identified these mindsets to be experimental and explorative, ambiguity tolerant, optimistic, and future-oriented. Together with the cognitive processes, they describe on how designers and innovators think (design cognition).

Design Outcome

Design outcomes can be separated into design outputs and design outcomes, as noted by Love in 2014. Design outputs are the direct results from the design work, such as the final product or service. "*Good design*" refers to a product or service that is functional and aesthetically pleasant. While functionality can be judged before the product or service launch, beauty as is often said to be in the eyes of the beholder, and it is difficult to fully ascertain an outcome without the perspective of users and related stakeholders. Design outcomes, by contrast, refer to consequences of a product or service once it is introduced, including social and cultural impacts, as well as environmental effects and economic consequences, which often take time to develop and assess. Organizations and clients who commission design projects are often very interested in the design outcomes. Because such outcomes change dynamically as they interact with environmental factors, it is difficult to assure that they will ultimately yield positive consequences. These dynamics influence the meaning that designers attempt to generate from their products and services, which affects stakeholder perception of the success of a product or service design, as discussed by Verganti in 2008.

The limitation of not fully understanding what makes good design contributes to the challenge of planning an optimal process and the difficulty of knowing how to evaluate both progress and output. Design is often judged not only after it is complete, but following a lag period where its broad impact can be assessed. Many design prizes are therefore given after a design became a design outcome. Other output never reach the design outcome stage, such as when they remain a design concept or prototype short of implementation.

Benefits of Design Thinking

Design thinking has been shown to provide several individual and organizational benefits:

- It encourages *creative problem-solving* and can lead to more innovative products. This is especially important in business, where new products, services, or processes can strengthen competitiveness.
- Fleming stated in 2004 that it fosters *collaboration*, as it brings together employees from different functions to deliver holistic outcomes. Research has shown that multidisciplinary teams, when managed well, can outperform homogeneous teams.
- It can provide organizations with a *competitive advantage*. Design-led organizations have been shown to outperform competitors. While design thinking cannot guarantee success, its focus on the human, combined with frequent testing and user involvement, reduces the risk of market failure.

Design Thinking in This Book

To this point, we have introduced and discussed what design and more specifically design thinking is. As we learned, the story of design thinking is quite complex, but the story of its development can help to understand how to use our proposed framework and tools. So, next we will cover how we see design thinking in this book. We will look at the design problem, designers, design method and cognition, as well as the design outcome.

Our AI design (AID) tools focus on problems related to the creation of physical or conceptual things. These things can be products, services, or processes. We do not focus solely on complex or wicked problems as AI has many capabilities (see Chapter 2) and ways in contributing to designing (see Chapter 3). For example, AI can be helpful in analyzing complex and large data sets (complex problem), but it can also create simple visualizations (easy problem). Hence, our AID tools can help to taggle complex but also simple design problems and subproblems.

Designers in this book are innovators or designers working on the creation of new processes, services, or products utilizing design thinking. While we wrote this book for innovators and novice designers, the AI design tools can be also applied by professional designers. In addition to the innovators and designers, AI is contributing to the design outcome. However, the current capabilities of AI (see Chapter 2) limit AI to the role of a contributor rather than that of an independent designer (see Chapter 3). The relationship between AI and design thinkers has often been viewed as that of a supervisor (design thinker) and subordinate (AI). However, as AI increases in complexity and people increase their understanding of how to work with AI, the connection becomes more of collaborators. We will elaborate on this relationship in Chapters 3 and 5.

Working with AI as a collaborator will require new skill sets for innovators and designers. We have two chapters designated to them. Chapter 4 will talk about the general skill sets required working with AI. Chapter 5 will provide specific guidelines for working with AI in the tools introduced in this book.

How does the design thinking or designerly thinking process changes? While we think we need to adjust the process, we do not agree with many from the engineering perspective that it should be dramatically different, like, for example, suggested by the Stingray model. We are in an in-between stage of AI in design, and we think that the most suitable process builds upon existing processes in organizations. This reduces the risk of failure but at the same time harvest the benefit from AI. Therefore, we organize our AID tools according to the simplified and standardized, but updated design thinking activities. AID tools support innovation through their use within design thinking activities. While many AID tools have utility across multiple design thinking activities, we have sorted the tools within specific activities to illustrate key points. Design thinking activities are behaviors and actions commonly used in design thinking process. We base the set of activities on an updated design thinking's five core phases: Prepare and Train, Empathize and Define, Ideate and Select, Prototype and Test, and Implement and Learn.

First, we do not lay out our AID tools in term of a process, but according to activities. The difference is that a process is a series of steps to reach a specific outcome and, so, the human-centered design thinking process suggested a specific way on how design problems are solved. This pre-described design thinking process has long been criticized within the field of design. As Jones described in his 1991 seminal work on design, "We sought to be open minded, to make design processes that would be more sensitive to life than were the professional practices of the time. But the result was rigidity: A fixing of aims and methods to produce designs that everyone now feels to be insensitive to human needs."

Each design problem and its context are different, requiring innovators to embrace a repertoire of design approaches. It will be up to the design innovator to decide upon the appropriate process and tools for the problem at hand. To get started, innovators can follow the sequence of activities laid out in this book. However, we believe it is important not to restrict design innovation by over-standardization of the process; instead, innovators should consider the full context of the design problem, including users, resources, and societal impact. Such consideration will likely involve iteration in multiple directions, as often suggested within the design discipline, or in a more linear preferred by many organizations for projects with a short timeline. The process of innovation may involve all design thinking activities discussed here, or only a subset relevant to the problem. For example, a solution-based focus approach might ignore initial research to start immediate prototyping, with ideas based perhaps on benchmarks gleaned from competitor organizations, or on the designer's intuition.

One consequence of the incorporation of AI in design thinking is that some new activities in design thinking emerge. First, in the prepare and train section, designers and innovators can prepare the way in which AI is integrated (e.g., train an AI assistant, as discussed in this book's appendix). This will take some time and effort to collect the right training data for the AI.

As a foundation for understanding the design thinking process, we believe it is helpful to start with a set of traditional activities, often grouped as stages or phases, but in reality, more flexible in their usage. Many readers will be familiar with similar processes and tools. We hope to encourage more design thinkers to explore the opportunities that AI provides for design. Below are the set of standard design thinking activities we will refer to, grouped into categories that are often sequential.

- Prepare & Train: These activities help the designer or innovator to enhance their understanding of the design context (e.g. who is my user, who are the stakeholders) and AI requirements (e.g. what AI is available, do I need to train an assistant, with what data?). The aim for these activities is to decide on the design direction, identify the enablers and potential limitations. While AI can support to reach the aim of these activities, AI will also require some attention. Time will be required to find a suitable AI tools and potentially train our specific AI assistant for this design project.
- Empathize & Define: In this activity group, AI and human designers collect and synthesize data generated from a variety of sources. The aim is to define a potential solution or problem on which to design. Here, AI can help to speed up the data collection (e.g. by transcribing and translating interviews) and analyzing part (e.g. by identifying themes from interviews), as well as more in terms of quantitative (e.g. interviewing humans and AI independently).
- Ideate & Select: Generate ideas from humans alone or working together with AI to select a potential solution. AI can support creation of more diverse ideas, help to record these ideas, and assist you to select the most promising ideas. After ideation, AI can create quickly some early concepts for internal communication, and help the team to advance selected ideas in the optimal direction.
- Prototype & Test: Develop a selected idea into a testable prototype. AI is specifically helpful in creating quick and cheap prototypes (e.g. simple visualizations) in the early stage but can also help in testing them and collecting human and AI feedback (as above in the synthesize and define section, AI can help us to collect and analyze data: here, to get a better understanding if our prototype works). Prototype and testing activities often cycle reciprocally with ideating and selecting, as ideas are quickly developed, discarded, improved, or replaced.
- Implement & Learn: Create the final concept for management to approve and learn from the activities and process. AI can help in the implementation and selling the idea internally. After the process is completed both, the design thinker and AI should seek reciprocal feedback to learn from the experience.

Summary

Traditional design thinking refers to how designers work and think to solve a given design problem and arrive at a preferred or optimized design solution. However, design thinking has been exported to other fields, and it is used to solve many types of problems, whether or not they have any relationship to traditional design. This created a picture in which many people (designers and innovators) use design thinking. Therefore, there are many different design thinking frameworks.

We adapted the standardized design thinking framework to incorporate AI. Within, we provide AID tools that can be applied according to the needs of innovators and designers. Whereas design novices or innovators may view it as a fixed guide, professional designers will treat it as a menu and chose what is appropriate for the given design problem.

References

Abram, D. (1997). The spell of the sensuous: Perception and language in a more-than-human world. Vintage Books, New York.

Borthwick, M., Tomitsch, M., & Gaughwin, M. (2022). From human-centred to life-centred design: Considering environmental and ethical concerns in the design of interactive products. Journal of Responsible Technology, 10, 100032

Burnett, D., & Evans, B. (2016). Designing your life. Alfred A. Knopf, New York.

Cross, N. (1982). Designerly ways of knowing. Design Studies, 3(4):221–227. https://doi.org/10.1016/0142-694X(82)90040-0

Cross, N. (1993). A history of design methodology. In: Vries M. J., Cross N., Grant D. P. (eds) Design methodology and relationships with science. Springer, Dordrecht, p 15–27.

Cross, N. (2011). Design thinking: Understanding how designers think and work. Berg Publishers Ltd, Oxford.

Dorst, K. (2011). The core of 'design thinking' and its application. Design Studies, 32: 521–532. https//doi:10.1016/j.destud.2011.07.006

Dorst, K., & Cross, N. (2001). Creativity in the design process: Co-evolution of problem–solution. Design Studies, 22: 425–37. https://doi.org/10.1016/S0142-694X(01)00009-6

Dorst, K., Dijkhuis, J. (1995). Comparing paradigms for describing design activity. Design Studies, 16: 261–274. https://doi.org/10.1016/0142-694X(94)00012-3

Fleming, L. (2004). Perfecting cross-pollination. Harvard Business Review, 82(9): 22–24.

Forshaw, T. (2024). The power of reasoning in design research: Deductive, inductive, and abductive approaches. Available via https://medium.com/stanford-d-school/the-power-of-reasoning-in-design-research-deductive-inductive-and-abductive-approaches-e1a4626aac65, Accessed 3 Sep 2025.

Giacomin, J. (2014). What is human centred design? The Design Journal, 17(4): 606–23. https://doi.org/10.2752/175630614X14056185480186

Gibbins, G. (2025). The ai-powered 'stingray model' for innovation. Available via https://www.boardofinnovation.com/blog/the-ai-powered-stingray-model-innovation/, Accessed 11 June 2025.

Graff, D., Clark, M. A. (2019). Communication modes in collaboration: An empirical assessment of metaphors, visualization, and narratives in multidisciplinary design student teams. International Journal of Technology and Design Education, 29: 197–215. https//doi.org/10.1007/s10798-017-9437-9

Hassi, L., Laakso, M. (2011). Design thinking in the management discourse: defining the elements of the concept. In 18th international product development management conference, Innovate Through Design, June 5–7, 2011. Delft, the Netherlands.

Jackson, A. P. (2024). Military Design Thinking: An Historical and Paradigmatic Analysis. Routledge, Milton Park.

Johansson-Sköldberg, U., Woodilla, J., Çetinkaya, M. (2013). Design thinking: Past, present and possible futures. Creativity and Innovation Management, 22(2):121–46. https//doi:10.1111/caim.12023

Jones, J. C. (1970). Design methods: Seeds of human futures. Wiley-Interscience, London.

Jones, J. C. (1991). Designing Designing. London: Architecture, Design and Technology Press (Phaidon), pp. 158-159.

Jones, P., & Kijima, K. (eds) (2019). Systemic Design: Theory, Methods, and Practice. Springer, Berlin.

Love, T. (2014). Design outputs and design outcomes. Available via https://www.love.com.au/index.php/25-design-outputs-and-design-outcomes, Accessed 3 Sep 2025.

Manzini, E., Coed, R. (2015). Design, when everybody designs: An introduction to design for social innovation. The MIT Press, Cambridge.

Norman, D. A. (2024). Design for a better world: Meaningful, sustainable, humanity centered (2nd ed.). The MIT Press.

Paton, B., & Dorst, K. (2011). Briefing and reframing: A situated practice, Design Studies, 32(6): 573–587, https://doi.org/10.1016/j.destud.2011.07.002

Rittel, H. W. J., Webber M. M. (1973). Dilemmas in a general theory of planning. Policy Sciences, 4(2): 155–169. https//doi:10.1007/bf01405730

Schön, D. A. (1983). The reflective practitioner: How professionals think in action. Basic Books, New York.

Simon, H. A .(1969). The sciences of the artificial. The MIT Press: Cambridge.

Steen, M. (2011). Tensions in human-centred design. CoDesign7(1): 45–60. https://doi.org/10.1080/15710882.2011.563314

Stickdorn, M. (2014). This is service design thinking. BIS Publisher, Amsterdam.

Thackara, J. (2006). The bubble: Designing in a complex world. MIT Press: Cambridge.

Verganti, R. (2008). Design, meanings, and radical innovation: A metamodel and a research agenda. *Journal of Product Innovation Management, 25*(5): 436–56. https://doi.org/10.1111/j.1540-5885.2008.00313.x

von Buuren, A., Lewis, J. M., & Peters, B. G. (2023). *Policy-Making as Designing: The Added Value of Design Thinking for Public Administration and Public Policy.* Policy Press, Bristol.

2

Artificial Intelligence: Foundations, Applications, and Future Directions

Artificial Intelligence (AI) can be defined as the ability of machines to exhibit behavior that appears intelligent—to analyze their surroundings, make decisions, and act autonomously toward specific goals. Once the subject of speculation in philosophy and science fiction, AI has evolved into one of the most transformative technologies of the modern age. It influences how we work, learn, design, communicate, and even make sense of the world.

From predictive text that anticipates the next part of the sentence to recommendation engines curating what you watch, read, or buy, AI is now woven into everyday experience. It organizes our inboxes, navigates our cities, assists in healthcare diagnostics, and creates new forms of art and music. What was once an abstract dream of building "thinking machines" has become a practical force reshaping industries and redefining the boundaries of human creativity.

This chapter demystifies AI by exploring its historical evolution, technological foundations, key breakthroughs, and future directions. Understanding where AI came from—and where it is heading—helps managers, designers, and innovators navigate its immense potential responsibly and effectively.

Historical Development of AI

Early Conceptualizations

Long before the term "artificial intelligence" was coined, the idea of intelligent machines fascinated thinkers, inventors, and storytellers. As discussed

© The Author(s), under exclusive license to Springer Nature Switzerland AG 2026

D. Graff et al., *Design Thinking with Artificial Intelligence*, Palgrave Executive Essentials,
https://doi.org/10.1007/978-3-032-10543-1_2

by Mayor in 2018, ancient myths featured mechanical beings animated by divine or human craftsmanship—from the bronze giant Talos guarding Crete in Greek legend to the Golem of Jewish folklore. These stories revealed an enduring human desire to create life from non-life, to build machines that could think or act with purpose.

In the 4th century BCE, the Greek mathematician Archytas of Tarentum designed a wooden pigeon that could reportedly fly using steam power—perhaps the first recorded automaton. Though primitive, it marked an early exploration of autonomy. Centuries later, mechanical engineers of the Islamic Golden Age, such as Al-Jazari, constructed intricate automata powered by water or gears, foreshadowing the programmable logic that would eventually define computing.

It wasn't until the twentieth century, however, that the dream of mechanical intelligence met the reality of electronic computation. As machines capable of performing arithmetic and logical operations emerged, so too did the belief that intelligence could be simulated through code.

Birth of Modern AI

The modern story of AI begins with Alan Turing's 1950 paper *Computing Machinery and Intelligence*, which posed the provocative question: "Can machines think?" As outlined by Hoffman in 2022, Turing proposed a practical experiment—now known as the Turing Test—to evaluate machine intelligence not by its internal workings but by its behavior. If a computer could converse with a human indistinguishably from another person, it could be said to exhibit intelligence. This marked a turning point: AI was no longer just philosophical but measurable.

In 1956, a small group of computer scientists gathered at Dartmouth College for a summer workshop that would later be recognized as the official birth of AI as a research field. Organized by John McCarthy, Marvin Minsky, Claude Shannon, and others, the conference introduced the term "artificial intelligence" to distinguish the field from earlier areas like cybernetics, as detailed by Moor in 2006. The goal was audacious—to make machines capable of human-level reasoning and learning.

The optimism of the era was contagious. Early AI systems, such as the *Logic Theorist* developed by Allen Newell and Herbert Simon, showed that computers could solve mathematical proofs and mimic aspects of human problem-solving. Researchers envisioned rapid progress toward general machine intelligence, believing it would only take a few decades to match human cognition.

Early Challenges and AI Winters

The enthusiasm of the 1950s and 1960s soon met hard limits. The computers of the time were slow, expensive, and memory-constrained. Even simple AI programs required immense computational resources. In the 1960s, leasing a computer could cost the equivalent of hundreds of thousands of dollars per month—an unsustainable barrier for experimentation.

By the early 1970s, progress had stalled. In 1973, the UK government commissioned the Lighthill Report, which concluded that AI research had failed to meet expectations. Funding was slashed, and similar cutbacks occurred in the United States. This period of reduced interest and investment became known as the first "AI winter."

AI research regained momentum in the 1980s with the rise of *expert systems*—rule-based programs that replicated the decision-making of human specialists. These systems achieved practical success in areas such as medical diagnosis and financial analysis. They relied on large databases of "if-then" rules combined with inference engines capable of drawing logical conclusions. For the first time, AI was generating commercial value.

Yet expert systems had limitations. They were brittle, expensive to maintain, and unable to handle uncertainty or context outside predefined rules. As computing advanced, these constraints once again tempered expectations. By the late 1980s, enthusiasm waned, and a second AI winter followed. But this time, the field didn't die; it transformed.

Emergence and Rise of Machine Learning

By the 1990s, a new approach began to redefine the field: *machine learning*. Instead of explicitly programming rules, researchers developed algorithms that could learn patterns and make predictions directly from data. This was a paradigm shift—teaching machines not by instruction, but by example.

Machine learning encompasses a range of methods. *Supervised learning* trains systems on labeled data. For instance, a spam filter learning from examples of "spam" and "not spam." *Unsupervised learning* uncovers hidden patterns in unlabeled datasets, useful for customer segmentation or anomaly detection. *Reinforcement learning* teaches systems through trial and error, rewarding correct actions and penalizing mistakes—the same principle that helps animals and humans learn.

The combination of better algorithms, more data, and increasing computing power made machine learning the driving force of modern AI. It gave rise to systems that could improve over time, a fundamental break from static, rule-based logic. AI was no longer merely simulating reasoning; it was adapting and evolving.

Deep Learning Revolution

The 2010s marked a profound leap in AI's capabilities through a subfield known as deep learning. Inspired by the structure of the human brain, deep learning uses neural networks, which are computational architectures composed of layers of interconnected nodes, or "neurons," that process and transform data as it flows through the network.

Although the concept dated back to the 1940s, deep learning became viable only when three key ingredients converged: massive datasets, powerful graphics processing units (GPUs), and new training techniques. The pivotal breakthrough came in 2012, when a neural network called AlexNet dramatically outperformed all competitors in the ImageNet competition, reducing image recognition errors by more than half. This moment proved that deep neural networks could achieve superhuman performance in visual tasks.

The implications were enormous. Within a few years, deep learning began powering speech recognition, natural language translation, recommendation systems, and self-driving technologies. These networks could identify objects in photos, understand spoken language, and generate coherent text. Unlike earlier systems that relied on human-defined features, deep learning models learned those features directly from data—discovering representations that even their creators couldn't always explain.

Deep learning's success was not magic but engineering at scale. As models grew deeper and data richer, their ability to generalize across domains increased. This era ushered in AI as a pervasive infrastructure for organizations, a foundation not only for digital products but for creativity, research, and decision-making itself.

Generative AI: Creating New Possibilities

Among the most remarkable recent advances in artificial intelligence is generative AI, which is systems capable not only of analyzing existing information but of creating entirely new content. Instead of classifying or predicting, generative models produce text, images, music, and even video that can rival human creativity. This shift from automation to imagination has opened vast new possibilities across industries.

Generative AI operates through deep neural architectures that learn the underlying structure of their training data. Once trained, they can generate novel variations that remain coherent and stylistically aligned with the source material. The results range from realistic images and fluent text to original musical compositions and cinematic video clips. For business leaders, this means creative workflows that once required weeks can now occur in seconds.

Natural Language Processing and Generation

Language is one of humanity's most sophisticated tools—and one of AI's greatest challenges. The subfield of Natural Language Processing (NLP) focuses on enabling computers to understand, interpret, and generate human language. Recent years have seen extraordinary breakthroughs thanks to transformer neural network architectures, which allow models to grasp long-range relationships between words and concepts.

Large Language Models (LLMs), such as GPT-style systems, are trained on vast datasets drawn from books, articles, and the internet. These models learn statistical relationships among words, enabling them to predict what comes next in a sequence. Though deceptively simple in principle, this predictive mechanism, scaled across trillions of parameters, gives rise to astonishing fluency and reasoning ability.

Such models now underpin a wide array of applications—conversational assistants, customer service chatbots, automated writing tools, and real-time translation services. They can summarize legal contracts, draft marketing copy, generate code, or simulate dialogue for design scenarios. Their versatility has redefined productivity across sectors. However, while these systems can produce highly convincing text, they do not possess true understanding—a reminder that human oversight remains essential in interpreting and validating AI-generated information.

Visual and Artistic Generation

AI's creative reach extends beyond words. Systems like DALL·E, Midjourney, and Stable Diffusion can generate digital images from textual descriptions, producing visuals that range from photorealistic to fantastical. When prompted with "a medieval town square on Mars," for instance, a model can conjure a coherent, visually compelling image that blends two vastly different contexts—medieval architecture and a Martian landscape.

These tools have become invaluable to designers, marketers, and artists. In product design, AI can visualize prototypes from conceptual sketches. In marketing, it can generate endless variations of campaign imagery tailored to different audiences. In entertainment, filmmakers use generative models to create storyboards and visual concepts at unprecedented speed.

The democratization of creativity also introduces new questions. Who owns an AI-generated image? How do we ensure authenticity in an era where fake visuals can be indistinguishable from real ones? And how will we define artistic originality when machines can synthesize styles across centuries of human culture? Addressing these questions will shape the future of creative industries.

Music and Video Generation

Generative AI has also made significant inroads into music and video production. In music, for instance, OpenAI's Jukebox system is a neural network model that composes raw audio music—including instrumental tracks and vocals—from scratch as stated by Zignuts in 2025. Whereas some earlier music-generation tools relied on symbolic representations (like musical notation), Jukebox works at the audio waveform level, capturing complexities of harmony, rhythm, and timbre across different musical genres.

Jukebox can continue an existing song, blend different musical styles, or create original compositions in high-fidelity audio as noted by Zignuts in 2025. Users of the system can specify a desired genre or even an artist style as a prompt, and the model will generate music in response. It is even capable of mimicking certain singers' voices with stylistic nuance. These capabilities make Jukebox a powerful tool for musicians seeking to experiment with new sounds or generate accompaniments.

Video generation presents an even greater challenge for AI, since a model must generate not just a single image but a sequence of frames that are spatially and temporally consistent. Nonetheless, progress is being made. For example, Google DeepMind's Veo 2 and OpenAI's Sora are two generative models that can produce short video clips based on text prompts or input images according to Awan in 2025.

Veo 2 is notable for its ability to generate videos in 4K resolution and for incorporating an understanding of physics—its generated videos portray motion and interactions that obey realistic physical principles, as Awan described in 2025. Sora, meanwhile, is optimized for speed and creativity, making it a practical tool for quickly generating video content without substantial quality loss, Awan also noted in 2025. Together, these tools hint at a future where animators, filmmakers, and content creators can leverage AI to generate or enhance video content, potentially transforming industries from advertising and entertainment to education and social media.

AI Applications Across Industries: Applied Business Examples

AI is already being applied in a multitude of industries. This section highlights several key sectors where AI is driving innovation and provides examples of how AI is being used in each context.

Healthcare

In healthcare, AI is driving innovations that improve diagnostics, treatment planning, and patient outcomes. AI systems can analyze medical images (such as X-rays, CT scans, or MRIs) to help detect diseases, predict patient outcomes by recognizing patterns in clinical data, and even suggest personalized treatment options based on an individual's unique health profile. Studies have shown that AI can match or exceed human experts in certain diagnostic tasks. For example, in some cases AI models have outperformed radiologists in detecting specific conditions from medical images, as described by Bajwa et al., in 2021. Beyond diagnostics, AI-driven predictive models can identify patients at high risk for complications, such as predicting which hospitalized patients are likely to deteriorate, which allows for early interventions. AI tools are also used to analyze genomic and biochemical data to aid in developing personalized medicine.

One concrete example is the use of AI to predict acute kidney failure in hospital intensive care units. Machine learning models can warn of kidney failure hours before clinical signs become evident, enabling doctors to take preventative measures and improve patient outcomes (Bajwa et al., 2021). Another example is AI-driven drug discovery: algorithms can sift through vast chemical databases to identify promising drug candidates and predict their effectiveness and safety profiles. This accelerates the research phase and can reduce the time and cost required to bring new drugs to market.

Design

AI is expanding the possibilities in creative design fields and making the design thinking process more efficient. AI allows creators to explore a greater variety of design options and iterate on ideas faster than ever before. We will elaborate on the use of AI in design in the following chapter.

For example, AI-powered software can generate novel fashion designs, architectural blueprints, or product prototypes based on a set of input parameters or by learning from existing design examples, as AdCreative.ai reported in 2024. Rather than replacing human designers, these tools act as collaborators—providing inspiration, suggesting variations, and automating routine aspects of design work.

In practice, designers are already using AI to augment creativity. In the fashion industry, a system like *ClothingGAN* can learn from thousands of existing clothing designs and then generate entirely new garment ideas as AIMultiple reported in 2025. In architecture and industrial design, AI algorithms are used to optimize design plans: for example, generating building layouts that balance structural integrity, cost, and aesthetic appeal, or suggesting product design modifications that reduce material waste while maintaining functionality.

Entertainment

The entertainment industry has quickly embraced AI to enhance content production and personalize user experiences. Streaming services such as Spotify, for example, use advanced algorithms to analyze users' viewing and listening histories in order to recommend content that each user is most likely to enjoy.

AI is also making inroads into film and video production. Machine learning tools can assist with script analysis, help in editing by automatically tagging scenes, or even generate visual effects. One cutting-edge example is the use of generative video models like Sora to create special effects or entire short scenes based on a simple textual description, according to AIMultiple in 2025. This could significantly reduce the time and cost needed for certain aspects of filmmaking.

In the video game sector, AI enables more immersive gameplay. Modern games use AI to generate content on the fly and create realistic behaviors. For instance, the game *Watch Dogs: Legion* uses an AI system to dynamically generate a large cast of unique non-player characters (NPCs). Each NPC in the game has distinct attributes and behaviors, making the game world feel more alive and varied for players, as noted by AIMultiple in 2025.

Marketing

AI has transformed marketing by allowing far greater personalization and efficiency in reaching customers. Machine learning algorithms can analyze large volumes of consumer data to identify patterns and preferences, which marketers use to craft and deliver highly relevant advertisements and messages to specific audience segments.

Many companies now use AI to generate marketing content and optimize campaigns. By leveraging AI content creation tools, a marketing team can quickly produce and test many variations of an advertisement or message. For example, one company reported that using an AI copywriting assistant helped reduce the time spent creating marketing content by 40% and saw campaign click-through rates increase by as much as 70%, as stated by AIMultiple in 2025. The AI system was able to tailor messages more precisely to what customers responded to, thus improving engagement.

AI is also revolutionizing online advertising through techniques like programmatic ad buying, where AI systems automatically bid on ad placements targeted to specific users in real time. These systems optimize advertising budgets by learning which strategies yield the best return on investment—ensuring that marketing messages reach the right audience at the right time through the best channels.

Urban Planning and Architecture

City planners and architects are adopting AI programs to help design smarter, more sustainable cities and buildings. AI can analyze complex datasets that include traffic patterns, energy consumption, sunlight exposure, and population movement to inform urban design decisions.

Using AI simulations, planners can generate and evaluate numerous design scenarios much faster than with traditional methods. For example, an AI system might propose multiple road network designs for a new city neighborhood, each optimized for different objectives like minimizing congestion or maximizing public transport efficiency. Similarly, architects can use AI to simulate how a building design performs under various conditions—identifying potential issues (like poor ventilation or insufficient natural light) before construction begins.

By optimizing resource use and anticipating environmental impacts, AI contributes to more sustainable urban development. It can recommend building designs that consume less energy, or city layouts that reduce commute times and improve quality of life for residents. In effect, AI augments human creativity and expertise in planning, making it possible to design spaces that better serve communities while respecting environmental and resource constraints.

Ethical and Societal Challenges of AI

As AI systems become more powerful and pervasive, it is crucial to address the ethical and societal challenges they pose. Ensuring that AI technologies are developed and used in ways that benefit humanity—while minimizing potential harms—requires careful consideration of several key issues, such as those outlined by Stewart in his 2024 ChatGPT-written report.

Accuracy and Reliability (Hallucinations)

One important challenge is the reliability of AI-generated information. Advanced AI models, particularly large generative models, can sometimes produce incorrect or entirely fabricated outputs while appearing confident and authoritative. This tendency is colloquially known as an AI "hallucination," where the system outputs information that sounds plausible but is actually false or nonsensical, as described by Stryker & Kavlakoglu in 2024.

These errors occur because such AI models are designed to generate content that statistically aligns with their training data—they have no inherent mechanism to verify factual accuracy. An AI might convincingly answer a question with incorrect information simply because that answer resembles valid patterns in the data it has seen. While a mistake like this might be relatively harmless in casual settings, it becomes a serious concern in high-stakes domains like healthcare, law, or finance, where decisions based on incorrect information can lead to real harm.

Addressing the hallucination problem will likely require a combination of approaches. Researchers are working on improving model architectures and training processes to reduce errors. There is also ongoing development of auxiliary systems that can fact-check or verify AI outputs against reliable external sources. In sensitive applications, the safest approach is to keep a human expert in the loop who can review and correct an AI's suggestions or conclusions.

Bias and Fairness

Another major challenge is ensuring fairness and avoiding bias in AI systems. AI algorithms can inadvertently learn and amplify biases present in their training data as noted by Ferrara in 2024. This can lead to discriminatory outcomes, especially in contexts like hiring, lending, criminal justice, or healthcare, where algorithmic decisions have significant impacts on people's lives.

For example, facial recognition software has been found to have higher error rates for women and individuals with darker skin tones, reflecting biases in the data used to train those systems as described by Ferrara in 2024. In another case, some AI-driven hiring tools were shown to favor resumes from men over equally qualified women, because they had learned from past hiring data where men were disproportionately favored.

Bias in AI can originate from biased data (historical or societal inequalities reflected in the training set), from biased assumptions built into algorithms, or from a lack of diversity among the people who design and test these systems. Addressing bias may require multiple steps: using more diverse and representative training data, applying algorithmic fairness techniques to detect and mitigate bias in models, and involving people from a variety of backgrounds in the development and evaluation of AI systems. We will explore this issue in more detail in later chapters.

Privacy and Surveillance

AI thrives on data—yet that same data can compromise personal privacy, as noted in the University of Southern California's 2024 report, *The ethical dilemmas of AI*. The proliferation of AI-powered surveillance systems can track individuals in public spaces without their consent, using sensors, cameras, and online activity measures to create vast datasets. This risks the use of personal information that people did not intend to share. Balancing innovation with individual rights demands robust data governance.

The challenge is to balance the benefits of data-driven AI innovations with individuals' right to privacy. Emerging techniques such as *federated learning* (which keeps data on local devices) and *differential privacy* (which obscures individual details) offer promising safeguards. But technical measures alone are not enough; strong legal and regulatory frameworks coupled with ethical norms are needed to define what constitutes responsible data use. In the age of AI, privacy is not just a legal concept—it is a cornerstone of human dignity.

Transparency and Accountability

Modern AI systems, particularly deep neural networks, often operate as "black boxes." Their decision-making processes are difficult to interpret even for their creators. When an AI denies a loan, misdiagnoses an illness, or flags a person for security screening, it can be unclear why. This opacity erodes trust in AI systems and complicates accountability for AI and its users. If AI makes an error, such as denying a home loan or misdiagnosing a patient, it may be unclear why the error happened or who is responsible for the decision.

Researchers are developing *explainable AI* methods that make systems more interpretable to shed light on AI's reasoning process. Equally important is governance: organizations must establish monitoring structures and clear lines of accountability for AI decisions. Transparency about how models are trained, what data they use, and how their performance is evaluated is essential to earning and maintaining public confidence. Stakeholders should be informed about an AI system's performance characteristics, including its accuracy rates, its potential biases, and the scenarios in which it might fail. This transparency allows users to make informed decisions about when to trust an AI system and when to apply additional human judgment.

The Future: Human-AI Synergy

Looking ahead, one of the most promising directions for artificial intelligence is the development of systems that enhance and collaborate with humans, rather than replacing them. This concept of human-AI synergy is based on the idea that humans and AI have complementary strengths that, when combined, can produce better outcomes than either could achieve alone.

AI systems excel at processing vast quantities of data, performing repetitive tasks consistently, and operating continuously without fatigue. Humans, by contrast, excel at creative thinking, emotional intelligence, moral reasoning, adapting to unforeseen circumstances, and drawing on common sense knowledge. By leveraging AI for what machines do best and leaving to humans what people do best, we can form effective partnerships.

In practical terms, human-AI collaboration is already taking shape. In medicine, for example, an AI system might quickly analyze diagnostic images or scan a patient's history to flag potential concerns, while a human doctor uses expertise and empathy to make final decisions and communicate with the patient. In customer service, an AI chatbot might handle routine inquiries, but human representatives take over for complex or sensitive interactions. These scenarios illustrate how AI can serve as a supportive assistant, boosting human productivity and decision-making rather than acting autonomously in isolation.

Future AI systems are likely to be designed with collaboration in mind. This could involve more natural interfaces that allow humans to interact with AI using speech, gestures, or visual cues. We may also see AI that can learn an individual user's goals and preferences over time, adapting its assistance to fit each person's style of working.

Even the concept of expert systems—originally envisioned as standalone decision-makers—may evolve into a collaborative paradigm. Rather than replacing human experts, tomorrow's expert systems might function as co-pilots for professionals, as reported by Milani in 2024. For example, an AI system could continuously learn from a human expert's decisions and feedback, while the human expert learns from the AI's recommendations and the data-driven insights it provides. In this way, both the AI and the human could improve over time by learning from each other's strengths.

Importantly, keeping humans involved with AI can also help address some of the ethical issues noted earlier. A human partner can override or correct an AI's mistakes, recognize nuances or context that an AI might miss, and ensure that decisions align with ethical norms and societal values. Conversely, AI can help humans by handling heavy data processing and providing unbiased analytical perspectives, which can complement human intuition and judgment.

Summary

The story of AI is one of imagination made real. From ancient myths to modern algorithms, humanity has long sought to understand and replicate its own intelligence. In just a few decades, AI has evolved from a theoretical curiosity to a pervasive force transforming every industry and aspect of life, changing how we work, create, communicate, and make decisions.

Deep learning and generative models have propelled machines into what not long ago would have seemed like science fiction, encompassing domains once considered uniquely human. Today's AI can carry on conversations, generate realistic images and videos from scratch, compose music, translate between languages, and assist in diagnosing diseases, among many other feats. Yet these advances come with challenges that demand vigilance: ensuring accuracy, fairness, privacy, and transparency in systems that increasingly shape our world.

The next frontier lies in collaboration. The future of intelligence is not artificial or human, but *augmented*—a partnership where technology amplifies our capabilities rather than replacing them. By embracing AI with both enthusiasm and responsibility, business leaders can harness it not just as a tool of efficiency, but as an instrument of insight, creativity, and positive change. With responsible development and deployment, artificial intelligence can be a powerful instrument for addressing some of humanity's most pressing challenges and for unlocking new levels of human potential in the years ahead.

References

AdCreative.ai. (2024, December 20). The intersection of art and technology: How AI is revolutionizing the creative design process. AdCreative.ai. https://www.adc reative.ai/post/how-ai-is-revolutionizing-the-creative-design-process

AIMultiple. (2025, April 4). Top 100+ generative AI applications with real-life examples. AIMultiple Research. https://research.aimultiple.com/generative-ai-appli cations/

Awan, A. A. (2025, February 17). Top 3 video generation models. KDnuggets. https://www.kdnuggets.com/top-3-video-generation-models

Bajwa, J., Munir, U., Nori, A., & Williams, B. (2021). Artificial intelligence in healthcare: Transforming the practice of medicine. Future Healthcare Journal, 8(2), e188–e194. https://doi.org/10.7861/fhj.2021-0095

Baktash, J. A., & Dawodi, M. (2023). GPT-4: A review on advancements and opportunities in natural language processing. arXiv preprint arXiv:2305.03195.

Ferrara, E. (2024). Fairness and bias in artificial intelligence: A brief survey of sources, impacts, and mitigation strategies. Sci, 6(1), 3. https://doi.org/10.3390/sci 6010003

Hoffmann, C. H. (2022). Is AI intelligent? An assessment of artificial intelligence, 70 years after Turing. Technology in Society, 68, 101893. https://doi.org/10.1016/ j.techsoc.2022.101893

Mayor, A. (2018). Gods and Robots: Myths, Machines, and Ancient Dreams of Technology. Princeton University Press. ISBN 9780691183510.

Milani, M. (2024). The future of AI: Expert systems will lead the next chapter. LinkedIn. https://www.linkedin.com/pulse/future-ai-expert-systems-lead-next-chapter -martin-milani-5ugxc/

Moor, J. (2006). The Dartmouth College Artificial Intelligence Conference: The next fifty years. AI Magazine, 27(4), 87–91.

Stewart, K. (2024, April 3). The ethical dilemmas of AI. USC Annenberg Relevance Report. https://annenberg.usc.edu/research/center-public-relations/usc-annenb erg-relevance-report/ethical-dilemmas-ai

Stryker, C., & Kavlakoglu, E. (2024, August 16). What is artificial intelligence (AI)? IBM. https://www.ibm.com/topics/artificial-intelligence

Zignuts. (2025). OpenAI Jukebox: AI music generator for raw audio composition. Zignuts Blog. https://www.zignuts.com/ai/openai-jukebox

3

The Use of AI in Design Thinking

Companies and individual innovators around the world are competing to discover the best way to leverage AI in designing innovative products and services. So far, despite its potential for transforming innovation processes, AI is often treated as simply as a tool with rudimentary functions of gathering and processing data. To realize AI's full potential for design thinking, we must consider not only the AI technology, but also how designers and innovators can adapt their methods and skills. In this chapter we explore the current perceptions, uses, and implications of AI use for the design field. We then offer a preliminary direction for leaders to take charge of the trajectory of AI use in their organizations.

There is a continuum of uses that describe on how AI can be adopted in design thinking. On one end, when AI is not given agency, we can describe AI as a tool used in the manner of other traditional software that designers and innovators are using (e.g., computer-aided design software, known as CAD). This is a very common way that AI is used in design thinking, based on our conversations with innovation firms and related studies, as noted by Clark & Graff in 2025. Here, designers and innovators remain in their dominant role, driving the work, and use AI only in a very simplified manner, such as a search engine or aggregator of simple instructions, without truly realizing the potential or benefits of AI. At the other extreme, firms might support AI in operating as an independent designer or innovator, completing tasks on its own with little input from human designers or innovators. However, this approach is very limited and more theoretical than practical in most situations. This is because as of this writing AI does not have the capability to take this

© The Author(s), under exclusive license to Springer Nature Switzerland AG 2026
D. Graff et al., *Design Thinking with Artificial Intelligence*, Palgrave Executive Essentials,
https://doi.org/10.1007/978-3-032-10543-1_3

initiative without significant errors or hallucinations, and in many cases is not sufficiently sophisticated or trained enough to add value as a full collaborator.

A middle ground may be found on interdependent teams with human designers or innovators that seek to collaborate with AI, each having supervised, complementary duties, and responsibilities. These collaborations are challenging, in that without appropriate tools, policies, and norms to guide the interaction, pairing AI with human teams may actually reduce performance as Vaccaro and colleagues noted in 2024. But with a perspective shift that enables organizational leaders and innovators to develop these policies, success is possible, as Kober emphasized in 2025.

Thus, given the capabilities of AI and the readiness of contemporary organizations, human-AI collaboration is the most beneficial model, as Wilson & Daugherty explained in 2018. Figure 3.1 illustrates our belief that great design thinking outcomes require human design thinkers with a profound understanding of the context, powerful AI programs and appropriate design methods. We note that the lack of any component—whether AI, human design thinkers, or the use of design methods—will lead to sub-optimal design outcomes. Before the arrival of AI in design thinking, the design knowledge and skill would be embedded in the human designer, however, now this expertise is extended and embedded in both AI and humans. As discussed in the previous chapter, we need to capitalize on AI-human synergies in design thinking. AI can bring its vast data processing power, while humans can utilize their emotional intelligence, moral reasoning, and adaptation to unforeseen circumstances. By leveraging AI for what machines do best and leaving to humans what they do best, we can form effective collaboration. However, this will require innovators and designers to adapt their design thinking tools and skills, as we will discuss in coming chapters of this book.

Our illustration depicts that design thinking which rely exclusively on the intersection of AI and design methods as potentially ineffective, labelled "inapplicable." In this event, AI takes over the whole design work (AI as designer), for example, via a single AI prompt. The resulting outcomes are often inapplicable because AI cannot fully understand and respond to the required context. Next, Figure 3.1 reveals that humans who use AI in design thinking without incorporating design methods likely achieve only gimmicky and "worthless" design thinking outcomes. The problem in this instance is that without design methods, AI cannot be used correctly in design, resulting in conceptualizations that do not respond, for example, to current user needs.

Finally, there are humans who do not use AI in design thinking, instead deploying their individual skills and knowledge through traditional design

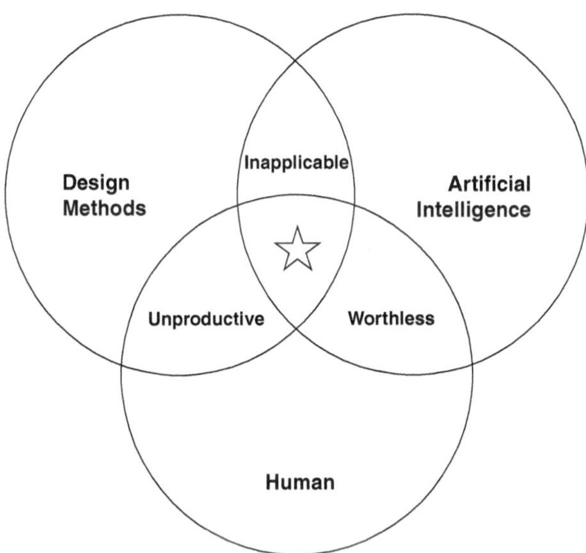

Figure 3.1   Great Design Requires AI, Human Designer Thinkers, and Design Methods.

methods. While this workstyle has achieved good design outcomes for many years, continuing without AI may incur opportunity cost, both in comparison to competitors and for the best quality design outcomes. Designing without AI may be relatively slow, "unproductive," and therefore expensive. It also limits designers and innovators to their own cognitive capacity and available work hours, whereas working with AI adds far-reaching possibilities to design work.

The perfect scenario may be when AI is integrated properly into design methods, used by a human design thinker with profound knowledge of the context. Here, AI enables innovators and designers to develop better products and services more quickly by shortening the research activity phase or improving information gathered in research. AI, for example, can be used to analyze more data and more quicky, but it can also be used to visualize quickly ideas to enhance understanding to make the process more effective and efficient. In that way, AI takes the role of a collaborator that supports the human in the design thinking process. Designers and innovators act as supervisors, guiding AI throughout the project. Further, the task of the human is to contextualize the outcomes of AI to make them more specific and relevant to the design thinking problem. To achieve this, we need updated design process tools, as well as new knowledge and skills, which we will discuss later in this book.

Current Perception of AI in Design Thinking

The emergence of AI appears in some ways similar to the internet boom of the 1990s. Both phenomena are technological advances that represent a major shift in how companies work and compete. However, while internet technology has been largely adopted and the transformation of work is almost complete, the emergence of AI has just begun and its future impact on how companies work and compete is still mostly unknown. Consequently, employees and companies alike struggle to fully understand and utilize AI.

In the field of design thinking, a plethora of new AI-based products and services can overwhelm designers and innovators, companies, and scholars who may not be able to keep up with the advancing technology. Consequently, and a bit ironically, designers work again like designers in the 1960s and 70s, when design thinking was much more improvised and, hence, designers developed their own tools and wrote their own design method books, such as Jones discussed in his 1970 text.

Design thinkers may be grouped into at least three distinct categories in response to this confusing situation. The first group, who we will call **technological futurists**, believe that AI in design thinking will have a powerful impact, nothing short of a revolution. This perspective may be held by those in design-related fields who may or may not have design training, such as engineers working in product development. This group is full of excitement for the innovative technology and paints a very bright picture of AI in design thinking. Its members are knowledgeable about AI but may lack in-depth design thinking knowledge and skills. They may use AI to augment or complement their limited capabilities, such as by using AI to sketch an idea into a graphic if they lack drawing skills. Many innovators using design thinking can also fall within this group. The advantage for them is that AI can help non-educated designers to overcome their weaknesses and improve their outcomes in a quick and substantial way.

The second group, **design traditionalists**, believes that AI in design thinking is insignificant, inconsequential, and over-hyped. This perspective is often raised by very experienced and professional designers who consider AI to be just another gimmick. To them, design thinking is not a prescribed scientific process that everyone can successfully follow, but is more of an artistic process that requires individual experience and depth of knowledge to succeed. They are suspicious of AI in design thinking, just as they have been skeptical about the hype for "design thinking" applied outside of the design discipline over the years. Design traditionalists consider their knowledge and skill to be superior to that of AI in terms of technical prowess, creativity, and the ability to relate to clients and user audiences. Therefore, they largely ignore the advances in AI and do not incorporate the new technology into their design processes. This prevents the design traditionalists from advancing their skills and knowledge. At the same time, they run the risk of designing in an unproductive manner that will potentially make it harder to compete in the future.

The third group, **AI agnostics**, does not know what to believe. This may be the largest of the three groups and includes design novices, many professional art-based designers, and those who have not seen how AI can or does improve their work output. While some of these AI agnostics actively seek to educate themselves, many remain passive and seem paralyzed. They may half-heartedly attempt to incorporate AI into their design thinking processes. Ironically, their lack of understanding AI's capabilities and operation may lead to its misuse; hence, the outcome of incorporating AI falls below their threshold for the trouble of using it. Consequently, this group often perceives AI as interesting but does not know how to incorporate it into their design thinking process.

Each of these groups, as well as other potential innovators, must be considered as we describe the use of AI in design thinking practice and its potential consequences in the short and long run. As we will expand upon next, limiting AI use primarily to the technological futurists could have negative consequences for design thinking in the near future as we could see more non-educated designers delivering most designed products and services. We will make some general suggestions for design thinking in the last chapter of this book to overcome these potential negative effects on the design field.

AI Use in Design Thinking Today

So, how is AI used in design thinking today? It varies considerably, depending on the country where the company or individual is located, the industry in which the firm competes, the designer's perception and experience with technology, as well as the types of tasks, among other factors, as noted by Clark and Graff in 2025. People use AI in their work for instrumental reasons, such as when they find that it rewards their efforts with improved performance through utility and ease of use, as noted by Marangunić and Granić in 2015. Additionally, more human reasons such as attitude, trust toward AI, and conducive cultural environments come into play. In some contexts, however, requirements for human interaction can still discourage the use of AI as highlighted by Kelly et al., 2023.

Innovators and designers interviewed as part of our research shared differing visions of AI utility, often depending on the company's location and regulatory environment, as described by Clark and Graff in 2025. On one hand, in some European countries, innovators, and designers stressed the importance of the human contribution to the design of a product or service. Their stories often included the view that AI should be limited in the design thinking process, both due to employment laws and design needs. In other countries, such as China or the USA, this seems less of a concern and the discussion shifts toward the positive implications of AI on design thinking. Perhaps not coincidentally the USA and China are also regarded as leaders in developing AI applications.

Furthermore, our research shows that there are differences among firms in their use of AI in design. Technology-affiliated companies, or companies within technology sectors seem to be more ready to apply AI in design thinking compared to companies from more traditional industries. As AI demands new work processes, traditional organizations are slower to adapt to the new environment compared to start-ups, which can more easily define new work processes.

It also appears that the design task is key determinant of AI use in design thinking. Some tasks, such as UX design, seem to rely much more on AI than, for example, industrial design. An Amazon website or Netflix homepage, for instance, is automatically adapted by AI, based on a consumer's previous behaviors, as Verganti, Vendraminelli, and Iansiti emphasized in 2020. In these cases, there is little work done by individual designers.

While these are all important factors describing the degree of AI use in design thinking, some other general observations apply. In what follows, we describe in more detail how AI is used, why AI is used, and who is using AI in design thinking.

AI Is Most Often Restricted to Use as a Tool

Our research showed that various types of AI (e.g. LLMs, image generators) are used throughout the design thinking process (from research activities to prototype to implementation) to varying degrees and proficiencies. These activities are rarely organized or standardized within companies. Instead, individual designers and innovators identify and decide for themselves which AI tool to use and how. This sporadic and often improper use of AI in design thinking is due to the lack of internal or external guidance. Few books provide detailed guidance on when and how to integrate AI into design thinking. We hope to address that deficiency in our work and this book.

Due to the lack of skills and knowledge on how to use AI in design thinking, designers and innovators (here we refer to AI agnostics) treat AI mostly as a tool rather than a collaborator. In other words, AI is currently treated in design thinking like any other traditional software. The process involves opening AI, using a function/feature/prompt, and directly assessing the outcome afterwards, and accepting or rejecting it. While this type of use is perfectly fine with traditional software, it limits the outcome AI can generate because it lacks contextual knowledge.

To fully benefit from AI in design thinking, many researchers believe that designers and innovators need to collaborate with AI as they would interact with other humans; more specifically, as they would supervise an employee. Like most supervisor–employee relationships, designers and innovators must get to know AI, and AI needs to get to know the human. This deeper use of AI in design thinking can be termed "**AI as a collaborator**," in keeping with the discussion above. In this model, designers take the role of a supervisor and guide AI in its design thinking tasks. However, the evidence for this type of collaboration in modern design organizations is scarce. We offer the tools and processes in this book to address this need. We will elaborate on this model in Chapter 4 (Reskilling of Design Thinkers in the Age of Generative AI) and Chapter 5 (Practical Guide to AID Tools).

The consequence of using AI only as a tool in design thinking is that the results are often limited and lack refinement (e.g., outcomes lack relevance without context). Designers and innovators who understand AI's limitations as a tool use it selectively—for example, when generic outcomes are "good enough" (e.g., for internal communication), when context matters less (e.g., analyzing large datasets within a specific scope), or when context can be explicitly defined (e.g., generating an Alibaba retailer homepage for a specific user).

However, designers and innovators unfamiliar with AI's limitations often feel disappointed with its outputs. This disappointment typically stems from overly high expectations of AI as a tool and a lack of understanding of how to use AI as a collaborator. Frustrated by underwhelming results, these designers and innovators (particularly AI agnostics) often abandon its use prematurely.

AI Is Used Predominantly to Improve Efficiency

When designers and innovators use AI as a tool, their focus is often less on enhancing creativity and more on improving efficiency. Most of these efficiency gains are linked to time savings and, consequently, the potential reduction of human effort in design thinking. For example, innovators can use AI programs to analyze large volumes of data, such as call center transcripts, to identify themes related to a research question. This saves time, reduces costs, and accelerates the project timeline. Similarly, AI can quickly generate a sketch to visualize an idea. While the sketch may not match the quality of a professional designer, it is often sufficient to illustrate a concept for internal communication. In short, designers and innovators commonly frame the value of AI in terms of time savings rather than its ability to inspire creativity.

There are several reasons for this emphasis on efficiency. First, using AI purely as a tool often limits its role in creative tasks, since the solutions it generates lack contextual depth and are less useful. In other words, it is easier to apply AI in areas where context matters less or can be controlled. Second, efficiency gains are easier to measure than increases in creativity, according to Hernández-Ramírez and Ferreira in 2024. Companies, therefore, prioritize AI applications that deliver tangible, quantifiable benefits, reinforcing its role in efficiency-driven tasks. Third, AI currently excels at analyzing existing data rather than generating truly novel ideas. Many AI applications still struggle to integrate context, which restricts the usefulness of their creative outputs.

Technologic Futurist Are Driving the Use of AI in Design

So, who are the designers and innovators using AI in design thinking? Early adopters are often engineering-based professionals who fall within the technological futurist group. These innovators typically have a background in engineering rather than art-based design, which better equips them to judge when and how to apply AI. This aligns with the technology acceptance model, outlined by Marangunić and Granić in 2015, which suggests that perceived usefulness strongly influences adoption. For engineering-oriented designers, AI is often seen as more valuable than it is for many art-based designers.

Their use of AI tends to serve two main purposes. First, they use AI to improve product or service design by analyzing large datasets. Where designers and innovators once relied on small samples of target populations, AI now allows them to examine much larger datasets, producing more detailed insights and greater confidence in results.

Second, technological futurists rely on AI for tasks they lack the skills to perform. These tasks often include traditional art-based design skills, such as sketching. Traditional designers and design agnostics are less likely to use AI in this way, albeit for different reasons. Traditional designers believe AI is not good enough and that engaging in activities like sketching contributes to their outcomes by immersing them in the design problem for an extended period. Design agnostics, on the other hand, often fail to use AI effectively due to a lack of understanding. As a result, the quality of outcomes does not meet their expectations.

Short-Term Consequences for Design

Now that we understand how AI is used in design thinking, primarily as a tool to improve efficiency and mostly by technological futurists, we can explore its short-term consequences. We believe that the current reliance on AI as a tool, focused largely on efficiency gains and concentrated within a specific group of designers and innovators, will make design thinking less innovative and more predictable. At the same time, we anticipate that more firms will integrate AI into their design thinking processes to cut costs and improve efficiency. This will likely reduce the demand for designers and innovators, particularly those specializing in art-based design. There is also a real possibility that many design outcomes will increasingly be created by non-educated designers applying design thinking in product and service development within organizations. In the following sections, we elaborate on these predictions.

Design Will Become More Dull

Let us begin by examining how we believe AI will influence design thinking outcomes in the short term, over the next few years. While AI will improve certain aspects of design thinking, it will also lead to negative consequences in others. Overall, we anticipate that design thinking outcomes will become more conservative and less innovative.

As mentioned, on the one hand, design thinking will get better. Design thinking will get better because AI allows us to identify "*objective*" problems and suggest neutral solutions. For example, AI enables the analysis of large amounts of data that was previously not possible. Take the example of a call center. Previously, designers and innovators would have chosen a sample of the call center calls with the hope that these were representative to the overall population (i.e., all call center calls). By analyzing all or more of the data, we can be more confident that the identified problem is significant, allowing for improvement in the service or product accordingly. AI proves most useful in scenarios involving objective measurement.

Therefore, AI can enhance design outcomes in specific scenarios. However, while these outcomes may be welcomed by consumers, they are likely to be quite predictable, as solutions often rely on patterns and majority preferences. Furthermore, design thinking processes will become faster. In the example above, data can be analyzed more quickly, and certain internal processes streamlined. This will lead to shorter development cycles and cost reductions in the creation of new products and services. Overall, the design thinking process will get faster and more cost-effective, encouraging more firms to adopt AI in their design thinking practices.

On the other hand, design thinking outcomes may deteriorate. Research shows that when humans collaborate with AI, designers and innovators may reduce their effort, resulting in good enough outcomes, as noted by Zhang et al., in 2021. This decline in performance is particularly evident in high-performing teams, where members rely on AI-generated outputs instead of putting in their full effort. Meanwhile, lower-performing teams may see slight improvements, narrowing the gap between performance levels. As a result, we anticipate reduced variance in design thinking outcomes, with fewer failures but also fewer instances of exceptional performance. In addition, the use of AI as a tool, with its focus on efficiency (as its current strength) rather than creativity (as its current weakness), will likely produce functional yet uninspiring products and services. This is rooted in the tendency of firms to prioritize certain solutions derived from AI-processed data over intuition-driven approaches. While this tension has existed in the past, the current abundance of data available for AI analysis could further diminish the role of designers' intuition.

Given the above, we believe that design thinking will get better in the sense of being more functional or relevant to the user, but less exciting and inspiring. In other words, we believe that design will be more similar, safe, and dull compared to today. We will see this development specifically among larger firms that will be more likely to use AI as a tool within their design thinking process.

Nevertheless, There Will Be More Firms Using AI in Design Thinking

Despite our prediction that design thinking will become less exciting and more predictable, many firms will still adopt AI in design thinking. The primary reason is simple: AI lowers costs and increases the speed of design thinking processes. As previously mentioned, speed and cost are measurable metrics, and in a competitive marketplace, these factors drive companies to implement AI in design thinking.

However, there will still be designers (particularly design traditionalists) and possibly "high-quality" design firms that charge a premium for their human design thinking work, relying more heavily on human input in the process. These companies and designers do not compete on cost but instead may position human-designed work as superior to AI-driven designs. Similar to the Arts and Crafts movement that emerged in response to industrialization, we anticipate a human-design movement reacting to the growing influence of AI in design thinking. This trend might even result in labels on products and services such as "100% human-designed" or "human-made." That said, only a small number of companies in niche markets are likely to resist integrating AI into their design thinking processes.

Fewer Art-Based Designers (Design Agnostics)

We predict that the efficiency gains in the design thinking process will result in an overall reduction in the number of designers and innovators employed. Some argue that these efficiency gains will enable designers and innovators to focus on higher value adding activities; however, it is not clear that such a direction will emerge. Compare this with the parallel argument made regarding workers in blue collar occupations in Western countries when manufacturing jobs shifted to China and other Asian countries. The idea then was that China would focus on low-quality and low-cost products, while Western manufacturers would focus on high-quality goods. In practice, this rarely materialized. Instead, China developed their own technology and industrial capabilities, which allowed them to compete in production of high-quality goods.

Similarly, the use of AI will likely result in efficiency gains for design thinking, such as shortened product development cycles and reduced employee hours, which lead to lower costs. To stay competitive, other firms will also incorporate AI in their design thinking processes to reduce costs. The cost savings will become a source of price competition, making it difficult for these efficiencies to benefit designers and innovators, particularly those early in their careers who may not get the opportunity to work on relatively simple designs which have been appropriated by AI.

This shift will increase demand for designers and innovators with AI skills (e.g., technological futurists), often those with engineering backgrounds or degrees from technical universities. Conversely, designers in the AI agnostic group are disproportionately likely to lose their jobs as their skill sets become less valued.

We also anticipate another boom for non-educated designers working in design thinking projects. Like the technological futurists, they have limited training in design and can currently benefit the most from AI, since AI can take over some of the skills, they are lacking. This could lead to a somewhat strange situation in which most designs will originate from non-educated designers. Their designs might be good enough for most purposes, leading to a complete revolution of design. The idea that everyone is a designer takes on a new meaning, enabled by AI.

In the next chapter, we will discuss the future skillset of designers and innovators. As with other technological advancements, one must consider which skills remain relevant, and which new skills become important with as the discipline transforms. This transformation will take time as individual designers and innovators gradually acquire the necessary skills.

Summary

This chapter provided an overview of the current perception and use of AI in design thinking, as well as an ideal situation for the relationship between AI and human designers and innovators. Current perceptions of the impact of AI on design thinking are mixed, ranging from a hyped view that everything will change and the future lies in AI to a very skeptical view that AI is just another fad unable to contribute productively to design thinking. As is often the case, the truth is somewhere in between.

The current use of AI in design thinking is largely limited to that of a tool. This narrow use wastes its potential impact and utility to innovators. While the future might hold the replacement of the human designer or innovator, this is not possible at the moment. Hence, we suggest the metaphor of AI as a collaborator to indicate that AI is more than a tool but not yet a full designer or innovator. This will require designers and innovators to develop new skills and gain more knowledge in order to successfully supervise AI. We will discuss this in the next chapter.

References

Clark, M., & Graff, D. (2025). AI & design collaboration: Not a full member (yet). In S. Dubrow &, S. Paletz (eds.) *AI in Teams*. Emerald Press, Leeds.

Hernández-Ramírez, R., & Ferreira, J. B. (2024). The future end of design work: A critical overview of managerialism, generative ai, and the nature of knowledge work, and why craft remains relevant. She Ji: The Journal of Design, Economics, and Innovation, 10(4): 414–40. https://doi.org/10.1016/j.sheji.2024.11.002

Jones, J. C. (1970). Design methods: Seeds of human futures. Wiley-Interscience, London.

Kelly, S., Kaye, S. A., & Oviedo-Trespalacios, O. (2023). What factors contribute to the acceptance of artificial intelligence? A systematic review. Telematics and Informatics, 77(February): 101925. https://doi.org/10.1016/j.tele.2022.101925

Kober, G. (2025). AI-first leadership: Embracing the future of work. Available via https://www.harvardbusiness.org/insight/ai-first-leadership-embracing-the-fut ure-of-work/. Accessed 10 Sep 2025.

Marangunić, N., & Granić, A. (2015). Technology acceptance model: A literature review from 1986 to 2013. Universal Access in the Information Society, 14(1): 81–95. https://doi.org/10.1007/s10209-014-0348-1

Vaccaro, M., Almaatouq, A., & Malone, T. (2024). When combinations of humans and AI are useful: A systematic review and meta-analysis. Nature Human Behavior, 8: 2293–2303. https://doi.org/10.1038/s41562-024-02024-1

Verganti, R., Vendraminelli, L., & Iansiti, M. (2020). Innovation and design in the age of artificial intelligence. Journal of Product Innovation Management, 37(3): 212–27. https://doi.org/10.1111/jpim.12523

Wilson, H. J., & Daugherty, P. R. (2018). Human + machine: Reimagining work in the age of ai. Harvard Business Review Press, Boston.

Zhang, G., Raina, A., Cagan, J., & McComb, C. (2021). A cautionary tale about the impact of ai on human design teams. Design Studies, 72:100990. https://doi.org/10.1016/j.destud.2021.100990

4

Reskilling of Design Thinkers in the Age of Generative AI

Design thinkers include professionals engaged in creative problem-solving and design processes, from graphic and UX designers to architects, product developers, marketing strategists, and others who employ design thinking. These individuals shape visual artifacts, user experiences, business models, and more. Today, they face another new wave of technological change as AI enters the workplace, particularly in its generative AI form (creating new content based on data patterns, rather than merely classifying or analyzing data). Much like past innovations like photography, CAD, or desktop publishing before it, generative AI is redefining workflows and required competencies. To remain relevant, design thinkers must adapt by reskilling—acquiring new tools, knowledge, and mindsets.

This chapter examines this imperative in three parts. The first part reviews historical precedents, showing that the need to reskill has always been integral to design practice. The next part outlines emerging areas of skill needed for the AI era, supported by academic and industry insights. The third part offers strategic recommendations for designers and organizations to navigate this transition, with examples from leading organizations and experts.

Reskilling Is Essential for Design Thinking Effectiveness

Technological and conceptual advances have always driven designers and innovators to acquire new skills. History offers many examples of designers and innovators adapting to disruptive tools or paradigms. Below we highlight five

© The Author(s), under exclusive license to Springer Nature Switzerland AG 2026
D. Graff et al., *Design Thinking with Artificial Intelligence*, Palgrave Executive Essentials, https://doi.org/10.1007/978-3-032-10543-1_4

concise examples spanning the nineteenth to twenty-first centuries where designers had to reskill in response to major innovations.

The Invention of Photography

Before 1839, creating a realistic image required a master painter. The debut of photography was a shock to the art and design world, prompting fears about the future of painting—although the often-quoted lament "From today, painting is dead!" attributed to Paul Delaroche is likely apocryphal as noted by Batchen in 1993. But artists adapted. Rather than emulate the camera, they pioneered new expressive movements—impressionism, symbolism, expressionism—emphasizing qualities the lens could not. As Edvard Munch said, he had *no fear of photography as long as it cannot be used in heaven and hell. I am going to paint people who breathe, feel, love, and suffer.* Some artists also learned to use photography as a tool, such as for reference images, blending aspects into their own creation process. Ultimately, painting did not die; it transformed, as stated by Mirzoeff in 2023. Designers and artists broadened their skillset, mastering the new medium or doubling down on uniquely human creative skills. Far from making artists obsolete, photography expanded the creative toolkit.

From Hand Drafting to Computer-Aided Design

For architects, engineers, and product designers, the advent of computer-aided design (CAD) software was revolutionary. Prior to the 1980s, technical designers spent years honing manual drafting techniques with pen and ink on paper, technical sketching, and physical blueprint production. In 1982, Autodesk released AutoCAD, one of the first widely adopted CAD programs for personal computers. Within a few years, CAD began replacing the drafting table. This shift demanded reskilling, encouraging architects and design engineers to learn to create and manipulate digital drawings on screen.

Designers who once used T-squares and drafting pencils now needed fluency in software commands, coordinates, and layers. The change was not merely technical; it altered design workflows and increased productivity and precision. Firms that adopted CAD could iterate faster and collaborate on digital files, leaving non-adopters at a disadvantage. CAD did not eliminate the need for architects or engineers, but it did change the skills profile of those roles dramatically.

Mastery of CAD commands, coordinates, and layers became essential—and firms that adopted quickly surged ahead. Later, 3D Building Information

Modeling (BIM) added further demands. CAD did not make architects obsolete, but it redefined their skill requirements (as stated by Pérez-Sánchez et al., in 2017), proving that reskilling enables survival through technological upheaval.

The Rise of Photoshop and Digital Publishing

Graphic designers underwent a major reskilling in the late twentieth century with the shift from purely print and analog methods to digital image editing and desktop publishing. The 1990s brought Photoshop, Illustrator, and desktop publishing software, revolutionizing graphic design. Techniques once demanding hours—photo retouching, darkroom photo processing, paste-up layouts—could be done in minutes, given the skill to run the software. Designers trained in analog methods either reskilled or risked irrelevance. Typographic and compositional principles persisted, but digital fluency became decisive. Firms that upskilled their teams gained a distinct edge. This episode parallels AI today: initially experimental, but quickly normalized and indispensable.

In parallel, Adobe Illustrator brought vector graphics to the desktop, and PageMaker/ InDesign enabled desktop publishing. Graphic designers had to learn these software tools to stay relevant in advertising, publishing, and media. Many mid-career designers went through training courses to master digital production. New design graduates entered the market with fluent computer skills, raising the bar for everyone. The outcome was a more efficient and experimental design process; innovators could prototype and revise artwork with unprecedented freedom.

This period shows how tool fluency became a critical part of design competence. Traditional typography and layout knowledge remained important but needed to be executed with new digital techniques. Firms that invested in reskilling their designers (or hiring digitally skilled ones) gained a competitive edge in the 1990s. This historical shift parallels today's AI tools: initially seen as novel, within a decade they became industry-standard. Designers and innovators once again learned that adapting to new software was part of their professional evolution.

Market Modeling and Simulation Tools

It is not just visual designers who have faced reskilling; business designers have also had to adapt. In the 1980s, the debut of spreadsheets like VisiCalc in 1979, Lotus 1-2-3 in 1983, and Excel in 1985 revolutionized strategy and financial design. Entire teams relearned workflows, replacing ledgers with formulas and scenario analysis, while business schools mandated spreadsheet proficiency. The shift enabled faster, data-driven decisions and expanded what strategists could achieve. Subsequent decades introduced specialized simulation software—from supply chains to financial risk—again requiring reskilling. In the 1980s, millions of copies of spreadsheet programs were sold, putting sophisticated financial and statistical modeling tools into the hands of people who, only a few years earlier, likely didn't even know what a spreadsheet was, as stated by Pallatto in 2013.

Entire departments had to reskill. Accountants and marketers learned to use Excel formulas instead of ledger books; business schools began requiring spreadsheet proficiency. This wave of reskilling was enabled by organizations investing in computer training and individuals realizing these digital skills were now core to their roles. By replacing paper-based workflows, spreadsheets also expanded what designers of business strategies could do—enabling rapid what-if analyses and data-driven decision making. Similarly, in the 1990s and 2000s, specialized simulation tools (for market research, financial risk, supply chain modeling, etc.) emerged, requiring analysts to acquire new technical competencies. The general pattern is that as analytical design tools improve, professionals must continuously update their skills.

History Tells Us to Reskill

To continue innovating, or at least to keep pace with competitors, designers have persistently adapted to new tools and paradigms through photography, printing presses, digital publishing, CAD, data modeling, and more. The pattern is clear: new technologies have not ever eliminated the need for designers, but instead demanded that they update their competencies. For each challenge, core creative problem-solving endured while the technical profile of the profession evolved. Generative AI and related AI programs are only the latest chapter in this ongoing story. Embracing history reminds us that adaptation is possible—and necessary.

Skills in the Generative AI Age

As generative AI systems such as GPT-5, DALL·E, and others integrate into design workflows, the profile of valuable skills is evolving. Designers and innovators now need to cultivate a blend of technical, cognitive, and collaborative abilities to work effectively with these programs. This section explores the key skill areas required in the generative AI era, drawing on academic research and industry reports to support each.

These emerging skills include working with AI as a collaborator, prompt engineering, problem decomposition for AI, curating AI outputs, and continuous learning. Importantly, many of these are extensions of classic design competencies rather than wholesale replacements. The ability to learn and adapt is itself becoming a critical skill, since the half-life of technical expertise grows shorter in the face of rapid AI advancement, as emphasized by Brynjolfsson et al., in 2018 and Fernández Vallejo in 2025.

Working with Machines: Shared Mental Models and AI "Theory of Mind"

Design thinkers increasingly find themselves working alongside AI assistants or even co-pilots, whether the AI is an image generation model creating concept art or a language model that suggests UX copy. To collaborate effectively with AI, designers and innovators need a mental model of how these AI programs "think." In cognitive science terms, this resembles developing a "theory of mind" for the AI—an understanding of its capabilities, limitations, likely biases, and modes of failure. Researchers in human–AI teams emphasize the importance of shared mental models between humans and AI for effective collaboration, as stated by cf. Andrews et al., in 2023.

In human teams, a shared mental model, meaning a common understanding of goals, tasks, and each other's roles, enables members to align efforts and communicate efficiently, which improves performance, as emphasized by Schmutz et al., in 2024. Similarly, when working with an AI system, a designer should cultivate an understanding of the AI's "knowledge" (what data it was trained on), its constraints (for example, an image model's difficulty with certain compositions, or a chatbot's tendency to output fluent but inaccurate text), and its decision logic (if interpretable). This allows the human to predict how AI will respond and plan accordingly—in essence, to trust but verify.

One aspect of this skill is data literacy: knowing that generative models are only as strong as the training data they learned from, and that they may reflect biases or gaps in that data. For instance, an AI image generator might produce biased results if its training images lacked diversity. A designer or innovator using such a system for marketing content must be aware of this and check outputs for fairness and inclusivity. The Nielsen Norman Group, a leading UX consultancy, advises that as AI becomes a "trusted collaborator," designers must assess the biases it may introduce, since AI algorithms "reflect the limitations and biases existing in the world" through their training data, as noted by Fernández Vallejo in 2025. In practice, this means building the habit of critically reviewing what the AI produces, rather than accepting it at face value—much like a senior designer or innovator might review a junior designer's work with an eye for what might be missing or misaligned.

Another facet is developing a collaborative mindset with AI. Rather than seeing AI as a mere tool, design thinkers can treat it as a collaborator that has a role in the design process. This aligns with what Wilson and Daugherty in 2018 describe as "collaborative intelligence," where humans and AI actively enhance each other's complementary strengths—the leadership, creativity, and social skills of humans combined with the speed and scalability of AI. This involves communicating goals clearly to the AI, often through prompts or parameters, and interpreting the AI's output in context. Some experts describe this as "AI stewardship," guiding the AI by setting the right constraints and providing feedback, as described by Verhulst in 2025. For example, a product designer might iteratively adjust prompts to get an AI-generated UI layout closer to a desired style, effectively coaching the AI. This requires patience, imagination, and an experimental approach. It also helps for designers to have a basic understanding of how AI models learn.

Prompt Engineering: Communicating with AI

Generative AI programs do not work autonomously; they respond to human prompts. Crafting effective prompts, the instructions or queries given to an AI to elicit a result, has become a pivotal skill often referred to as "prompt engineering." In the context of design thinking, prompt engineering might involve describing a visual style in text to an image generator, scripting a scene for an AI to render, or asking a chatbot to generate copy in a specific tone. The goal is to communicate intent in a way that yields useful output. This requires understanding both the language and the logic that the AI model responds to.

Prompt engineering has gained such prominence that it is even being described as a profession in its own right, at least in the short term. AI prompt engineering topped the World Economic Forum's 2023 list of future jobs, with OpenAI's Sam Altman describing it as a remarkably high-impact skill, as stated by Acar in 2023. Early adopters in design and marketing are already showcasing "magic prompts" that produce impressive results from text-to-image models or ChatGPT-like systems. This enthusiasm underscores a reality: those who know how to speak the AI program's language can unlock exponentially more value from it. For design thinkers, even if prompt engineering does not remain a standalone job in the long run, it is certainly a key competency now, much like how knowing keyboard shortcuts or coding simple scripts can supercharge one's use of software.

In practice, prompt engineering involves careful wording, providing context, and sometimes giving step-by-step instructions to guide the AI. For example, a UX writer using a generative text model to draft interface microcopy might prompt: *"You are an expert UX writer. Write five alternative tool-tip texts for a file upload button, in a friendly and concise tone, at most five words each."* Such a prompt gives the AI a role, context, specific task, style guidance, and constraints. Getting adept at this requires trial and error; the design thinker learns which phrases or parameters produce the best outcomes, much like adjusting knobs on a complex machine. This is a new type of design thinking vocabulary to master; one composed of keywords and phrases that the AI interprets effectively.

Recent analyses caution, however, that prompt engineering as a discrete skill might be a temporary advantage. As AI models improve in interpreting intent, and as user interfaces for AI become more sophisticated, the need for elaborate prompt engineering could diminish. A Harvard Business Review analysis argues that the more enduring skill will be the ability to formulate problems well, rather than simply writing clever prompts, as noted by Acar in 2023. In other words, if you know exactly what problem you are trying to solve, you can prompt AI or any tool more effectively. This involves clarity in defining the design goal and success criteria. At present, prompt engineering is closely tied to problem formulation, breaking down a request in a way the AI can process and respond to.

For validation, LinkedIn data shows a surge in demand for prompt engineering know-how. AI literacy skills, including prompt engineering and proficiency with tools such as ChatGPT, have increased more than sixfold in demand in one year, according to a 2025 World Economic Forum report (World Economic Forum & LinkedIn Economic Graph, 2025). Furthermore, more than half of hiring managers in one survey said they would not hire a candidate who lacks AI literacy skills, which include the ability to craft prompts that yield useful results. These indicators reinforce that prompt engineering is becoming a baseline competency for knowledge workers, designers included.

Mastering prompt techniques can significantly amplify a designer's productivity and the quality of AI-generated content. It is a skill learned through practice: by iteratively refining prompts and observing the AI's responses, people designers train themselves to "speak AI" more fluently.

Breaking Goals into Tasks for AI: Problem Decomposition and Orchestration

Another critical skill in the generative AI era is the ability to decompose high-level design thinking goals into a sequence of tasks that either a machine or a human can execute. AI programs tend to perform best on specific, narrowly defined tasks, such as "generate 10 logo concepts in a flat illustration style" or "draft a user persona description based on these data." They are less effective at intuitively addressing broad goals such as "design me a successful product" without guidance. Therefore, designers must play the role of orchestrators, mapping out processes where AI is used for what it does well, and human insight is applied where it is needed.

This skill is essentially problem-solving and project scoping elevated to new importance. In the past, a design thinker might informally break down a project into steps such as research, ideation, prototyping, testing, and refinement. Now, with AI in the mix, the design thinker deliberately considers which of those steps can be accelerated or enhanced by AI, and how to set that up. For instance, a service designer might break a challenge into sub-tasks such as:

1. Generate a range of journey map diagrams using AI based on different customer data points
2. Use AI to summarize user research transcripts to identify pain points
3. Manually synthesize the AI outputs with domain knowledge to propose solutions
4. Use AI to create visuals or scenarios illustrating those solutions
5. Conduct human-led final evaluation and storytelling

Each step is well defined so that either the AI or the service designer knows exactly what to do. Experts highlight that problem formulation is paramount in leveraging AI. A recent summary by Mollick et al., 2024, in Harvard Business Review put it succinctly: "Without a well-formulated problem, even the most sophisticated prompts will fall short." This means the designer must clearly articulate the problem and its sub-problems. Key sub-skills include diagnosing the core issue, breaking a complex challenge into manageable parts, and reframing the problem if needed. These are classic design thinking abilities, but they now apply not only to understanding users or markets but also to instructing AI. You must first determine exactly what you want the AI to do before worrying about how to ask it. In practical terms, if a project goal is to "increase e-commerce conversion rate through better UI," the designer might deconstruct this into smaller problems such as "improve product page layout," "optimize call-to-action phrasing," and "streamline checkout flow." Each of these can be tackled in part with AI assistance, for example by generating alternative layouts, suggesting button text, or analyzing drop-off points from data.

Being an effective orchestrator with AI also involves workflow design, meaning knowing how to intersperse AI tasks with human judgment. Generative AI often produces drafts or sets of options that require human selection and refinement. The designer or innovator should be adept at setting up this iterative loop. For example, an AI might generate 50 rough logo ideas. The designer then evaluates and selects five promising ones, asks AI to elaborate variations of those five, and finally polishes the top choice by hand. In this way, the broader goal of "get a great logo" is broken into an orchestrated sequence of AI generation and human curation steps. In a sense, the designer is now part creator and part project manager, while the AI functions as a collaborator executing specific tasks.

To support this skill, organizations can document best practices that clarify where AI fits into design processes. For example, IBM has developed "AI design guidelines" for its teams, outlining at which stages AI programs can be applied. Designers and innovators also benefit from familiarity with multiple AI programs, since this allows them to select the right program for each subtask, such as using a text generator for content ideas or an image generator for visuals. This connects to the idea of tool fluency, which will be discussed later in this section.

Shaping AI Outputs into Coherent Narratives and Designs

AI can produce an abundance of content-images, text, layouts, and code but quantity does not equal quality or coherence. Researchers and industry experts have identified curation and editing of AI-generated output as an emerging critical skill for designers as argued by Tsipursky in 2024; Fernández Vallejo in 2025; and Zhang et al., in 2025. One of the emerging skills for designers is acting as a curator and editor of AI-generated output. In other words, design thinkers must take often disparate or rough outputs from AI and shape them into polished, contextually appropriate narratives or designs that serve the project goals. This requires traditional design judgment, storyboarding ability, and an eye for detail, applied in new ways.

An analogy can be made to the role of an editor in writing or a curator in art. When an AI generates dozens of variations or a long piece of content, someone must decide what is on target, what to discard, and how to weave the pieces together into a cohesive result. Rather than creating every element from scratch, the design thinker now guides, selects, adapts, and integrates AI contributions.

Concretely, this skill might involve reviewing multiple AI-generated design concepts and picking the best elements from each, then combining them into one stronger design. It might involve taking an AI-drafted text and editing it heavily to align with brand voice and logical flow, or using AI to generate data charts and then rearranging those charts into a compelling presentation storyline. Narrative assembly is often key: AI can provide the pieces, but the human must arrange those pieces meaningfully. For instance, an AI might output a set of user persona descriptions given some data, but the design thinker needs to package those personas into a narrative that the product team can easily grasp and act on. That could mean editing the AI text for clarity, adding insights the AI missed, and presenting it in a persona template that ties back to design goals.

Another aspect of this skill is imparting human empathy and context to AI outputs. AI does not inherently understand emotional subtleties or cultural context the way humans do. Designers and innovators therefore ensure that outputs resonate with real user needs and feelings. This curator role aligns with what Wilson and Daugherty in 2018 describe as humans needing to "sustain" AI outputs—ensuring responsible use and contextual appropriateness. They also balance innovation with practicality when refining AI outputs. AI can generate wild ideas or overly recognize solutions that look good in isolation but may not be feasible. The human design thinker applies domain knowledge and practical constraints to filter those. A curator mindset means not just choosing the most visually appealing output, but the one that best meets the project's requirements and can be implemented. In product design, this could mean selecting an AI-suggested design that respects accessibility guidelines and technical constraints, even if another suggestion looked flashier. The designer's trained judgment is critical here, recognizing what ideas to push forward and what to set aside.

This shift from creation to curation has been highlighted by industry observers. Tsipursky in 2024 argues that as generative AI becomes more proficient at producing ideas, the human role shifts toward selecting, refining, and promoting the most valuable concepts—a transition from creators to curators. In the design world, early evidence of this is seen in how agencies are using AI. Many firms have internal processes where junior designers, or now AI, generate a broad range of concepts, and senior designers then curate and refine the best ones for presentation to clients. The senior designer's skill in storytelling—explaining why a particular concept works is as important as ever. Generative AI does not replace that; if anything, having more initial options means the designer must be even more decisive and narrative-focused to avoid confusion.

Continuous Learning and Tool Fluency

Finally, an overarching skill that enables all others is the commitment to continuous learning and maintaining fluency in emerging tools. Designers and innovators who thrive will be those who view learning as a lifelong endeavor and who can quickly become competent with new software or AI systems.

Data strongly supports this need. A report by Boston Consulting Group notes that the average half-life of professional skills is now less than 5 years, and in fast-changing fields it may be as short as two and a half years according to Goel & Kovács-Ondrejkovic, 2023. This means that roughly half of what you learned five years ago may already be outdated. Generative AI illustrates this well. A designer who learned a prototyping tool or programming language a few years ago might now find it partially replaced by AI-driven tools that require different knowledge. Designers must therefore be prepared to refresh and upgrade their skills frequently. World Economic Forum's Future of Jobs analysis in 2020 projected that 50% of all employees would need reskilling by 2025 due to technology adoption as stated by World Economic Forum in 2020, a figure that likely rose further with the 2023 AI breakthroughs. Moreover, the World Economic Forum's analysis found that about 40% of the global workforce will need to reskill in the next three years because of AI and automation as noted by World Economic Forum in 2025. These figures underscore that continuous learning is not simply a personal aspiration but an economic imperative.

For design thinkers, tool fluency specifically means being comfortable trying and using new software, plugins, and AI services as they appear. For example, if a new generative layout tool emerges that can auto-generate UI code from sketches, a forward-looking designer will experiment with it, take an online tutorial, and consider how to integrate it into their workflow. This does not mean chasing every new tool at the expense of depth. It means cultivating a versatile toolkit. It is similar to being multilingual: the more "languages" or tools you speak, the more options you have to solve problems. And if one language falls out of use, you learn the next one. In design history, those who knew only one software often struggled when it was replaced, while those with the meta-skill of learning new tools could transition smoothly.

Continuous learning also involves staying updated on conceptual developments, not just tools. As AI ethics and regulations grow in importance, designers and innovators should educate themselves on responsible AI principles. As new methodologies emerge, such as AI-driven design thinking, they should attend workshops or read up to understand them. Many organizations support this by providing training budgets, time for courses, or access to e-learning platforms. Forward-looking innovators also take initiative by enrolling in Massive Online Open Courses, commonly referred to as MOOCs, participating in design thinking communities, or working on personal side projects to recognize new skills.

Crucially, continuous learning is as much a mindset as it is an activity. It requires humility-the recognition that there is always more to learn and curiosity. A designer or innovator may hold an MBA and have 20 years of experience, but in the face of AI they become a student again. Those who embrace this will find learning rewarding, while those who resist may feel increasingly anxious as the gap widens. Cultivating a growth mindset, where each new tool learned is seen as an investment in adaptability, helps reduce the fear of obsolescence. From a strategic perspective, companies are also recognizing continuous learning as a core competency. McKinsey's research shows that leading companies in AI adoption are significantly more likely to invest in talent development and ongoing training for their workforce as stated by Relyea et al., in 2024.

These organizations understand that tools alone do not create value; it is the people skilled in using them who do. Design thinkers should therefore take advantage of any upskilling programs offered by their employers, and managers should treat reskilling as a strategic priority rather than a one-time event. Building a learning culture across organizations will support individual designers in continuous skill development. As new AI tools appear, a continuously learning designer will quickly evaluate their usefulness, learn to use them if relevant, and integrate them into their repertoire. This adaptability may be the single most important skill in the long run, because it ensures that the designer's abilities remain aligned with whatever the future of design may hold.

Reskilling Strategies in the Generative AI Age

Facing the rapid changes brought by generative AI, design thinkers and the organizations that employ them need clear strategies to reskill and upskill. It is not enough to identify what new skills are needed; one must also implement how to gain those skills effectively and adapt roles accordingly. This section provides research-backed recommendations for reskilling in the AI era. The insights are drawn from sources such as the World Economic Forum, IBM, McKinsey, and design-focused organizations, as well as lessons from previous technology transitions. These strategies can guide both individual designers planning their career development and business leaders shaping workforce training. Key recommendations include: leveraging domain expertise, keeping up with tools continuously, collaborating across disciplines, building AI literacy for all, focusing on uniquely human skills, and staying user-centered and ethical in design.

Leverage and Deepen Your Domain Expertise

In a world of powerful general-purpose AI, an innovator's domain-specific knowledge becomes a critical differentiator. Domain expertise refers to a deep understanding of a particular field or industry for example, an automotive UI designer's knowledge of driver behavior or a financial services marketing designer's grasp of customer psychology in banking. Staying rooted in a domain (and expanding that expertise) is a strategic move because it provides the context in which AI programs perform best under human guidance. AI may provide rapid options, but it takes a domain-savvy designer to judge what solutions make sense in the real world. As one tech consulting firm phrased it, automation and "Human AI" should put innovation power directly in the hands of those who understand problems best.

Research by global consulting group McKinsey & Company supports the value of combining AI skills with domain know-how, as noted by Relyea et al., 2024. They note that organizations should develop not just general AI fluency but also deep expertise in their field. A designer with technical prompt writing skill is less valuable than, for example, a UX designer who knows e-commerce, enabling her to use AI to create better shopping experiences. We further suggest that innovators should develop proficiency in multiple areas, moving from what is referred to as a "t-shaped" skillset (deep knowledge in one area shown as a vertical line on a graph) to a more "pie-shaped" set of expertise domains. This is consistent with calls by designers, such as Lee in 2025, to draw on interdisciplinarity to address challenging innovation problems. For instance, our UX designer might add understanding of consumer psychology to their e-commerce and AI knowledge, furthering their utility to resolve retail strategy dilemma. This approach capitalizes on what AI currently lacks: contextual understanding.

From a career perspective, doubling down on domain expertise also insulates designers and innovators from being easily replaced. AI can produce competent generic designs but often misses niche requirements. A public-sector service designer, for example, knows the policy constraints and social factors that an AI will not consider unless explicitly instructed. That kind of insight comes from experience and continuous learning in the domain, which designers should treat as a lifelong journey. Moreover, domain experts can play key roles in training and fine-tuning AI systems. Many companies already involve their experienced designers in refining AI models, whether by feeding them proprietary data or providing evaluation feedback. An AI guided by domain experts will learn more relevant patterns. Maintaining domain expertise is therefore not just about using AI, it is also about improving it.

Embrace Continuous Learning and Keep Up with Tools

As emphasized earlier, continuous learning is both a skill and a strategy. To reskill effectively in the AI age, design thinkers and their organizations must integrate ongoing learning into daily routines. This involves proactive steps such as taking courses on new design software infused with AI, attending webinars or conference talks on AI in design thinking, experimenting hands-on with new tools, and learning from peers. The World Economic Forum identifies active learning and learning strategies as top skills for the workforce of the future, stressing that employees must update skills frequently as roles evolve.

Forward-looking companies create structured "learning paths" for designer-curated sets of courses or projects that build AI-related competencies over time. Some establish internal guilds or communities of practice where designers share tips on using AI in projects, fostering peer-to-peer learning. McKinsey's 2024 report recommends treating reskilling as a continuous change management initiative, not a one-off training session as stated by Relyea et al., in 2024. Leaders should communicate that learning is part of the job and even a criterion for advancement. Organizations also need to provide resources and time for learning. For instance, major technology companies have launched AI upskilling initiatives for their employees, recognizing that approximately 40% of workers will need significant skills upgrades due to generative AI.

A practical approach is to integrate learning into everyday work. For example, when starting a new design task, consider whether an AI program might help and learn it in the context of that project. This way the learning is immediately applied. Another helpful tactic is to maintain a personal curriculum. Keep a list of tools and skills you want to learn, along with resources to explore and a way to track your progress. Treat it like a personal development Kanban board to keep goals visible and manageable.

Collaborate Across Disciplines and Hybridize Skills

AI is blurring the lines between traditionally siloed roles. A UX designer might now work closely with a data scientist to fine-tune an AI model for personalization, while a graphic designer might collaborate with a machine learning engineer to develop a custom image generator for a brand. A key strategy is therefore to embrace interdisciplinary collaboration. Designers and innovators should not only deepen their own domain (as discussed in previous recommendations) but also develop an appreciation for adjacent fields and be willing to work in cross-functional teams more than ever.

Collaboration across disciplines means breaking down barriers between design, engineering, data science, marketing, and other functions to jointly create value with AI. A report by the Nielsen Norman Group envisioned "radical interdisciplinary collaboration" enabled by AI, where "cross-functional teammates could engage with your domain in ways that seem impossible today, while you simultaneously gain the ability to contribute meaningfully to theirs," as argued by Pablo Fernández Vallejo in 2025.

In practical terms, AI programs can act as a kind of universal translator between experts. For instance, a designer can use an AI program to generate preliminary code for a prototype, edging into engineering, while an engineer might use an AI-driven design tool to create a draft interface, stepping into design. They then refine each other's work collaboratively.

At the organizational level, one practical strategy is to form "fusion teams." These are small groups created for a specific project and intentionally composed of members from different departments. For example, a digital innovation task force might include a designer, a data scientist, a marketer, and an IT specialist. IBM highlights fusion teams as a way to accelerate AI adoption and drive innovation, since they combine perspectives and can iterate quickly. Designers in such teams serve as user advocates and creative synthesizers, while also learning technical constraints and opportunities directly from colleagues.

Build AI Literacy and Fluency Across the Team

A fundamental strategy for reskilling in the AI era is to ensure AI literacy for yourself and your team. AI literacy means understanding at a conceptual level how AI works, what its capabilities and limitations are, and how to critically evaluate and interact with AI outputs. It does not require coding AI algorithms from scratch (unless that is your role), but it does require being conversant in AI. For design thinkers, this might include knowing the difference between a generative model and a rule-based system, understanding terms such as neural networks, training data, bias, and overfitting, and being aware of the ethical issues AI can raise.

AI fluency goes beyond knowledge to hands-on comfort. Designers and innovators should integrate small uses of AI into their daily work to build confidence. For example, use an AI writing assistant to draft an email or apply a simple script to sort data, then reflect on the result. Over time, interacting with AI becomes second nature. Organizations can support this by incorporating AI programs into standard toolkits, but with guidance. If a company adopts a generative image library, for instance, designers should receive a tutorial on how to query it effectively and how to evaluate outputs responsibly. The goal is to remove fear and mystery through regular exposure.

Another essential part of AI literacy is ethical and critical awareness. Design thinkers must understand issues such as algorithmic bias, privacy concerns when user data trains models, and intellectual property questions around AI-generated content. Guidelines published by organizations like the World Economic Forum, Google's AI Principles, or IBM's Trustworthy AI framework are useful resources. Designers can translate these into practical actions, such as ensuring human review of AI outputs in sensitive scenarios or initiating team discussions on inclusivity: Are our AI-driven design decisions fair to all user groups?

AI literacy should be seen as a baseline expectation for everyone on the team, not just one expert. Some companies are already treating it this way. Global banks and consulting firms, for example, have launched company-wide AI awareness programs, similar to how basic computer literacy was taught in the 1990s. Design leaders could advocate for including "AI 101 for designers" in professional development plans. An AI-literate team can harness tools effectively, avoid costly mistakes, and signal to employers and clients that they are forward-thinking professionals who understand the emerging landscape.

Focus on Uniquely Human Skills and Values

While designers sharpen their technical skills, it is equally strategic to cultivate the uniquely human attributes that AI cannot yet replicate. These include creativity, empathy, intuition, leadership, and ethical judgment. Numerous reports conclude that as AI takes over routine tasks, human soft skills will become more important, not less, according to World Economic Forum & LinkedIn Economic Graph from 2025.

For design thinkers, this means doubling down on the human-centered mindset of creativity and empathy. By engaging directly with users and grounding design in lived experiences, designers ensure that end results are meaningful and compassionate. AI outputs can provide options, but only human insight can interpret user stories, cultural context, and emotional resonance. IDEO, long known for its human-centered ethos, often emphasizes storytelling and user journeys. Those narratives come from understanding people's experiences-something AI cannot authentically achieve.

AI can also be used as a creative provocation rather than a replacement. A designer or innovator might look at an AI-generated concept and ask: "What is a completely different approach the AI did not consider?" In this way, AI stimulates imagination rather than constrains it.

Leadership and communication are other human skills that grow in importance. As teams integrate AI, someone must lead decisions about how and when to use it, how to interpret its suggestions, and how to explain the design direction to clients or executives. Designers who can articulate why a design works, including how AI contributed, will excel. Storytelling remains a vital tool. While AI may generate slide templates, it will not craft the compelling vision that convinces stakeholders. That responsibility remains human.

Summary

The age of generative AI presents both a challenge and an opportunity for design thinkers. The challenge is clear: many tasks that designers and innovators once performed can now be partly automated, and the skills in demand are shifting. Yet history and current research show that those who adapt will not be replaced. Instead, they will enhance their roles and often find even greater creative scope with AI as a partner. The opportunity is to elevate the role of the designer into that of strategist, curator, and visionary who harnesses AI's power. By reskilling in the technical, cognitive, and interpersonal areas discussed, designers can continue to deliver unique value that AI alone cannot.

Design as a discipline has always lived at the intersection of technology and humanity. Generative AI does not change that—it only changes the tools at hand. As this chapter outlined, reskilling is not a new phenomenon for designers. It has always been part of the profession's evolution. Those entering the field or currently practicing should take heart: by *staying flexible, learning continuously, and keeping user needs front and center, they can* navigate this latest transformation successfully. In practice, a designer or innovator in 2025 might have begun to learn to brainstorm with a GPT-based ideation partner, use an image generator for mood boards, or rely on AI analytics for user insights. At the same time, they will spend more energy orchestrating solutions, telling compelling stories, and ensuring that the final design resonates on a human level.

For leaders managing design teams or products that involve design thinking, the mandate is to support and steer these reskilling efforts. Encourage designers and innovators to acquire new skills, provide them with training and tools, and foster a culture where human creativity and AI efficiency reinforce one another. Businesses that do this will likely see their design function become more agile and influential in the AI era, driving innovation that competitors who neglect reskilling cannot match.

References

Andrews, R. W., Lilly, J. M., Srivastava, D., & Feigh, K. M. (2023). The role of shared mental models in human-AI teams: A theoretical review. *Theoretical Issues in Ergonomics Science, 24*(2): 129–175. https://doi.org/10.1080/14639 22X.2022.2061080

Batchen, G. (1993). The naming of photography. History of Photography, 17(1), 22–32. https://doi.org/10.1080/03087298.1993.10442589

Brynjolfsson, E., Mitchell, T., & Rock, D. (2018). What Can Machines Learn and What Does It Mean for Occupations and the Economy? AEA Papers and Proceedings, 108, 43–47. https://doi.org/10.1257/pandp.20181019

Goel, S., & Ondrejkovic, O. K. (2023). Reskilling for a Rapidly Changing World. Boston Consulting Group. https://www.bcg.com/publications/2023/ reskilling-workforce-for-future

Lee, S.-H. (2025). From computation to curation: Expanding the boundaries of design practice. Design Studies, 101, 101357, https://doi.org/10.1016/j.des tud.2025.101357

Mirzoeff, N. (2023). An Introduction to Visual Culture (3rd ed.). Routledge. https:// doi.org/10.4324/9780429280238

Mollick, E., Cremer, D. D., Neeley, T., & Sinha, P. (2024). Generative AI: The Insights You Need from Harvard Business Review. Harvard Business Review Press.

Oguz, A. Acar. (2023, June 6). AI Prompt Engineering Isn't the Future. Harvard Business Review. https://hbr.org/2023/06/ai-prompt-engineering-isnt-the-future

Fernández Vallejo, P. (2025, January 3). Redefine Your Design Skills to Prepare for AI. Nielsen Norman Group. https://www.nngroup.com/articles/prepare-for-ai/

Pallatto, J. (2013, August 28). 30 Years Ago: PC Spreadsheets Bring Number Crunching to the Masses. eWEEK. https://www.eweek.com/enterprise-apps/30-years-ago-pc-spreadsheets-bring-number-crunching-to-the-masses/

Pérez-Sánchez, J. C., Mora-García, R. T., Pérez-Sánchez, V. R., & Piedecausa-García, B. (2017). From CAD to BIM: A new way to understand architecture. 45–54. https://doi.org/10.2495/BIM170051

Relyea, C., Maor, D., & Durth, S. (2024). Gen AI's next inflection point: From employee experimentation to organizational transformation. McKinsey & Company. https://www.mckinsey.com/capabilities/people-and-organizational-performance/our-insights/gen-ais-next-inflection-point-from-employee-experimentation-to-organizational-transformation

Schmutz, J. B., Outland, N., Kerstan, S., Georganta, E., & Ulfert, A.-S. (2024). AI-teaming: Redefining collaboration in the digital era. Current Opinion in Psychology, 58, 101837. https://doi.org/10.1016/j.copsyc.2024.101837

Tsipursky, G. (2024, August 28). The Generative AI Revolution Elevates Idea Curation Over Creation. https://www.wsb.com/blog/generative-ai-and-idea-curation//?utm_source=chatgpt.com

Verhulst, S. (2025). Data Stewardship Decoded: Mapping Its Diverse Manifestations and Emerging Relevance at a time of AI (arXiv:2502.10399). arXiv. https://doi.org/10.48550/arXiv.2502.10399

Wilson, H. J., & Daugherty, P. R. (2018). Collaborative intelligence: Humans and AI are joining forces. Harvard Business Review, 96, 114–123.

World Economic Forum, & LinkedIn Economic Graph. (2025). WorkChange Report: AI is Coming to Work.

World Economic Forum. (2020). The future of jobs report 2020. https://www.weforum.org/publications/the-future-of-jobs-report-2020/

World Economic Forum. (2025). The future of jobs report 2025. https://www.weforum.org/publications/the-future-of-jobs-report-2025/

Zhang, K., Zhang, X., Wu, W., Wu, S., Cai, S., & Shen, H. (2025). Redefining design competence: A framework for equipping product designers in the generativeAI era. The Design Journal, 28(3), 452–474. https://doi.org/10.1080/14606925.2025.2462862

5

Practical Guide to AID Tools

So far, we covered the concepts of design thinking (Chapter 1) and AI (Chapter 2), why to incorporate AI in design thinking (Chapter 3), and the skill set required to successfully collaborate with AI now and in the near future (Chapter 4). Beyond the general perspective on the skill sets to work with AI in design thinking, this chapter offers more specific guidance on how to use AI with the AID tools presented in this book. As shown in a report by Boston Consulting Group in 2024, only 6% of organizations have started to train their employees to use AI, as argued by Goel & Ondrejkovic in 2023. Therefore, we believe that we need to provide more specific guidance on how to use the AID tools in this book.

There is always a risk with specific guidance in a topic that is progressing so fast, as some suggestions might become obsolete relatively soon. Therefore, we tried to strike a balance between specific, executable suggestions, and more general guidance to make this chapter relevant for a longer period. Nevertheless, you need to search continuously for updates and changes in the AI environment and, consequently, how to interact with it.

The AI environment is characterized by new AI programs entering the market e.g., DeepSeek in 2025, some systems becoming obsolete for example, discontinued tools, and existing systems improving and integrating new capabilities (e.g., from GPT-3.5 to OpenAI o1). Table 5.1 illustrates these advances by showing how features changed between AI system upgrades, namely from ChatGPT 3.5 to OpenAI o1.

OpenAI not only improved the outcomes but also enhanced its interface and feature set by making it multimodal. All of this happened in only 2 years. We can only imagine what will be possible in the future. The consequence of

© The Author(s), under exclusive license to Springer Nature Switzerland AG 2026

D. Graff et al., *Design Thinking with Artificial Intelligence*, Palgrave Executive Essentials,
https://doi.org/10.1007/978-3-032-10543-1_5

Table 5.1   Upgraded Capabilities of OpenAI (adapted from McKinsey & Company, 2025)

GPT-3.5	OpenAI o1
• Introduced in Nov. 2022	• Introduced in Dec. 2024
• Text only	• Text and image (multimodal)
• Fair reasoning (bottom 10% of bar examination)	• Advanced reasoning (top 10% of bar examination)
• Limited contextual understanding	• Enhanced contextual understanding

this rapid and continuously changing AI environment is that one must keep up to date with advances in AI, recognizing both new systems and upgraded capabilities.

We divided the specific guidance into three parts, similar to the structure of design thinking. These parts are knowledge (selecting AI, understanding AI, and keeping up to date), skills (prompting and AI assistants), and cognition (critical thinking), all of which are required to work successfully with AI in design thinking. While we discuss them as individual items, they are highly interrelated.

Selecting Your AI

Selecting your AI to work with is as much about performance and costs as it is about personal choice and preference. While we can identify and present some objective criteria for AI programs, we cannot make the choice for you. Identifying the right AI program is far more complex than buying traditional software, where costs and performance are usually the main factors. Choosing an AI is more like choosing your team members. You are not only interested in hiring the smartest person, but also in someone who fits well with the existing team. The same applies to AI. We can identify objective criteria, such as costs or test results on specific tasks, but we do not know your subjective requirements and preferences. Hence, we will not suggest one AI but urge readers to find the system that fits them best. Over time, you may even build a team of AIs depending on your tasks.

Several factors will influence your choice of one AI program over another. Some of them will be straightforward, such as costs (older versions may be good enough and cheaper for your tasks than the newest version), availability, or data confidentiality. Another objective factor is the quality of responses to questions that have a clear right answer. These are often expressed in test scores. Keep in mind that the overall best AI system may not be the best for you. It may be too expensive or not perform well in the areas most relevant to you. To get an overview of different capabilities, you can consult the resources provided in this book, such as the 113 unique AI programs listed later. However, the older this book becomes, the less accurate the list will be, so you should also search online for updated comparisons.

More difficult to judge are the outcomes where no single right answer exists. For example, if AI generates product ideas, the value of the results will depend on subjective user preferences. Different AIs may generate very different designs, even with the same prompt, depending on factors such as the training data (see discussion in Chapter 2).

For such subjectively assessed outcomes, training data matters a great deal because the system uses it to statistically predict results. For example, if an AI is trained primarily on German, Chinese, or American datasets, its outcomes will reflect those cultural contexts. People quickly recognized, for instance, that DeepSeek provided different answers to world events than OpenAI. For design, cultural differences shape what is considered "good design," and AI systems will reflect these differences. Consequently, individuals will develop preferences for particular AIs, potentially leading each person to have a unique "preferred" AI.

We recommend starting with one of the large, generic AI systems but also training your own AI assistant over time. Everyone has preferences in style or worldview, and training an AI on these preferences can produce results that align more closely with your expectations. However, it is important not to build AI assistants that think in only one way, as this risks limiting perspectives. Projects often benefit from multiple viewpoints. Therefore, we suggest training different assistants for different tasks or even deliberately training an AI to provide outcomes that contradict your preferences, prompting new ways of thinking about a problem. We will discuss how to use an AI assistant in this section, and later in this book we provide an AID tool designated to building an AI Assistant and dedicate a complete Appendix 1 to building your own assistant.

AI is not merely a computer tool. It is a collaborator. Human designers and innovators need to identify the "right" AI just as they would choose the "right" colleague to join a project. In the near future, we suggest that human resource experts should be involved in identifying and "hiring" the right AI and helping to train it, rather than leaving this decision solely to information technology professionals. In the last section of this book, we provide a brief overview of the most common AIs for design thinking. Explore their capabilities, see what fits your requirements best, and begin experimenting with them.

It is also important to note that unlike human learning, machine performance can fluctuate with updates. While upgrades may improve overall capabilities, they can also introduce mistakes that did not occur in earlier versions. Research indicates that users sometimes misjudge AI after an upgrade, assuming that because it was correct before, it must still be correct now, as noted by Bansal and colleagues in 2019. Any AI update can therefore change your preferred system. This is another reason to stay informed about developments in the AI environment. In this respect, AI differs from humans, who build on previous knowledge and rarely become weaker in one area when they acquire new skills.

Understanding AI

To use any AI successfully, we need to understand how it works (see also Chapter 2), how it arrives at its outcomes, and how good and reliable those outcomes are. As we have established, each AI is different, and designers and innovators who collaborate with AI need to understand these differences. This understanding applies from perspectives both of the AI and of the design thinker. Generally speaking, humans may not always understand or predict AI's outcomes, which can lead to reduced trust and limited use of AI as stated by Amershi and colleagues in 2019. At the same time, AI needs to recognize the human conception of the task and their expectations as mentioned by Norman in 2013 in order to produce relevant results. Humans often judge AI outcomes to be poor when they first attempt to use AI with a simple or naïve prompt that leaves the machine guessing about intent. The result is frequently dismissed as worthless. So, how do we achieve a shared understanding between design thinkers and machines?

Much of this mutual understanding is captured in the concept of shared mental models, where members of a human team hold knowledge in common about their tasks and relationships. This helps the team predict each other's needs and behavior, thereby improving performance, as supported by Cannon-Bowers and her colleagues in 1993. Shared mental models do not just emerge; they develop through interaction over time. Many researchers now argue that this concept could also be applied to human–AI teams. Andrews and colleagues in 2023 proposed a conceptual model that explicitly incorporates AI into this framework.

How can this be achieved in practice? In a human team, members talk with each other, introduce themselves, and share expectations and goals. In human–AI collaboration, however, the process must be adapted, because AI and humans develop understanding in different ways. For the machine to grasp your intent and purpose, humans must incorporate this information into their prompts. Clear prompting signals to AI the type of outcome you expect. Specific guidance on this can be found later in the prompt section of this chapter. We have also many examples prompts within our AID tools to help beginners to gain a better understanding about prompting.

At the same time, researchers are working on ways for AI to build an understanding of its collaborators' mental models. This work falls under the term *machine theory of mind*, which refers to a machine's ability to model the human mind, as stated by Rabinowitz and colleagues in 2018. Such advances will improve human–AI collaboration in the future as noted by Yang and colleagues in 2023. Until then, we must include our own mental model in the prompts.

For humans to better understand AI outcomes, we can return to the guidance in the previous section. Training an AI assistant so that its outputs align more closely with your expectations is one approach. In addition, researchers are actively working to increase the transparency and explainability of AI systems, which is seen as crucial for developing shared mental models as argued by Endsley in 2023.

AI Assistant

Assistants can help you with many tasks. Broadly, there are two groups of tasks where AI assistants can support you. First, they can assist with administrative work such as managing calendars or drafting emails. Second, they can help with design-related tasks, for example conducting interviews or supporting research. We will begin with administrative task work before moving to design task work. In this section, we provide directions on how to use AI assistants. In the appendix "AI Assistants in Design Thinking," and within our AID tools section, we go into more detail on how these helpers can support design thinkers, and how to develop your own.

Here are some examples of administrative tasks that AI assistants can perform:

- Manage your schedule: Check your calendar, tell you what is coming up, or add new events on command.
- Handle emails: Read and summarize emails or draft responses and new emails via voice or text requests.
- Help with coding: Support you with basic programming questions or generate simple code snippets when you are learning to code.

- Write content: Draft a blog post, create designs, or generate other text content. Over time, you can train AI so that the machine learns your style and preferences.
- Keep you up to date: Scan the internet and report back about new and upcoming AI services and general developments.

In the past, programming skills were needed to develop an AI assistant. Today, however, there are companies that allow you to create one without any coding experience. This is one of the rapid advances in the AI environment: it enables anyone, even without IT knowledge, to build and benefit from their own AI assistant.

AI assistants can also support many design tasks (see details in Appendix 1 "AI Assistants in Design Thinking"). Artificial intelligence is rapidly transforming design workflows across UX/UI, graphic, product, interior, service design, and design research. Modern AI assistants can automate routine work, generate creative content, and even simulate human feedback. We will explore this function of AI assistants in greater depth in the next chapter. For now, here are some examples of design thinking tasks that AI can support:

- UX research and user testing
- Ideation and mood boards
- UI/UX design and prototyping
- AI assistants in Collaborative design sessions

AI Prompting

Leveraging generative AI in design thinking requires more than simply verbalizing a request. This section introduces advanced strategies for making the most of generative AI in design thinking. It explores the intersection of AI and human creativity, offering practical prompting techniques to enhance innovation and problem-solving in business contexts. We have divided the section into three parts: the S.T.A.R. Method in Design Thinking, Bias Mitigation, and Iterative Prompting for Continuous Improvement.

The S.T.A.R. Method in Design Thinking

To unlock AI's full potential, design thinkers must master prompts that interweave domain knowledge—design types such as characters in game design,

UX research and design, style systems, and design briefs with target audience and deliverable requirements—with clear strategic intent.

Building on Scotland's STAR framework published in 2023, we enrich each stage with design-thinking–specific parameters. STAR stands for situation, task, appearance, and refine.

- Situation provides the context (e.g., project goals, user segment, brand positioning).
- Task describes AI's role and the type of deliverable.
- Appearance dictates style, tone, and format of the response.
- Refine specifies any constraints or special requirements.

Below are two examples of how to apply each aspect of the STAR framework.

1. Design Example: Quick Poster

   - Situation: A non-profit organization needs a social-media poster announcing a community clean-up.
   - Task: Draft a poster layout.
   - Appearance: Bold headlines in Montserrat, illustrative icons, brand colors (green #10B981, white).
   - Refine: Include date/time and location: "WED., May 21, 2025, 9–12 am, Kendall Square, Building 999." Deliver as print-ready, 4:3 ratio, 300 dpi.

The complete prompt could look like:

"Create a social-media poster for a nonprofit's community clean-up. Use bold Montserrat headlines, illustrative icons, and the brand colors green (#10B981) and white. Include date/time, locations, which is "WED., May 21, 2025, 9-12am, Kendall Square, Building 999"; deliver as print-ready with 4:3 ratio at 300 dpi."

2. Design Example: Icon Library

   - Situation: Our product team needs a cohesive icon library for a health-tech website.
   - Task: Act as a digital illustrator to draft icons.
   - Appearance: Nine line-style icons. Follow a 24 px grid and use 2 px strokes. Align each icon with Material Design principles.
   - Refine: Annotate any non-black elements with sRGB hex codes.

Tip: You can reference existing prompt collections on Ideogram for shape consistency and naming conventions

The complete prompt could look like:

"Generate 9 cohesive line-style icons for a health-tech mobile website. Follow a 24 px grid and use 2 px strokes. Align each icon with Material Design principles. Export as PNG files at 24×24 px artboards. If you introduce any colors beyond black, annotate each element with its HEX code."

Bias Mitigation

Human-centered design demands ethical AI use. Below we identify common bias types in generative tools and offer frameworks and advanced mitigation tactics.

Common biases

- Data bias: Training sets that under-represent design contexts lead to skewed suggestions. *Example:* A color-palette generator trained on Western art history omits skin-tone palettes suitable for darker complexions, such as discussed by Buolamwini and Gebru in 2018.
- Algorithmic bias: Model objectives amplify normative aesthetics. *Example:* A layout AI optimizing for "highest engagement" consistently favors minimalistic Scandinavian styles, marginalizing other traditions.
- Interpretation bias: Teams accept AI personas or style guides uncritically. *Example:* Designers adopt AI-generated personas without validating diverse user interviews, leading to non-inclusive user journeys.
- Feedback-loop bias: Recursive learning solidifies initial biases. *Example:* A recommendation engine keeps suggesting flat-design mock-ups because past selections favored that trend.

Ethical frameworks for assessment

- FATTER (Fairness, Accountability, Transparency, Trustworthiness, Explainability, Resilience): From Google's AI fairness principles of 2021. *Design thinking example:* Require an explanation of why an AI chose a particular icon set, ensuring equal representation across cultural motifs.
- 4D Ethical Assessment (Detect, Document, Debias, Decide): Based on IBM's AI Fairness 360 methodology, published by Bellamy and colleagues in 2018. *Design thinking example:* Detect with Fairlearn to audit color-contrast outputs; document via model cards describing training image datasets; debias by adversarial reweighting of under-represented

design styles; decide through a cross-functional ethics review before deployment.

There are several strategies to prevent or mitigate AI biases. Broadly, they fall into pre-processing, in-process, and post-hoc methods.
Pre-processing

* Reweighting: Adjust the influence of training samples so that under-represented groups—and, in our context, under-represented design styles—receive proportionally greater impact during learning, as discussed by Kamiran & Calders in 2012. *Concrete example:* If only 10 percent of your icon library reflects non-Western motifs (e.g., South Asian mandalas, West African Adinkra symbols), assign those examples higher weights so the loss function "pays more attention" to them.
* Synthetic data: Augment your corpus with realistic artificial examples to fill gaps. GAN-based augmentation can enrich low-resource domains, according to Antoniou, Storkey, and Edwards in 2017. *Design practice:* Train a conditional GAN on festival branding assets—such as Diwali rangoli designs and Chinese New Year lanterns—then generate additional mock-ups. Merging these synthetic samples with authentic data diversifies the training set so a generative UI tool draws on a broader palette of cultural aesthetics.

In-process

* Adversarial debiasing: Train an icon-generation model alongside a style-bias classifier to minimize discriminatory patterns, as stated by Zhang and colleagues in 2018. *Workflow:* One AI (the "artist") creates icons; another (the "critic") tries to guess each icon's style origin—Western or non-Western. When the critic succeeds, the artist updates to confuse it next time. Over repeated rounds, the artist learns to blend styles so well that the critic cannot tell them apart, yielding a richer, fairer mix of styles for multicultural icon libraries.

Post-hoc

* Subgroup calibration: Tailor decision thresholds or output rankings for different demographic clusters to ensure equitable performance, per Pleiss and colleagues in 2017. *Design tooling:* Measure an "aesthetic quality score"

for mock-ups across segments (age groups, cultural backgrounds, accessibility needs), then adjust thresholds for "acceptable" outputs per segment.

- Impact analysis: Systematically stress-test outputs under worst-case or edge-case conditions before rollout, as supported by Raji and colleagues in 2020. *Example:* For a web-UI generator, use corner-case prompts—"design a navigation bar readable by users with 20/200 vision," "create icons that function at 8 px"—and evaluate results against WCAG 2.1. Document failure modes, quantify non-compliance rates, and iterate on prompts or model settings.

Iterative Prompting for Continuous Improvement

Prompts are not static commands; they are living blueprints refined through disciplined feedback loops. By adopting Chain-of-Thought (CoT)–style prompting, teams guide large language models to surface their reasoning steps at a high level, turning AI from a simple tool into a collaborator.

Structured Workflow Example: "Analyze 50 User Interview Transcripts to Identify the Top Three Pain-Point Themes."

1. Extract mentions of emotional cues such as "frustration" or "delight."
2. Cluster excerpts by functional topic: onboarding, navigation, responsiveness.
3. Rate each cluster on frequency and sentiment intensity.
4. Recommend three UX interventions, prioritized by expected impact versus implementation effort.

Three strengths of using CoT:
1. Transparency and traceability: High-level reasoning steps can be audited and validated at each stage of insight generation.
2. Progressive refinement: With each iteration, tune your prompt—clarify definitions, adjust sentiment thresholds, or reshape cluster labels—using output-quality metrics such as Cohen's κ for theme agreement.
3. Cross-functional alignment: Codifying each step fosters shared understanding among researchers, designers, and stakeholders, so data-driven recommendations land with credibility.

   - "navigation bar readable by users with 20/200 vision," "create icons that function at 8 px"—and evaluate results against WCAG 2.1. Document failure modes, quantify non-compliance rates, and iterate on prompts or model settings.

Critical Thinking

When working with AI, humans need to remain critical, especially in relation to the generated outcomes. As illustrated in previous chapters, some AI-generated outputs may be hallucinations or may rely on stereotypes, making them less useful or even harmful to the user. Remaining critical becomes more difficult the more we rely on AI. Research has shown that excessive reliance can reduce critical thinking, as users begin to accept AI outcomes as correct without proper evaluation, as expressed by Gerlich in 2025. One way to overcome this challenge is to resist the temptation of superficial use. Instead, users should engage deeply and critically with both the process and the results. The process must be informed by the user, while the AI's outcome and reasoning should be evaluated for credibility and relevance.

Critical thinking refers to the human ability to make reasoned decisions based on analysed and assessed information. It is not only essential for design thinking, but also for academic success, professional competence, and informed citizenship, as noted by Halpern in 2010. Over-reliance on AI can reduce critical thinking through *cognitive offloading* according to Gerlich's statement in 2025. Cognitive offloading occurs when individuals lighten their mental workload by outsourcing it to external tools, as state by Risko & Gilbert in 2016. With Google and other tools, knowledge is instantly available, making it less important to remember facts and more important to know where to find them, as emphasized by Sparrow, Liu, & Wegner in 2011. However, this shift carries a cost: reduced cognitive engagement and weakened skill development according to Gerlich noted in 2025. In design especially, meaningful outcomes depend on deep understanding and sustained engagement with the problem and solution.

The negative effects of over-reliance on AI are particularly strong among younger participants who have grown up using external tools for cognitive offloading. Therefore, we need to purposefully educate both students and practitioners to thoughtfully and critically collaborate with AI as stated by Gerlich in 2025. This is especially relevant as AI is increasingly used in tasks ranging from virtual assistants to search engines.

There are several ways to remain critical when using AI. One approach is to compare AI outputs against reliable outside sources. Another is to establish quality criteria beforehand and iteratively refine the outputs until they meet those standards (see https://tlconestoga.ca/critical-thinking-with-ai-3-approaches/). These are simple but effective ways of ensuring that critical thinking remains central when working with AI.

Summary

Working with AI tools requires training and experience. It begins with selecting the AI you want to work with. This decision should be based on both objective factors (e.g., accessibility, costs, general performance) and subjective ones (e.g., preferences in outputs or style). The choice of AI may change over time as your collaborator evolves through updates or as new systems emerge. Staying updated with the evolving AI environment is essential.

One recommendation is to develop your own AI assistant. We dedicate an appendix and one AID tool in this book to this topic, because there are many ways an AI assistant can be used and many ways to build one. Broadly, AI can serve as an assistant for administrative tasks such as calendar management, as well as a collaborator in a wide range of design thinking activities.

We also incorporated a section on prompt engineering. We decided against devoting a full chapter to this area, as prompting strategies are evolving rapidly and the way we interact with AI may change in the future. That said, the broad strategies for writing specific prompts and for mitigating bias are likely to remain relevant for some time. Writing effective prompts will continue to require practice and training.

References

Amershi, S., Weld, D., Vorvoreanu, M., Fourney, A., Nushi, B., Collisson, P., Suh, J., Iqbal, S., Bennett, P. N., Inkpen, K., et al. (2019) *Guidelines for Human-AI Interaction.* In Proceedings of the 2019 Chicago Conference on Human Factors in Computing Systems. ACM.

Andrews, R. W., Lilly, J. M., Srivastava, D. & Feigh, K. M. (2023). The role of shared mental models in human-AI teams: a theoretical review, *Theoretical Issues in Ergonomics Science, 24*(2): 129–175. https://doi.org/10.1080/14639 22X.2022.2061080

Antoniou, A., Storkey, A. & Edwards, H. (2017). Data augmentation generative adversarial networks. arXiv preprint arXiv:1711.04340.

Bansal, G. et al. (2019). Updates in Human-AI Teams: Understanding and Addressing the Performance/Compatibility Tradeoff. Proceedings of the AAAI Conference on Artificial Intelligence, 33(01): 2429–2437. https://doi.org/10.1609/aaai.v33 i01.33012429

Bellamy, R. K. E., Dorado, S., Hutchinson, B., et al. (2018). AI Fairness 360: An extensible toolkit for detecting, understanding, and mitigating unwanted algorithmic bias. arXiv preprint arXiv:1810.01943.

Buolamwini, J. & Gebru, T. (2018). *Gender Shades: Intersectional Accuracy Disparities in Commercial Gender Classification*. Proceedings of the 1st Conference on Fairness, Accountability and Transparency, 81: 77–91.

Cannon-Bowers, J. A., Salas, E., & Converse, S. (1993). Shared mental models in expert team decision making. In N. J.Castellan, Jr. (Ed.), *Individual and group decision making: Current issues* (pp. 221–246). Lawrence Erlbaum Associates, Inc., New Jersey, USA.

Norman, D. (2013). The Design of Everyday Things. Revised and expanded edition. Basic Books, New York.

Endsley, M. R. (2023). Supporting human-AI teams: transparency, explainability, and situation awareness. *Computers in Human Behavior, 140*, 107574.

FakeClients.com. Instant client briefs for creative professionals. https://fakeclients.com/

Gerlich, M. (2025). AI Tools in Society: Impacts on Cognitive Offloading and the Future of Critical Thinking. Societies, 15(1), 6. https://doi.org/10.3390/soc15010006

Google AI. (2021). AI Principles: Fairness. Retrieved from https://ai.google/principles/

Halpern, D. F. (2010). Halpern Critical Thinking Assessment: Manual; Schuhfried GmbH: Middling, Austria.

Kamiran, F., & Calders, T. (2012). Data preprocessing techniques for classification without discrimination. *Knowledge and Information Systems, 33*(1), 1–33.

Pleiss, G., Raghavan, M., Wu, F., Kleinberg, J., & Weinberger, K. Q. (2017). On fairness and calibration. In *Advances in Neural Information Processing Systems, 30*, 5684–5693.

Rabinowitz, N., Perbet, F., Song, F., Zhang, C., Eslami, S. A., & Botvinick, M. (2018). Machine theory of mind. In International Conference on Machine Learning. (pp. 4218–4227). PMLR. ArXiv abs/1802.07740.

Raji, I. D., Smart, A., White, R. N. & Mitchell, M. (2020). *Closing the AI accountability gap: Defining an end-to-end framework for internal algorithmic auditing*. In Proceedings of the 2020 Conference on Fairness, Accountability, and Transparency (pp. 33–44).

Risko, E. F. & Gilbert, S. J. (2016). Cognitive Offloading. *Trends Cognitive Science. 20*, 676–688. http://doi.org/10.1016/j.tics.2016.07.002

Scotland, C. (2023) The STAR Method. Retrieved from https://colinscotland.com/the-star-method

Sharpen.design. Open-ended project prompts for design creativity. https://sharpen.design/

Sparrow, B., Liu, J., Wegner, D. M. (2011). Google effects on memory: Cognitive consequences of having information at our fingertips. *Science, 333*, 776–778. http://doi.org/10.1126/science.1204531

Thinking. Societies 2025, 15, 6. https://doi.org/10.3390/soc15010006

Yang, S. C.-H., Folke, T., & Shafto, P. (2023). The inner loop of collective human–machine intelligence. *Topics in Cognitive Science*, *0*: 1–20. https://doi.org/10.1111/tops.12642

Zhang, B. H., Lemoine, B., & Mitchell, M. (2018). Mitigating unwanted biases with adversarial learning. In Proceedings of the 2018 AAAI/ACM Conference on AI, Ethics, and Society (pp. 335–340).

Section II
AI in Design Thinking Activities, Tools, and Use-Cases

The heart of this book is found in the AID (Artificial Intelligence Design) tools in this section. The AID tools originate from a simple question—how can AI improve design thinking processes and outcomes? In addressing this, we borrowed and adapted a wide variety of traditional design process tools to through incorporating AI. The AID tools grew through the ingenuity and hard work of university students in a course taught by this book's first author, supported and further developed by the co-author team. Students were tasked with creating tools and applying them to real-world challenges, resulting in a large variety of AID tools, approaches, and illustrative use-cases.

As the students found, many AID tools have utility across multiple design thinking activities, and their output reflected that. To highlight some key uses of various tools and cases, in the following chapters we have sorted the tools within specific activities.

AI Design Thinking Activities

Each design problem and its context are different, and this will require innovators to design differently. It will be up to the designers to decide what the appropriate process and tools are. For design thinking novices, you can follow the sequence of activities laid out in this book: Prepare and train, emphasize and define, ideate and select, prototype and test, and implement and learn. However, more advanced designers and innovators should take the design problem and its context in consideration when deciding on how to design.

This might be iterative as often suggested within the design discipline, or linear as preferred within many organizations. It may involve all activities listed, or only some. For example, we can have a solution-based focus approach and ignore initial research, starting with prototyping our ideas based on our intuition instead. Alternatively, one could do the research to identify the underlying problem.

One consequence of the incorporation of AI in design thinking is that some new activities in design thinking emerge. First, in the prepare and train section, designers can prepare the way in which AI is integrated (e.g. train an AI assistant). This will take some time and effort to collect the right training data for the AI. In addition, in implement and learn activities, it is not only for the human to learn but also for the AI, specifically when you work with a personalized AI assistant. This will require the human designer to support this learning process.

We use the traditional activities within the design thinking process, sometimes called stages or phases, as a foundation. Many readers will be familiar with the process and tools. By doing so, we hope that we can convince more design thinkers to explore the opportunities AI provides for design. Below is a summary of the activities.

- Prepare & Train: Understand the design context (e.g. who is my user, who are the stakeholders) and AI requirements (e.g. what AI is available, do I need to train an assistant, with what data?). The aim for this phase is to decide on the design direction, identify the enablers and potential limitations. While AI can support to reach the aim of these activities, AI will also require some attention. Time will be required to find a suitable AI tools and potentially train our specific AI assistant for this design project.
- Empathize & Define: AI and human design thinkers collect and synthesize human, and AI generated data. The aim is to define a potential solution or problem on which to design on. Here, AI can help to speed up the data collection (e.g. by transcribing and translating interviews) and analyzing part (e.g. by identifying themes from interviews), as well as more in terms of quantitative (e.g. interviewing humans and AI independently).
- Ideate & Select: Generate ideas from humans alone or working together with AI to ideate and select a potential solution. AI can support you to create more diverse ideas, help to record these ideas and assist you to select the most promising ideas. After the ideation, AI can create quickly some early concepts for internal communication and help the team to advance the selected idea in the right direction.
- Prototype & Test: Develop a selected idea into a testable prototype. AI is specifically helpful in creating quick and cheap prototypes (e.g. simple

visualizations) in the early stage but can also help in testing them and collecting human and AI feedback (as above in the synthesize and define section, AI can help us to collect and analyze data: here, to get a better understanding if our prototype works). Prototype and testing activities often cycle reciprocally with ideating and selecting, as ideas are quickly developed, discarded, improved, or replaced.

- Implement & Learn: Create the final concept for management to approve and learn from the activities and process. AI can help in the implementation and selling the idea internally. After the process is completed by both, the design thinker and AI should share reciprocal feedback to learn from the experience.

The Design Thinkers Role in AID Activities

As mentioned in Chapter 3, AI cannot be viewed as a full independent designer thus far. We believe AI is a collaborator. It is more independent (e.g., AI is more flexible as it can adapt to new data and environment compared to traditional software which is more static and rigid) than traditional software and, hence, need to be worked with differently. We have given tips throughout the book and specifically Chapters 4 and 5 discusses skills and best practices on how to work with AI.

So, what is the designer thinker's role? We suggest that the designer thinkers should enact the role of a supervisor. Designers or innovators are supervising AI and only if they manage AI well, AI can deliver fast and great outcomes for them. This requires the human designer to give AI specific instructions via prompts, control performances and support learning. You cannot rely on AI to do your job independently yet.

As we laid out in the previous chapter. AI has its flaws, and designers need to help AI overcome these challenges. Among others, you need to refine the outcomes of AI with better prompts to make sure that the results are relevant. You need to identify potential biases so to eliminate them in potential solutions. You need to provide AI tools with the context and intend needed so that it is possible to deliver relevant outcomes. You need to train the AI assistant and provide feedback so that the AI tool can learn and improve the performance. While we see AI as a tool, it is a different tool compared to other more traditional software. Hence, we suggest that the interaction between design thinkers and AI is more of a supervising role.

AID Tools

We planned for the creation of our AID tools by first identifying the most useful and commonly published design thinking tools. Then, we instructed college students to integrate AI in design thinking tools for use them in projects. After successful use, the new or adapted AID tool was further tested, refined, and written up as a guide. We are sharing the most relevant and easy to use 41 AID tools in this book, and will publish further tools and examples on our website (www.ai-designthinking.com/).

Each AID tool is formatted in a similar way. First we provide the brief description of the AID tool, including its purpose. We highlight the benefit or advantage of using AI with the traditional design thinking tool (e.g., cheaper, faster, or more creative). This is followed with a step-by-step "how-to" guide on using the AID tool, including a variety of options and tips for use. Please note that the AID tools presented in this section are intended to showcase possibilities, especially to help those new to AI-assisted design. For this reason, we offer many sample prompts and tips, including multiple AI platforms and detailed workflow steps, meant to illustrate the range of what is possible, spark ideas, and build confidence. Not every platform or step must be used in a given project; think of each tool as including a menu of options rather than a fixed recipe. For your projects, you may choose to use only one or two of the suggested AI programs, to skip steps that don't fit your context, or to combine elements from different tools. As you gain experience, adapt freely: substitute tools, simplify workflows, and develop approaches that suit your team, timeline, and project needs. The goal is not to follow instructions perfectly, but to integrate AI in ways that genuinely improve your design thinking process, as well as honing your expertise for a changing AI environment.

We sorted the AID tools within the core sets of design thinking activities outlined in Chapter 1: prepare & train (Chapter 6), empathize & define (Chapter 7), ideate & select (Chapter 8), prototype & test (Chapter 9), and implement & learn (Chapter 10). Design thinkers can work with AID tools that are specifically in line with their chosen activity. While many projects may begin with prepare & train activities, it is equally possible to lead with tools in the ideate & select section. This provides flexibility suitable for design, whether with or without AI in each activity, keeping the design process both creative and efficient.

In addition to the AID tools, we include use cases which illustrate how AI tools can be used within each design thinking activity. These use cases were adapted from design thinking projects where students worked in small teams to solve a design challenge. Building on the students' initial drafts, our author team further developed and refined the use cases to provide a helpful illustration for our readers.

6

Prepare & Train: AID Tools and Use Cases

The aim of the AID tools in the prepare and train activity section is to improve our understanding of the design problem and context in which we design. The basic question is on how we want or can design. It helps us later to see what needs to be done, how and why. This chapter explores how AI can responsibly support nine foundational tools of design thinking: AI Agent (6.1), Peers Observing AI (6.2), Stakeholder Map (6.3), Problem Statement (6.4), Opportunity Map (6.5), AI-Assisted Definition of Success (6.6), Value Hypothesis (6.7), Critical Items Diagram (6.8), Jobs to Be Done (6.9), and two use cases, (6.10) Designing a Smarter Street Trash Bin for Shanghai with AI, and (6.11) Designing a Futuristic Poster with AI.

We offer a variety of AID tools with a standard set of information to help the reader: AID description, suggested AI Program, benefits of AI for this design tool, application instructions, tips, strengths, and weaknesses. The use cases are based on real-world design challenges, addressed by university student teams, focused on important aspects of using AI in design thinking. They reflect their real experiences in using AI and AID tools, as applied to these challenges.

The Work Instructions in each section include concrete domain examples—such as healthcare, education, mobility, and sustainable fashion. These are chosen deliberately to illustrate how the same AI-enabled method adapts across contexts. For instance, in healthcare, AI may highlight patient pain points to sharpen problem statements; in education, it models success criteria for digital learning platforms; in mobility, it maps complex stakeholder dynamics around bike-sharing; and in sustainable fashion, it tests

© The Author(s), under exclusive license to Springer Nature Switzerland AG 2026

D. Graff et al., *Design Thinking with Artificial Intelligence*, Palgrave Executive Essentials, https://doi.org/10.1007/978-3-032-10543-1_6

hypotheses about consumer willingness to pay. By anchoring AID tools in realistic examples, the chapter shows how AI's role can be both pragmatic and adaptable.

It is important to recognize, however, that AI's integration into design methods is not without risk. Left unchecked, it can obscure nuance, reinforce biases, or dilute the interpretive richness of design practice. Scholars have emphasized that design's strength lies in reframing problems and generating meaning, not just optimizing processes (Dorst, 2011; Verganti, 2009). AI can support these goals only if it is harnessed thoughtfully.

Taken together, the methods in this chapter present AI as an amplifier of design thinking's core strengths. AI can process complexity, uncover patterns, and generate alternatives—but designers remain the empathizers, sense-makers, and ethical stewards of the process. When combined, these roles position AI not as a threat to design thinking's integrity, but as a chance to reinvigorate it with new possibilities.

6.1 AI Agent

Description of the Tool

This tool will guide designers and innovators in setting up an AI Agent for design thinking using n8n, a no-code automation platform. We will cover the basics of design thinking (in accessible terms), show how AI can support the key phases of ideation, research, and prototyping, introduce n8n and its role in automation, and provide step-by-step instructions (with examples) to build an AI-driven workflow. Along the way, we'll integrate with Google Docs to document outputs, present practical use cases, and include tips, definitions, and diagrams to clarify concepts.

In simple terms, an AI agent is an AI system given a goal or role, which can perform multiple steps or use tools to achieve that goal. In n8n, the AI agent might be configured as a series of nodes (or a special AI Agent node) that works with an AI model and possibly other utilities. This has advantages over the more basic Application Programming Interface (API) that developers often use to integrate AI capabilities into their application code. Specifically, unlike a basic AI API, an agent can make decisions, call different functions (e.g., search an API, then summarize), and carry on a multi-step interaction to complete a task. Don't be intimidated by the term—in our workflow, our "AI agent" will simply be the orchestrated set of AI actions that help in ideation, research, and prototyping.

Figure 6.1   AI Agent. A multidisciplinary team collaboratively configuring an AI agent, visualized through a shared, holographic brain interface that represents collective reasoning, human–AI interaction, and decision-making in an organizational setting. AI generated image created with Ideogram, Inc., Ideogram.ai, 3.0, 2025.

Introducing n8n: A No-Code Automation Platform

Harnessing AI for design thinking is powerful, but doing so effectively often means integrating various tools and orchestrating a process (for example, getting AI outputs and putting them into a document for the team to review). This is where n8n comes in. n8n is a workflow automation platform that lets you connect apps, APIs, and services using a visual, no-code interface. Think of it as a flexible digital assembly line for your software tools: you can chain together actions (nodes) like building blocks to automate tasks and data flows.

Some key points about n8n:

* No-Code/Low-Code: You create workflows in n8n by dragging and dropping nodes (each node represents an action or trigger) and connecting them, rather than writing complex code. This makes it accessible to non-programmers, yet it's very powerful for those who know a bit of coding (you can add custom code if needed). It gives technical teams the flexibility of code with the speed of drag-n-drop.

- Integrations: n8n has 400+ built-in integrations (and growing) with popular apps and services—from Google Docs to Slack to databases—as well as generic nodes like HTTP Request (Note: HTTP Request is a technical term for how one application talks to another over the web. An HTTP Request may be thought of as sending a message to an online service to request information or trigger an action. This functionality allows you to connect your workflows to virtually any web-based tool or service through its web Application Programming Interface, abbreviated API) for any web API. This means you can automate across your entire stack. For example, n8n can take an output from an AI service and automatically save it to a Google Doc, send a notification on Slack, or add data to a spreadsheet, all in one flow.
- Self-Hosted or Cloud: You can run n8n on your own server (it's source-available) or use n8n Cloud. Either way, you maintain control of your data—a plus for businesses concerned about privacy. Setup is straightforward (cloud sign-up or a Docker install for self-hosting).
- Flow Logic: n8n isn't just linear sequences; it supports logic like branching (if/else), loops, and even waiting for events. This allows creation of complex workflows. For instance, you could incorporate an approval step (have a human review AI output) before continuing the automation.

For our purposes, n8n will serve as the glue to build an AI agent for design thinking. The AI itself (e.g., a GPT-5 model) is one piece of the puzzle—n8n will trigger the AI at the right times, feed it the appropriate prompts, and then route the outputs to wherever they need to go (like documentation in Google Docs). Essentially, n8n lets us create a custom AI-powered assistant that fits our process.

Building Your AI Agent Workflow in n8n (Step-by-Step)

In this section, we will set up a practical workflow in n8n that utilizes an AI model to assist in the ideation, research, and prototyping phases of a design thinking project. We'll also integrate with Google Docs to record the results of each phase for easy sharing and review.

By following these steps, you'll not only create a working AI helper for your design thinking project, but also learn the fundamentals of how n8n orchestrates different tools together. To make it concrete, we assume that our team is working on the design thinking challenge: "How might we improve the coffee shop experience for customers?" We'll use the AI agent to brainstorm ideas, gather some quick research insights, and draft a simple prototype concept, documenting everything in a Google Doc. You can adapt the same workflow to your own design questions. Before you begin, ensure you have access to n8n (either via n8n Cloud or a local instance) and accounts/API access for any external services:

For the AI, you'll need an API key from an AI provider (e.g., OpenAI for ChatGPT). Sign up on the OpenAI platform and generate a secret API key if you haven't already. For Google Docs integration, you'll need a Google account and to authorize n8n to access it (n8n will handle this via OAuth when you add the Google Docs node—you don't have to manually get a token, just be ready to log into Google and grant permission).

Now, let's build the workflow:

* Create a New Workflow in n8n. After logging into n8n, click the "New Workflow" button (in n8n Cloud, it's typically on your dashboard; in self-hosted, you'll see a blank canvas upon opening the editor). This opens the visual workflow editor. Give your workflow a name, like "Design Thinking AI Agent". You might also want to save it right away. Initially, you'll have an empty canvas with a single Start node (the Start node simply signifies where the workflow begins when triggered manually).
* Add a Trigger Node. We need a way to start our AI agent workflow. For simplicity, we'll use a Manual Trigger (so we can run it on demand while building). In the nodes menu, search for "Manual" and drag the Manual Trigger node onto the canvas. Connect the Start (or trigger) to the next node by drawing a line—in this simple case, connecting from the Manual Trigger's output (If you don't see a Start node, the Manual Trigger itself can act as the starting point.)—Optional: In a real deployment, you could use other triggers. For example, a Schedule Trigger could run the workflow at a certain time (perhaps every morning during a design sprint). Or a Webhook trigger could start the flow when someone sends a specific web request. n8n even has a Chat Trigger if you want the agent to work interactively through chat. But to keep things straightforward, manual execution is fine for now.

Activity 1 – Ideation: Add an OpenAI Node for Idea Generation

* Integrating AI. n8n has a built-in OpenAI node that makes it easy to connect to models like GPT-3.5, GPT-4, or GPT-5. Find and add the OpenAI

node (or specifically, the OpenAI Chat node, if available, since we'll want the chatbot style completion).

- Configure the OpenAI node: In the node's settings, you'll specify the model and prompt. For example, choose "GPT-3.5-Turbo" as the model (or GPT-5 if you have access and need more advanced output). In the Prompt field, we'll enter the instruction for ideation. Since we want lots of creative ideas, a good prompt might be: "You are a creative design thinking assistant. Generate a list of five innovative ideas to improve the coffee shop experience for customers, with a one-sentence description for each." We ask for a list of five to keep it manageable (you can adjust the number).

- Credentials: The first time you use the OpenAI node, n8n will prompt you to set up credentials. Click "Create New" or select your existing OpenAI API credential. To create a new one, you'll need to paste in your OpenAI API Key (and optionally your Organization ID) that you obtained from OpenAI's website. Once saved, n8n will use this key to authenticate when calling the AI. (Don't worry—the key is stored securely in n8n.) After adding the key, test the node by clicking "Execute Node"—it should send the prompt and return a list of idea texts. You'll see the AI's response in the node's output.

- Example output: The AI might return something like: "Express Checkout App—A mobile app allowing customers to preorder and skip the line." "Interactive Waiting Display—A screen that shows the coffee brewing process with fun facts." "Personalized Greetings—Baristas greet regulars by name and preference via a smart system." "Coffee Workshop Corner—Customers can learn latte art or coffee trivia while waiting." "Ambient Entertainment—Headphone stations with curated playlists or short podcasts."

  - These are hypothetical, but you can see the kind of creative ideas an AI can generate on the fly.

Under the hood: When you run this node, n8n is sending your prompt to OpenAI's API and getting the response. This happens in real time during workflow execution. The node output will include the AI's text, which we can use in subsequent nodes.

Activity 2 – Research: Add a Node for Quick Research Insights

After generating ideas, it's useful to have some background research to inform which ideas are worth pursuing. We'll use the AI again, but in a slightly different way—perhaps to get pros/cons or relevant facts.

You Have a Couple of Options Here:

Option A: Use the OpenAI node again with a different prompt. For instance, we can feed it one of the ideas and ask for an analysis: "Considering the idea of an Express Checkout App for a coffee shop, list some potential benefits and challenges of this idea." This will yield a short pros/cons list or discussion, generated from the AI's general knowledge. To do this, you can add another OpenAI node and in its prompt, reference the output of the first node. n8n allows you to use output data from previous nodes via expressions. For example, you might write: "For the idea: {{$node["OpenAI"].json["text"]}}, provide some quick market research or known facts that support or refute it." (This uses n8n's expression syntax to plug in the idea text.)

Option B: Use a specialized research tool. If you want actual up-to-date information (because language models might be limited to their training data), you could integrate a tool like an HTTP Request node (a connector for web services and APIs) to call a search API (e.g., Google's Custom Search API or a service like SerpAPI) and then have the AI summarize the results. This is more advanced, so for now we'll stick to Option A for simplicity.

Let's Go with Option A in Our Workflow:

Add another OpenAI Chat node (or reuse the existing one by branching, though using separate nodes in sequence is simpler to start).

Connect the output of the first OpenAI node (ideas) to this new node, so it runs afterward.

Set up the prompt. If we want to focus on one idea, we could specify: "You are a research assistant. The idea is: {{$node["OpenAI"].json["text"][0]}}. Give a brief analysis of this idea's feasibility or any relevant data (e.g., have other coffee shops done this?)." Here, {{$node["OpenAI"].json["text"][0]}} would grab the first idea from the previous output. Alternatively, ask generally: "Provide a quick market insight for improving coffee shop experiences—e.g., what do customers complain about most in coffee shops?" This more general prompt might yield broad info like "Customers often cite long wait times and order inaccuracies as top issues." Feel free to experiment with the wording.

Use the same OpenAI credentials. Run the node to test the output.

Result: The AI might output a paragraph or list with research-like insight. For example: "Self-service ordering apps have been adopted by major chains (Starbucks, Dunkin') and tend to reduce wait times by ~10%. However, some older customers prefer human interaction. Many complaints in coffee shop reviews focus on long lines during peak hours and lack of personalization." While not guaranteed to be 100% accurate, this gives the team some immediately useful context and talking points, drawn from the AI's knowledge base.

Activity 3 – Prototyping: Add a Node to Draft a Solution Concept

Now we have ideas and some supporting info, the next step is to propose a prototype or concept to test. We'll use the AI to combine everything into a brief concept description or blueprint. Add yet another OpenAI node (our third use of AI in this flow).

Prompt for prototyping: We want the AI to propose how to implement one of the ideas in a quick-and-dirty way. For instance, using the Express Checkout App idea, we prompt: "As a prototype, describe how the 'Express Checkout App' idea could work. Include what the app would do and how it improves the customer experience, in 2–3 sentences." This should yield a concise description of a prototype solution.

If you prefer a more visual prototype, you could ask for steps: "Outline the steps to create a simple prototype of this idea that we could test in one week." The AI might respond with steps like "1. Draft wireframes of the app interface. 2. Set up a dummy ordering page… 3. Have staff simulate receiving mobile orders…", which could guide your real prototyping tasks.

Another option: if you had integrated an image-generation AI, you could use n8n to get a UI mockup, but that would involve a different node or API (for example, DALL·E via OpenAI or an HTTP node to Midjourney's API, which is beyond a beginner scope). So, we'll stick to text description.

- Execution: Set the OpenAI node's prompt accordingly, and run it. The output might be something like: "Prototype concept: A mobile app where customers can place orders and pay before arriving. The app generates a pickup code and the order goes straight to baristas. For testing, we could use a simple web form as the 'app' and have a dedicated pickup shelf for mobile orders to simulate the experience." This provides a tangible direction for a prototype that can be built out.
- Integrate with Google Docs for Documentation. With our AI agent generating results for each phase, we want to capture these outputs in a document so the design team can review and build on them. We'll use the Google

Docs node to automate this. Add a Google Docs node to the canvas and connect the output of the prototyping AI node to it (so it runs last).

- Authenticate Google Docs: The first time you use Google Docs in n8n, you'll need to create credentials. In the Google Docs node, choose "OAuth2" and follow the prompts to sign in with your Google account and authorize n8n (This grants n8n permission to create or edit docs on your behalf. You can revoke access any time via your Google account's settings.).
- Once connected, you can select your Google Docs credentials for this node.
- Configure the Google Docs action: Decide how you want to store the info. A simple approach is to create a new document summarizing the outputs. For example:
- Resource: Document (meaning we'll work with whole documents).
- Operation: Create (to make a new doc).
- Title: Give the document a name, e.g., "Coffee Shop Design Sprint—AI Outputs".
- Content: Here we compile what to put in the doc. We can write a template and insert data from our nodes. For instance:
- Design Challenge: How might we improve the coffee shop experience for customers?
    - **AI-Generated Ideas:**
    - {{$node["OpenAI"].json["text"]}}
    - **AI Research Insights:**
    - {{$node["OpenAI2"].json["text"]}}
    - **Prototype Concept:**
    - {{$node["OpenAI3"].json["text"]}}
- In this snippet, replace OpenAI, OpenAI2, OpenAI3 with the actual node names in your workflow (n8n might name them "OpenAI", "OpenAI1", "OpenAI2" by default). The expressions {{$node[…]…}} pull the text output from each AI node. We also added some markdown-style bold headings for readability in the document.
- This configuration will create a Google Doc with the design challenge at top and sections for the ideas, research, and prototype. Save the node settings.
- Run the Google Docs node: When you execute this node (or the whole workflow), it should create the doc in your Google Drive. Check your Google Drive for the new document. You can open it and verify that the content matches the AI outputs. The text might need some formatting or cleanup (AI outputs can be verbose or not perfectly formatted as lists), but you have the core content automatically documented.
- Test the Entire Workflow. Now that all pieces are in place, do a full test run. In n8n, you can click "Execute Workflow" to run from the start through

all nodes in sequence. Watch as each node executes—you should see the Manual Trigger kick off, then the first AI node generate ideas, the second AI node do research, the third propose a prototype, and finally the Google Docs node create the document. If all goes well, you'll end up with a nicely populated Google Doc containing the results of all three phases. If a node fails or something doesn't work:

- Check the error messages. Common issues might be an authentication problem (e.g., wrong API key or missing Google creds) or hitting usage limits on the AI API. You can debug by executing nodes one at a time. For example, disable the later nodes and just run the OpenAI node to ensure it is returning output as expected.

- Make sure your expressions referencing other nodes are correct. n8n's expression editor (accessible by clicking the gear icon next to a field and selecting "Add Expression") can help pick the right output data.

- Refine Prompts and Workflow Logic (Iterate). Building an AI agent is an iterative process. You might realize you want the AI to generate more ideas, or format them as bullet points. You can tweak the prompts accordingly (e.g., add "-" before each idea in the prompt to force a bullet list, or ask for a numbered list). Perhaps you want to loop through each idea and get research on all of them, not just the first—that could be done with a Split In Batches or looping construct in n8n, iterating the research node over each idea. That's a bit advanced, but keep in mind it's possible. For now, maybe limit to one idea or manually run research multiple times for different ideas. You can also add a human review step if desired. For instance, you might insert a pause (using the Wait node or Webhook response technique) after the AI generates ideas, so a person can pick which idea to research, then feed that selection into the next step. N8n is very flexible in this way.

- Save and Activate the Workflow. Once you're happy with the setup, save your workflow. If you want it to run automatically (say you used a Schedule Trigger to get daily idea inspiration), you can activate it. Activation in n8n means the workflow will listen for its trigger events in the background. In manual trigger mode, activation isn't needed because you run it manually. But if you had, for example, a trigger like "when a Google Form is submitted, run this workflow", you'd activate it so that it continuously waits for that event.

Congratulations—you've built a functioning AI agent to assist with your design thinking project! You can now use it whenever your team embarks on a new project: just update the design challenge in the first prompt, run the workflow, and you'll get a fresh Google Doc with brainstormed ideas, research pointers, and a prototype concept outline.

Tips for AI Workflows

Before we conclude, let's summarize some useful nodes in n8n that you're likely to use when building AI agents and provide a few final tips on prompt design and workflow management:

- Trigger Nodes: As discussed, nodes like Manual Trigger, Cron (Schedule) Trigger, Webhook Trigger, or Chat Trigger start your workflow. Pick based on how you want to initiate the AI agent (manually, timed, or event-driven).
- AI Nodes: The OpenAI suite of nodes (which includes Chat models, completion models, etc.) is central for text-generating tasks blog.n8n.io. n8n also integrates with other AI services (e.g., Google's PaLM via a Gemini node, or using the HTTP node for custom AI APIs). Choose the AI that fits your context—for most, OpenAI's ChatGPT models are a good default due to their versatility.
- Function and Transform Nodes: Function (Code) nodes or Set nodes can manipulate data between steps. For example, if you want to format the AI output or extract a part of it, you can use a Function node with JavaScript to do so. Merge or Wait nodes handle control flow—e.g., wait for two parallel AI calls to finish then merge results.
- HTTP Request Node: This is your gateway to any web service that n8n doesn't have a built-in node for. You might use HTTP Request to call a specific API (like a news API for research data, or a Figma API to create a design asset). Coupled with an AI, you could fetch real data then have the AI summarize or interpret it ideou.com.
- Google Docs, Sheets, or Slides Nodes: These allow you to output or fetch information from the Google Workspace, which is great for documentation. For example, a Google Sheets node could log each idea in a spreadsheet with columns for "AI idea" and "team feedback" so you can track which ideas were chosen. Google Slides integration could even let an AI create draft slide content for a concept presentation.
- Collaboration Nodes: Nodes for Slack, Teams, or email can notify team members of outputs. You could have n8n post the top 3 AI-generated ideas into a Slack channel automatically, inviting the team to discuss. This way, the AI agent's work is immediately injected into your existing collaboration channels.

Prompt Engineering Tips

- Be clear and specific about what you want. If you need a list, say "List 5 ideas..."; if you want a certain format, instruct the AI accordingly (e.g., "in 2 sentences," or "as a bullet list").
- You can give context in the prompt. We often started with a role or scenario: *"You are a creative assistant..."* Setting context helps the AI tailor its style.
- If the output isn't what you expected, iterate on the prompt. Sometimes adding an example in the prompt can help (few-shot prompting), but that uses more tokens—usually not needed for our usage.
- Remember that AI can produce incorrect or irrelevant info. Always review the outputs. As a business leader, encourage your team to see AI suggestions as *suggestions*, not gospel truth.

6.2   Peers Observing AI

Description of the Tool

Peer observation is a learning method where design thinkers improve their own skills by watching how others engage with tools and processes. Applied to AI, Peers Observing AI highlights the creative and technical strategies individuals use when collaborating with generative AI. By studying how peers craft prompts, iterate on outputs, and adapt to AI feedback, participants refine their own techniques while gaining new perspectives on creativity and problem-solving. This approach democratizes learning: experts gain fresh insights by watching novices, while beginners accelerate their understanding by modelling expert behaviors.

Why Use AI in Peers Observing AI

Observing peers using AI accelerates collective learning. AI systems like text-to-image generators are highly sensitive to input phrasing and iteration and watching how others experiment exposes new approaches that may not emerge individually. Peer observation helps participants refine prompt engineering, discover unconventional workflows, and develop collaborative norms for human–AI co-creation. This method turns AI into both a tool and a shared learning environment.

Figure 6.2   Peers Observing AI. Multiple users simultaneously interacting with and comparing embodied AI agents across devices, illustrating collaborative evaluation, configuration, and shared decision-making in human–AI systems. AI generated image created with Ideogram, Inc., Ideogram.ai, 3.0, 2025.

Suggested AI Programs

- MidJourney: Text-to-image generation, ideal for exploring prompt phrasing and iteration.
- DALL·E: OpenAI's text-to-image generator, accessible and flexible for group use.
- ChatGPT 5 (LLM): Simulates peer reflection, generates "prompt alternatives," and assists in documenting observations.
- Runway Gen-2: Creates AI-driven video prototypes for observing multimodal creativity.
- Google Data Studio (Looker Studio): Visualizes peer observation data, highlighting common strategies and differences.

Work Instructions

1. Form teams and define the shared challenge.

    (a) Divide participants into groups of 2–4. Provide a clear creative brief, for example: "Design alternatives to single-use plastic bags using

MidJourney." Prompt, for example, MidJourney: *"Eco-friendly packaging inspired by traditional crafts and biodegradable materials."*

   (b) Possible outcome: Teams produce varying visual directions (woven baskets, algae-based packaging, foldable fabric carriers), setting the stage for comparison.

2. Generate multiple AI outputs per team.

   (a) Ask each team to create five finalized visuals. Encourage iteration by prompting MidJourney: "Reframe the concept to emphasize cultural aesthetics—show eco-bags influenced by Japanese origami."

   (b) Possible outcome: One team produces foldable origami-style carriers, while another interprets the same prompt as modular shopping containers.

3. Observe and document peer interactions with AI.

   (a) While teams generate visuals, observers record process details. Use ChatGPT 5 to guide notetaking: *"List keywords used, describe how prompts evolve, and note reactions to AI feedback."*

   (b) Possible outcome: Documentation shows Team A refining prompts by adjusting material descriptors ("biodegradable plastic" $\rightarrow$ "compostable corn starch"), while Team B experiments with stylistic cues ("minimalist design," "heritage patterns").

4. Present results and compare workflows.

   (a) Each team shares their outputs and explains their creative choices. Use ChatGPT5 to draft comparative notes: *"Summarize how Teams A, B, and C approached the same theme differently, and highlight at least two unique prompt strategies per team."*

   (b) Possible outcome: Presentations reveal one group prioritized aesthetics, another emphasized usability, and a third innovated on material science cues.

5. Visualize insights collaboratively.

   (a) Consolidate observations into Google Data Studio. Prompt: *"Visualize shared keywords across teams, clustering them into themes such as materials, aesthetics, and function."*

   (b) Possible outcome: The visualization shows "sustainability" terms dominate across teams, while cultural cues appear in only one group, sparking discussion on overlooked creative dimensions.

Limitations and Tips

One limitation is that AI outputs may overshadow the observation process—participants focus on the images rather than on how prompts were crafted. To counter this, facilitators should emphasize documenting peer decision-making and use AI (like ChatGPT 5) to structure observation logs.

Another limitation is the risk of unequal participation, where confident members dominate the process while others remain passive observers. A useful practice is to rotate roles—every participant alternates between creating prompts and observing peers—ensuring shared ownership of learning.

Finally, peer observation can reproduce biases if all groups use similar strategies. To avoid homogeneity, encourage deliberate experimentation with unusual prompt structures or alternative AI tools. No threshold for learning/observing position (who is learning and who is observing). Even if you're an AI expert, observing beginners' experiment with AI can provide new insights.

6.3 Stakeholder Map

Description of the Tool

A stakeholder map visually represents individuals, groups, or organizations with vested interests in a design or innovation project. It helps teams identify who will be affected, who holds influence, and how various actors are interconnected. The purpose is to ensure that all relevant stakeholders are considered, power dynamics are clarified, and tailored engagement strategies are developed.

The traditional three-step process includes brainstorming stakeholders through cross-functional team sessions, prioritizing using the influence-interest matrix with four-quadrant plotting and engaging through tailored communication strategies. Advanced models include the Salience Model (power, legitimacy, urgency), Network Maps for relationship visualization, and Dynamic Mapping for lifecycle updates. The influence-interest matrix categorizes stakeholders into four quadrants: high influence/high interest (manage closely), high influence/low interest (keep satisfied), low influence/high interest (keep informed), and low influence/low interest (monitor).

Figure 6.3   Stakeholder Map. A stakeholder map illustrating the diverse individuals and roles involved in an AI-enabled system, emphasizing the networked relationships, influence structures, and multi-level participation shaping design and decision-making processes. AI generated image created with Ideogram, Inc., Ideogram.ai, 3.0, 2025.

Why Use AI in Stakeholder Maps

AI enhances stakeholder mapping by automating discovery and revealing hidden dynamics. Entity recognition can mine reports, news, or communication records to identify stakeholders that humans might overlook. Sentiment analysis of communications tracks shifts in support or resistance, while network analysis reveals influence pathways across groups. These capabilities provide faster, broader, and more dynamic maps, leaving human designers to interpret meaning and set priorities.

Suggested AI Programs

- Simply Stakeholders: AI-driven stakeholder sentiment analysis and interactive 3D network maps.
- ClickUp Brain: Provides AI-enhanced templates and automation for stakeholder mapping.
- Insight7: Extracts patterns and data analytics to reveal stakeholder influence.

- TSC.ai: Builds network maps from large-scale databases.
- Lucidchart with AI: Automatically generates diagrams and relationship visuals.

Work Instructions

1. Brainstorm and seed initial stakeholders.

   (a) Start with human-led brainstorming of known actors in a new city-wide electric scooter project (e.g., riders, city officials, local businesses). Then, prompt ChatGPT 5: *"Based on urban mobility projects, suggest additional stakeholders—formal and informal—who may influence adoption or regulation."*

   (b) Possible outcome: AI highlights overlooked actors such as insurance companies, neighborhood safety groups, and repair shop owners, broadening the map beyond the obvious.

2. Define categorization criteria with AI support.

   (a) Humans establish criteria such as influence and interest. Next, feed descriptions into Insight7: *"Group these stakeholders into an influence–interest matrix and explain why each was placed in a given quadrant."*

   (b) Possible outcome: The AI clusters city officials under "high influence/high interest," places casual riders under "low influence/high interest," and justifies each categorization with references to mobility regulations or adoption incentives.

3. Visualize relationships and hidden dynamics.

   (a) Upload communication data (meeting notes, local news mentions, social media posts) to Simply Stakeholders. Prompt: *"Map connections and detect sentiment toward scooter adoption among these stakeholders."*

   (b) Possible outcome: The visualization shows strong positive sentiment from young commuters and negative sentiment from local resident associations, with city council members appearing as bridges between both groups.

4. Refine with human interpretation and AI iteration.

   (a) Review AI outputs and adjust where nuance is missing. Prompt ChatGPT 5: *"Generate three alternative visual narratives explaining the tensions between commuters, residents, and policymakers."*

(b) Possible outcome: Narratives frame the conflict as either (1) innovation vs. safety, (2) economic growth vs. neighborhood stability, or (3) youth mobility vs. intergenerational equity. These framings help teams decide which story best captures stakeholder dynamics.

5. Update dynamically with ongoing monitoring.

   (a) Integrate Lucidchart with AI to refresh maps as new data arrives. For example, prompt: "*Update the stakeholder map weekly using recent news and council agendas. Highlight shifts in sentiment and new actors entering the debate.*"

   (b) Possible outcome: The system flags that insurance providers have shifted from neutral to supportive after new liability frameworks are introduced, prompting the design team to increase engagement.

Limitations and Tips

One limitation when using AI to create stakeholder maps is the risk of inaccurate or incomplete data. Automated tools may identify stakeholders incorrectly, miss less-visible actors, or overstate influence based on noisy inputs. To mitigate this, teams should start with comprehensive and validated information—such as reviewed organizational charts, meeting notes, or verified public records—before inputting data into AI systems.

Another limitation is the difficulty of analyzing complex stakeholder relationships. AI may reduce nuanced, multi-layered connections into overly simple diagrams, leading to a distorted picture of influence and interest. A useful approach is to break down the analysis into smaller steps, feeding AI with context-specific subsets of data (e.g., regulators vs. community groups).

A further limitation lies in the AI's limited ability to grasp project-specific context. For instance, it might misinterpret the urgency of a local advocacy group's influence if it only sees general patterns from past cases. To address this, teams should provide explicit background details about the project—including scope, cultural setting, and stakeholder roles—when prompting AI. Additionally, team members should critically review and supplement AI's analysis with lived knowledge, ensuring that context-sensitive nuances are not lost.

6.4   Problem Statement

Description of the Tool

A problem statement in design thinking is a meaningful, actionable, and human-centered declaration that synthesizes observations about users into a focused direction for innovation. It acts as the compass of the design thinking process: clarifying what matters most, framing the challenge to be solved, and anchoring ideation to genuine user needs. By shaping the "why" behind a project, the problem statement creates both possibility and optimism for generating solutions while offering a reference point against which ideas can be tested.

One common framework is the Point of View (POV) statement, structured as: [User] needs [need] because [insight]. This format foregrounds the human perspective, linking users' unmet needs with the underlying insight that makes the problem worth solving. It strikes a balance between being broad enough to invite creativity and narrow enough to remain manageable. Supporting tools such as Empathy Mapping or How Might We (HMW) statements (which can be found later in this chapter) often precede the problem statement, helping teams distil field research into clear and actionable directions.

Why Use AI in Problem Statement

AI provides opportunities in the problem statement by opening new possibilities for speed, scale, and insight. Data analysis capabilities have significantly advanced with AI programs. For example, sentiment analysis can process thousands of social media posts, reviews, and surveys to identify user emotions and attitudes. Behavioral pattern recognition allows teams to detect subtle and often overlooked user behaviors. Additionally, large-scale data processing enables the analysis of massive interview datasets within minutes, a task that would otherwise take days or weeks. Enhanced synthesis is another area where AI proves valuable. Data visualization tools can transform complex datasets into clear, interpretable visual representations, helping teams make sense of overwhelming information. Predictive analytics allows designers to analyze historical data to anticipate future user needs and trends. Furthermore, AI-driven pattern recognition can uncover correlations between seemingly unrelated data points, offering deeper insights for problem framing.

Figure 6.4 Problem Statement. A design team engaged in structured discussion around an open problem, highlighting uncertainty, divergent perspectives, and collaborative sense-making during early-stage decision-making and problem framing. AI generated image created with Ideogram, Inc., Ideogram.ai, 3.0, 2025.

Suggested AI Programs

- ChatGPT 5 (or other LLM platforms): Useful for synthesizing interview transcripts, re-framing raw observations into candidate POV statements, and generating exploratory "How Might We" variations.
- MonkeyLearn: A no-code NLP (Natural Language Processing) platform for sentiment analysis, keyword extraction, and clustering survey responses.
- Qualtrics Text iQL: An NLP-powered survey analysis tool that uncovers themes and hidden insights in open-text responses.
- Quid: Provides large-scale data visualization to identify user clusters, trends, and thematic patterns.
- Tableau with Einstein AI (Salesforce): Combines visualization with predictive analytics, projecting user needs from past behaviors.
- Hotjar: Captures real-time user behavioral data through heatmaps, session recordings, and feedback widgets.

Work Instructions[1]

1. Capture and preprocess user data with AI monitoring.

   (a) Here we use a healthcare example. Healthcare teams can configure AI-driven systems to continuously capture patient feedback from post-visit surveys and online forums.

   (b) Tools such as MonkeyLearn can classify incoming patient reviews as "scheduling issues," "treatment concerns," or "staff communication." This creates a real-time pipeline of categorized feedback for rapid analysis.

2. Use AI for large-scale data categorization.

   (a) Once feedback is collected, NLP (Natural Language Processing) tools such as Qualtrics Text iQ can cluster thousands of open-text survey responses.

   (b) A hospital might discover that "waiting time" and "doctor availability" appear as dominant themes, while "clarity of diagnosis" emerges as an unexpected but critical concern. AI reduces the manual effort of coding and surfaces patterns that matter for problem framing.

3. Visualize and explore patterns.

   (a) Visualization platforms like Quid or Tableau with Einstein AI can then map these categories into interpretable diagrams.

   (b) In healthcare, a Quid map might show "clarity of diagnosis" strongly connected to "anxiety" and "follow-up compliance." This makes visible the relational dynamics between patient emotions and systemic processes.

4. Translate AI outputs into candidate statements with LLM support.

   (a) Using ChatGPT 5, design teams can convert clustered insights into draft POV (Point of View) statements. For instance: "Patients with chronic conditions need clearer explanations of diagnostic results because uncertainty undermines adherence to treatment."

   (b) Multiple versions can be generated and compared for scope, tone, and actionability.

5. Validate insights with human empathy and finalize.

---

[1] In applying AI to problem statement development, it is useful to show how this process plays out across multiple domains. In "Work Instructions," each step uses a fresh domain example to demonstrate the mechanics.

(a) AI-generated clusters and drafts must be checked against real stories. Doctors and nurses review transcripts of patient interviews to confirm whether the AI's clustering reflects genuine lived experiences.

(b) If "clarity of diagnosis" is identified as an issue, professionals can verify it by listening to actual patient accounts of confusion after appointments, ensuring the problem statement resonates authentically.

(c) Using ChatGPT 5 or other LLM platforms, the validated statement is then consolidated into a clear POV that guides further design. This might be: "Patients with complex treatment plans need transparent and simple explanations because medical jargon leads to misunderstanding and reduced adherence."

Limitations and Tips

A key limitation is that AI can process data but cannot feel empathy. A sentiment analysis tool may reveal that users are "frustrated" or "anxious," but it cannot capture the lived experience behind those emotions. Designers must therefore revisit raw stories and quotes, weaving human empathy back into the AI-generated clusters to prevent superficial framing.

Another limitation is the risk of generic or shallow insights when using generic datasets. Off-the-shelf models may over-generalize, producing insights that lack contextual depth. To counter this, teams should customize AI pipelines with domain-specific data—for instance, training on interviews and feedback collected directly from their user base.

Finally, AI outputs can overwhelm with volume rather than clarity. Visualization dashboards may generate endless clusters or patterns, leaving teams unsure of where to focus. A useful strategy is to apply the "How Might We" lens immediately after AI synthesis. By converting clusters into HMW questions, teams ensure outputs translate into action rather than confusion.

6.5   Opportunity Map

Description of the Tool

An Opportunity Map is a structured framework for identifying, visualizing, and prioritizing areas where innovation can create value. It helps teams move beyond isolated ideas to systematically explore unmet customer needs, gaps in the current market, and under-served user groups. The process usually includes:

1. Collecting customer stories and contextual observations.
2. Conducting gap analysis to find where expectations exceed existing solutions.
3. Recognizing patterns across user segments and contexts.
4. Breaking large opportunities into smaller, solvable components.

By layering opportunities on dimensions such as feasibility, impact, and strategic fit, teams create a visual map that clarifies where to focus innovation resources.

Why Use AI in Opportunity Map

AI strengthens opportunity mapping by scanning vast data sources in real time (e.g. news, patents, social media, and consumer behavior) to uncover unmet needs and weak signals. It helps detect trends earlier, identifies gaps between expectations and current solutions, and forecasts which opportunities have the highest potential impact. While AI accelerates discovery and prioritization, human judgment ensures cultural relevance and strategic alignment.

Suggested AI Programs

- AlphaSense: AI-driven business research and financial intelligence.
- Trend Hunter AI: Identifies early-stage cultural and market trends.
- Crayon: Competitive intelligence platform with AI-based tracking.
- Quantilope: Consumer research tool with predictive analytics.
- GWI Spark: Provides consumer insights via natural language queries.

Work Instructions

1. Configure AI systems for trend scanning.

    (a) Begin with broad exploration. Prompt Trend Hunter AI, for example in our healthcare case: *"Identify three emerging consumer health trends in vitamins and supplements, focusing on sustainability and personalization."*

Figure 6.5 Opportunity Map. A cross-functional team collaboratively synthesizing information under a shared, data-rich visualization, representing collective sense-making, alignment, and convergence toward informed design and strategic decisions. AI generated image created with Ideogram, Inc., Ideogram.ai, 3.0, 2025.

    (b) Possible outcome: AI highlights micro-dosing supplements, plant-based packaging, and AI-guided personalized vitamin plans. These signals frame the opportunity landscape.

2. Conduct AI-supported gap analysis.

    (a) Feed customer reviews from e-commerce platforms into Quantilope. Prompt: "Detect gaps where consumer expectations are unmet compared to current supplement offerings."

    (b) Possible outcome: AI surfaces repeated frustrations such as "unclear dosage guidance" and "plastic-heavy packaging." These pain points become raw opportunities for design.

3. Analyze competition and adjacent innovations.

    (a) Use AlphaSense or Crayon to scan industry reports and patents. Prompt: *"Summarize competitors' recent innovations in personalized supplements. Highlight areas of saturation versus white space."*

(b) Possible outcome: AI finds many players in DNA-based supplement personalization but fewer offering eco-friendly distribution systems. This identifies under-served niches.

4. Forecast feasibility and impact.

(a) With Quantilope, simulate adoption scenarios. Prompt: "*Model the adoption likelihood of eco-friendly supplement packaging among 18–35-year-olds in the South Africa market.*"

(b) Possible outcome: AI predicts high short-term adoption if costs stay competitive but notes logistical risks. This sharpens the feasibility-impact assessment.

5. Generate and visualize the opportunity map.

(a) Bring insights into GWI Spark. Prompt: "*Organize identified opportunities into a matrix by feasibility (low/high) and potential impact (low/high). Output in table form.*"

(b) Possible outcome: The AI map shows "AI-guided personalization" in the high-impact/high-feasibility quadrant, while "biodegradable capsules" fall under high-impact but lower feasibility. Human review adjusts final placements before sharing with stakeholders.

Limitations and Tips

One limitation is that AI-identified opportunities may lack cultural or contextual relevance. For example, an opportunity flagged as promising in one region may not fit local lifestyles elsewhere. Teams should validate findings with on-the-ground user research to ensure relevance.

Another limitation is that AI predictions depend heavily on historical data quality. If past datasets underrepresent certain consumer groups, forecasts may be skewed. Designers should supplement AI with fresh, diverse data to avoid narrow conclusions.

6.6   AI-Assisted Definition of Success

Description of the Tool

Defining success in design thinking establishes measurable criteria that integrate traditional project management factors with human-centered considerations. Unlike conventional metrics that emphasize time, cost, or efficiency alone, design thinking emphasizes dimensions such as desirability, feasibility, viability, and sustainability. This holistic approach ensures that solutions not only function technically and economically but also resonate with users and remain viable over time. This framework typically involves four dimensions:

- Desirable: Do people want or value the solution?
- Feasible: Can it be designed and delivered effectively?
- Viable: Does it create more value than it consumes?
- Sustainable: Can the solution be maintained and evolved throughout its lifecycle?

Best practice includes developing a multi-layered framework with success criteria (tangible outcomes), success factors (conditions enabling success), critical success factors (whose absence would cause failure), and KPIs (quantitative measures tracking progress). By aligning all stakeholders on these aspects, defining success provides a shared compass that guides projects through the uncertainties of design and innovation.

Why Use AI in Define Success

AI strengthens the define success activity by offering predictive analytics, scenario modelling, and metric optimization. It helps design teams simulate trade-offs across desirability, feasibility, viability, and sustainability, while aligning diverse stakeholder priorities. AI can surface benchmarks, forecast risks, and cluster qualitative inputs into coherent criteria. Importantly, it accelerates synthesis without replacing the nuanced, human-driven process of deciding what success truly means.

Suggested AI Programs

- Claude (or other LLMs): Effective for synthesizing long stakeholder requirement documents, identifying recurring priorities, and reframing them as measurable success dimensions.
- Microsoft Power BI with AI: Enables automated KPI tracking through customizable dashboards and predictive performance monitoring.

Figure 6.6   AI-Assisted Definition of Success. A diverse team collectively defining success criteria, illustrating alignment around shared goals, evaluation metrics, and values that guide human–AI system design and assessment. AI generated image created with Ideogram, Inc., Ideogram.ai, 3.0, 2025.

- Tableau with Einstein Analytics (Salesforce): Offers scenario modelling and forecasting, helping teams test different success frameworks.
- IBM Watson Studio: Provides machine learning tools for outcome prediction and advanced risk analysis.

Work Instructions

1. Preparation with AI-assisted data gathering.

    (a) Here we illustrate with an education example. Begin by orienting the team with evidence from related projects. Prompt Claude with: "Summarize three Education Technology case studies where success was measured in both learning outcomes and adoption rates. Identify recurring criteria and missed opportunities."

    (b) *Possible outcome: Claude returns a summary highlighting "student comprehension gains," "teacher adoption rates," and "cost per learner" as recurring success measures, while also flagging overlooked factors such as emotional engagement. This output informs the team's starting point before brainstorming.*

2. Collaborative brainstorming and clustering.

   (a) Invite human stakeholders to list their ideas first, then use AI to synthesize. Input into Claude or ChatGPT 5: "Cluster the following criteria into desirability, feasibility, viability, and sustainability categories. Suggest one new criterion for each cluster, based on industry benchmarks."

   (b) *Possible outcome: The tool categorizes "student engagement" under desirability, "teacher training resources" under feasibility, "affordability per student" under viability, and "IT support" under sustainability. It also proposes "equitable access" as an additional sustainability metric.*

3. Scenario modelling for feasibility and viability.

   (a) Use Tableau with Einstein Analytics for "what-if" analysis. Upload project parameters and simulate scaling from 500 to 50,000 students. Prompt: "Model scenarios for user growth and show which KPIs are most at risk when scaling."

   (b) Possible outcome: The model forecasts that scaling risks lowering "personalization quality" while sharply increasing server costs. This insight adjusts feasibility and sustainability targets.

4. Refining criteria with benchmark comparisons.

   (a) *In IBM Watson Studio (or Claude, ChatGPT 5), run: "Compare our draft success criteria with current benchmarks in educational technology. Highlight missing or underweighted metrics."*

   (b) *Possible outcome: The AI suggests adding "monthly active learners" as a stronger engagement KPI than "daily active users," aligning with real-world EdTech usage cycles.*

5. Validating alignment and documenting criteria.

   (a) *Finally, check resonance with human stakeholders. Prompt Claude or ChatGPT 5: "Draft three alternative success statements integrating desirability, feasibility, viability, and sustainability. Phrase them in accessible language for teachers and administrators."*

   (b) *Possible outcome: The team receives candidate statements such as: "Success means achieving a 20% improvement in student comprehension scores within a 12-month pilot, while ensuring equitable access across schools and reducing per-student costs by 10%." After review, one is finalized as the guiding statement.*

Limitations and Tips

A limitation of AI in defining success is that it cannot fully capture cultural or subjective dimensions of success, such as the sense of pride or community felt by teachers and students. To address this, teams should combine AI-generated KPIs with qualitative measures, such as teacher reflections or student narratives, ensuring human meaning remains central.

Another limitation is the risk of overfitting success metrics to historical data, which may not apply to innovative or unprecedented projects. AI might emphasize "test score improvements" because past projects valued them, but new goals—like fostering creativity—might be overlooked. Teams should explicitly introduce aspirational or future-oriented success factors that AI cannot infer from precedent.

A further limitation lies in stakeholder misalignment when over-relying on AI clustering. While AI can highlight overlapping priorities, it may miss subtle differences in language or intent. For example, "accessibility" for policymakers may mean affordability, while for teachers it means usability. Teams should therefore run facilitated discussions to clarify meanings after AI synthesis.

6.7 Value Hypothesis

Description of the Tool

A Value Hypothesis is a structured assumption about whether a product or service delivers enough value for customers to justify purchasing or using it. It defines what customers will pay, what problem is solved, and what outcomes are achieved. A common formulation is: "[Client] will spend [cost] to purchase our [product/service] to solve their [specific problem]." This tool aligns with Lean Startup methodology, guiding teams through:

- Hypothesis formation (based on customer discovery),
- Validation (through MVPs, A/B testing, or pilot launches),
- Behavioral analysis (tracking usage and purchase data).

Figure 6.7   Value Hypothesis. A team articulating value hypotheses, representing the formulation and alignment of assumptions about user, organizational, and societal value that inform human–AI system design and evaluation. AI generated image created with Ideogram, Inc., Ideogram.ai, 3.0, 2025.

By clarifying assumptions early, the Value Hypothesis minimizes risk before heavy investment in development.

Why Use AI in Value Hypothesis

AI enhances value hypothesis testing by accelerating customer insight generation. It can analyze vast amounts of feedback, detect hidden value propositions, and generate candidate hypotheses. AI also strengthens validation: predictive models forecast adoption likelihood, while A/B testing platforms automate iterative experiments. Crucially, AI speeds up cycles of assumption → test → refinement, letting teams focus on strategic judgment rather than repetitive analysis.

Suggested AI Programs

- Optimizely: AI-enhanced experimentation and hypothesis testing.
- VWO (Visual Website Optimizer): AI-powered A/B and multivariate testing.

- Evolv AI: Uses machine learning to optimize customer experiences across variations.
- Hotjar AI: Provides behavioral insights via heatmaps and AI-driven session analysis.
- Google Optimize: Runs controlled experiments with automated recommendations.

Work Instructions

Sustainable Fashion Example

1. Generate initial value hypotheses with AI.

   (a) Start by gathering customer sentiment around sustainable clothing. Prompt ChatGPT or other LLMs: *"From these 500 customer reviews, generate three value hypotheses about why people buy sustainable fashion."*

   (b) Possible outcome: AI suggests: (1) "Eco-conscious consumers will pay 20% more for recycled fabric jeans to reduce environmental impact," (2) "Urban professionals will purchase modular clothing to reduce wardrobe clutter," (3) "Young buyers will pay a premium for transparent supply-chain fashion to support ethical labor."

2. Refine hypotheses with customer segmentation.

   (a) Feed the draft hypotheses into Hotjar AI with behavioral data. Prompt: *"Map which customer segments resonate with each hypothesis based on browsing and purchase data."*

   (b) Possible outcome: Data shows that premium-paying eco-conscious buyers cluster in the 25–34 age group, while transparency resonates strongly with Gen Z customers.

3. Design experiments using AI-powered testing tools.

   (a) Set up A/B tests through Optimizely or VWO. Prompt: "Run a test comparing interest in recycled denim vs. modular clothing, measuring click-throughs and cart additions."

   (b) Possible outcome: Optimizely reports a 15% higher engagement with re-cycled denim messaging, indicating stronger traction for that hypothesis.

4. Forecast adoption with predictive analytics.

   (a) Use Evolv AI to model likely customer adoption. Prompt: *"Predict purchase likelihood for recycled denim jeans priced at a 20% premium, based on historic sales data."*

   (b) Possible outcome: AI forecasts a 35% adoption rate in eco-conscious clusters, but warns adoption falls sharply outside that segment.

5. Iterate and consolidate into a tested hypothesis.

   (a) After analyzing outcomes, refine the statement. Final example: "*Eco-conscious millennials will spend 20% more on recycled fabric jeans to reduce environmental impact, provided style remains competitive.*"

   (b) This tested value hypothesis becomes the foundation for MVP development and scaling decisions.

Limitations and Tips

One limitation is that AI-generated hypotheses require human validation. Without domain expertise, AI may propose ideas that sound logical but lack cultural or contextual fit. Teams should validate AI suggestions against field interviews and real purchasing data.

Another limitation is the risk of overlooking nuanced customer segments. Automated clustering may merge distinct groups under broad categories (e.g., "eco-conscious buyers"), masking differences in age, geography, or lifestyle. To address this, segment hypotheses explicitly by demographic or psychographic factors before testing.

A further limitation lies in the investment needed for testing infrastructure. Effective AI-powered validation (e.g., A/B testing, behavioral analytics) requires tools, data pipelines, and staff training. Smaller teams can adopt lighter setups (e.g., Google Optimize with survey-based validation) to test hypotheses affordably.

Finally, ethical considerations arise in using customer data for hypothesis development. Collecting and analyzing behavioral data must comply with privacy standards and be transparent to users. Teams should clearly communicate how data is used and seek consent where required.

6.8 Critical Items Diagram

Description of the Tool

A Critical Items Diagram helps design thinking teams identify and prioritize the most decisive elements for project success. It synthesizes findings from earlier research and observation phases, filtering out secondary details to highlight user pain points, core needs, and mission-critical functions. By focusing on "what matters most," the diagram provides a structured base for ideation and prototyping, ensuring the team directs effort toward elements with the greatest impact.

Traditional approaches involve functional decomposition (breaking a system into its essential parts), assessing the potential impact of failure, and clustering critical functions into a shared visualization. This tool helps teams agree on the few essential items that should drive design, aligning perspectives before creative exploration begins.

Why Use AI in Critical Items Diagram

AI accelerates the Critical Items Diagram by processing large volumes of qualitative and quantitative data. It identifies recurring pain points in user behavior, clusters them into themes, and highlights high-impact areas that may otherwise be overlooked. Beyond analysis, AI can suggest experience improvements, forecast emerging issues, and simulate user interactions for refinement. In short, AI acts as a collaborator that makes prioritization more evidence-based and responsive.

Suggested AI Programs

- Notion AI / ChatGPT 5: Analyze user feedback and convert it into clustered insights.
- RiskWatch: AI-driven platform for risk assessment and critical failure identification.
- LogicGate: Provides workflow automation and AI-based risk prioritization.
- Palantir Foundry: Advanced analytics for mapping critical dependencies in complex systems.

Work Instructions

Urban Mobility Example

1. Set up AI tools and define objectives.

    (a) Begin by clarifying the project's focus. For a bike-sharing service redesign, prompt ChatGPT 5: *"From survey data and app reviews, extract recurring issues that affect user experience in urban bike-sharing."*

Figure 6.8   Critical Items Diagram. A collaborative analysis session where a multidisciplinary team reviews a critical items diagram to understand relationships, information flows, and decision dependencies within a complex system. AI generated image created with Ideogram, Inc., Ideogram.ai, 3.0, 2025.

(b) Possible outcome: AI surfaces pain points such as "unclear pricing," "bike availability at peak hours," and "confusing app navigation." These become candidate critical items.

2. Collect and cluster user inputs with AI support.

(a) Invite team members to add their own observations. Then, feed combined inputs into Notion AI: "*Cluster these issues into themes and highlight which appear most frequently across user groups.*"

(b) Possible outcome: AI groups issues into clusters: Pricing Transparency, Availability Reliability, App Usability. This simplifies the raw data into clearer categories.

3. Visualize relationships and dependencies.

(a) Move to a platform like Miro or Palantir Foundry. Prompt: "Map dependencies between pricing, availability, and navigation. Show how failure in one area impacts the overall user journey."

(b) Possible outcome: The visualization shows that availability reliability has the strongest downstream impact on satisfaction, linking to both trust and repeat usage.

4. Refine and prioritize critical items.

   (a) Ask ChatGPT 5: "Propose three 'How Might We' questions that focus on the most impactful clusters."

   (b) Possible outcome: AI generates: "How might we ensure bikes are always available during peak hours?" and "How might we simplify navigation for first-time riders?" These reframe insights into design opportunities.

5. Iterate and validate with AI simulations.

   (a) Run quick scenario tests using RiskWatch or LogicGate. Prompt: "*Simulate the impact if availability reliability improves by 20%. Which user satisfaction metrics improve most?*"

   (b) Possible outcome: AI predicts higher retention and reduced complaints, validating availability as the most critical focus.

Limitations and Tips

A key limitation is that AI lacks intuition and empathy. While it can highlight pain points, it cannot sense emotional weight (e.g., frustration from embarrassment at failing to unlock a bike in public). Teams should always validate AI outputs with user stories and direct observation.

Another limitation is data dependency. If the training data or feedback pool is biased toward certain user groups, the diagram may overemphasize their concerns. To counter this, collect inputs from a diverse set of users before analysis.

Finally, resource constraints may hinder adoption. Advanced platforms like Palantir Foundry can be costly for smaller teams. A practical solution is to combine lightweight tools (ChatGPT 5 + Notion AI + Miro) to achieve similar outcomes at lower cost.

6.9 Jobs to Be Done (JTBD)

Description of the Tool

The Jobs to be Done (JTBD) framework emphasizes that customers "hire" products or services to make progress in their lives. Instead of focusing on demographic categories or product features, JTBD asks: What task is the user trying to accomplish? The framework often uses a three-part formula: Situation—Motivation—Expected Result, expressed in the structure "When I [situation], I want to [motivation], so I can [expected result]."

By shifting the focus to tasks and outcomes, JTBD helps teams uncover unspoken needs, align design with user intent, and inspire innovations that directly support progress in real contexts.

Why Use AI in Jobs to Be Done

AI enhances JTBD analysis by accelerating discovery, structuring inputs, and surfacing hidden motivations. Large language models can quickly organize interviews into the JTBD template, while sentiment analysis identifies emotional drivers behind user actions. AI also supports simulated user responses, enabling teams to probe "what jobs exist but are unserved" more deeply. By compiling and clustering these findings, AI helps teams map entire customer journeys and identify opportunities for differentiation.

Suggested AI Programs

- Insight7: AI-powered transcription that extracts recurring themes and organizes them into JTBD-style task statements.
- Notably AI: Provides ready-made templates and automation for JTBD analysis, reducing setup time.
- ChatGPT 5 (or other Large Language Model platforms): Useful for drafting JTBD canvases, generating hypotheses, and simulating user perspectives.
- Helio: A research platform with AI features for rapid user testing and JTBD task framing.
- Qualtrics with AI: Enables advanced survey design and open-text analysis to uncover hidden jobs.

Work Instructions

1. Identify the situation with AI-supported data gathering.

   (a) Begin by collecting transcripts from student interviews about online learning. Prompt Insight7: *"From these transcripts, extract situations where students describe friction or unmet needs in remote classes."*

   (b) Possible outcome: AI highlights statements such as *"When I attend late-night classes after work..."* or *"When I try to review recorded lectures..."* These situations seed the JTBD framework.

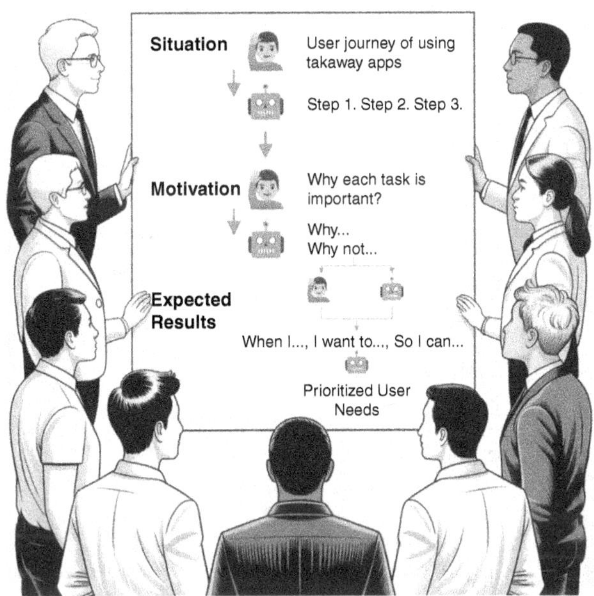

Figure 6.9 Jobs to be Done (JTBD). A structured framework linking situation, motivation, and expected results to translate user journeys into prioritized user needs, illustrating human–AI–supported sense-making and requirements definition in design processes. Figure partially generated by ideogram.ai in August 2025 and edited in Sketch.

2. Probe motivations through AI-driven inquiry.

   (a) Use ChatGPT-5 to ask follow-up "why" questions. Prompt: "*For each situation above, generate 3 probing 'why' questions to uncover the deeper motivation behind the task.*"

   (b) Possible outcome: For the late-night class example, AI generates: "*Why do you prefer late-night sessions?*" → "*Because I balance study with work commitments.*" This reveals the motivation of time flexibility.

3. Structure responses into JTBD statements.

   (a) Apply the formula When I. . ., I want to. . ., so I can. . .. Prompt: "Rewrite the extracted situations and motivations into structured JTBD statements."

   (b) Possible outcome: "*When I attend late-night classes after work, I want shorter lecture segments, so I can stay focused and retain knowledge despite fatigue.*"

4. Organize insights into a JTBD template.

   (a) Upload structured responses into Notably AI. Prompt: "*Compile the data into a three-column table with Situation, Motivation, and Expected Result.*"

(b) Possible outcome: The tool outputs a JTBD table where each row represents one distinct job to be done, allowing quick comparison across learners.

5. Synthesize and innovate using AI.

(a) Finally, use Helio or ChatGPT 5 to cluster similar jobs and propose opportunities. Prompt: "Identify 3 patterns across the JTBD table and suggest possible product or service innovations."

(b) Possible outcome: AI suggests innovations such as "adaptive micro-lectures," "AI reminders for revision," or "collaborative night-time study groups." These become candidates for prototyping.

Limitations and Tips

One limitation is that AI may generate overly generic JTBD statements if inputs are vague. To avoid this, teams should provide transcripts rich in context and prompt AI with specific task-related details. Human review ensures statements retain authenticity.

AI clustering may bias toward dominant patterns, overlooking smaller but high-value jobs. Teams should scan for minority voices in the dataset and deliberately test whether niche but impactful tasks—such as accessibility needs—are fully represented.

6.10 Prepare & Train Use Case: Designing a Smarter Street Trash Bin for Shanghai with AI

Our challenge: to create a functional street bin that also enhances Shanghai's visual identity.

Shanghai is a city that prides itself on its modern image, yet in many neighborhoods trash bins are unevenly distributed, typically lacking a distinctive design. To meet our challenge, we explored how AI could support the entire design-related process: identifying best locations, defining the core functions, and shaping the trash bin's appearance.

We began by using large language models like **ChatGPT** and **Perplexity** to research the current state of trash bins in Shanghai and study existing design examples. Perplexity's ability to provide cited sources helped us quickly gather reliable data, while ChatGPT assisted in refining our ideas and proposing directions when the next step was unclear. This early research stage allowed us to prepare and define key priorities for our project: mobility, visual appeal, and integration with the city's style.

Our final concept was a mobile trash bin designed for the Bund waterfront walkway, a popular visual attraction for both tourists and locals of the Shanghai skyline on display across the Huangpu River, highlighting the city district's signature Art Deco elements with a modern anthropomorphic form. The bin would move autonomously on tracks, navigating busy pedestrian areas during peak hours and using image recognition or electronic signals to approach users when needed. We used **Midjourney** to generate a variety of visual sketches, testing different color schemes, shapes, and proportions. While the AI-generated imagery gave us a strong aesthetic starting point, it also revealed a limitation that AI could not deliver functional engineering details or resolve all design constraints.

The team worked in a reciprocal process, with all members involved in both constructing prompts and evaluating AI outputs. Reviewing results together helped us merge the best AI suggestions with human insight. ChatGPT often proposed decision-making frameworks that helped us weigh trade-offs, but we found this needed adaptation to fit cultural expectations and practical use. One unexpected benefit was that communicating with AI required us to translate abstract ideas into clear language, which clarified our own thinking and improved internal communication.

AI helped us prepare by accelerating decision-making by synthesizing fragmented inputs into coherent options and reducing the time spent verifying feasibility. For example, we could compare multiple proposals within minutes instead of hours, quickly ruling out designs that were impractical or misaligned with our goals. However, we also saw where AI fell short. It could not fully capture the nuances of user behavior, nor could it account for the emotional and cultural resonance that makes a public design feel truly local. We realized that we needed to spend more time training our AI, developing stronger and more detailed prompts, and perhaps utilizing an AI assistant.

The final design concept balanced AI's strengths in rapid visualization and information processing with our own ability to adapt, contextualize, and humanize the outcome. The mobile bin's Art Deco-inspired curves and friendly "pixel eye" features gave it personality, while its autonomous movement addressed functional gaps in waste disposal during high-traffic times.

Key Learnings

- AI excels at gathering data, generating concepts, and speeding up iteration.
- Human oversight ensures cultural fit, functional feasibility, and emotional resonance.
- The act of "prompting" AI sharpens design thinking by forcing clarity in communication.

Final Reflection

This project confirmed that AI works best as a partner, not as a replacement. By combining AI's ability to rapidly process information with our understanding of place, people, and culture, we created a design that was both imaginative and grounded in reality. The process has given us a model for using AI in future urban design challenges, ensuring technology and human creativity work in harmony.

6.11   Prepare & Train Use Case: Designing a Futuristic Poster with AI

Our challenge: to create a fresh, futuristic, and visually striking poster to promote a publishing event for this book.

The poster must communicate our theme clearly while standing out in a crowded space. We wanted bold fonts, dynamic layouts, and imagery that hinted at technological creativity. None of us were professional graphic designers, and while we had ideas about the style, translating them into a polished design was another matter.

To begin, we tested different ways of working with AI. We set up four design pathways that varied the role of AI, ranging from completely AI-generated posters to designs created entirely by humans, and two mixed approaches in between. This structure allowed us to consider where AI excelled, where it fell short, and how human creativity could bridge the gaps.

The most surprising insight came early in the process. Using **ChatGPT** to refine our prompts drastically improved our efficiency. Instead of spending hours manually searching for typefaces or visual references, we could describe our vision and have **GPT** generate lists of futuristic font ideas, style suggestions, and pattern concepts in seconds. This meant we could move past vague ideas and quickly zero in on specific visual directions.

We then used **Midjourney** to turn these refined prompts into poster imagery. By specifying details such as color schemes, focal points, and even grid system requirements, we could push the visuals closer to our intended style. However, we discovered that AI struggled with certain design fundamentals, especially text layout. Specific words used in instructions matter! When we asked for a grid system, the AI often interpreted it literally, producing intersecting lines rather than balanced compositions.

Our team process was sequential but highly collaborative. Each member proposed initial ideas, which were then tested through AI-generated visuals. We reviewed every output together, voting on which elements worked best. In the pure AI pathway, the results were visually rich but often lacked logic in image arrangement and text placement. In the collaborative pathway, AI provided main images, logos, and fonts, while humans manually arranged them into a coherent layout. This hybrid approach proved the most successful, combining AI's speed and variety with human judgment in structure and readability.

The final poster used AI-generated patterns and typography suggestions but was assembled manually to ensure clarity and balance. It achieved our goal of a clean, modern, and futuristic look while still feeling approachable. AI had accelerated the ideation and asset creation stages, freeing us to focus our energy on refining the layout and ensuring the message came through clearly.

Key Learnings

- AI is a powerful tool for generating prompts, visual elements, and design inspiration, but it struggles with complex layout logic.
- Hybrid workflows, where AI produces components and humans assemble them, yield the best results.
- Effective prompting is critical; the more specific we were, the closer the outputs matched our vision.

Final Reflection

This project showed us that AI's value in design lies not in replacing the designer, but in enhancing the designer's toolkit. By handling repetitive or time-consuming tasks like asset creation and style exploration, AI allowed us to experiment more and make better creative decisions. In future projects, we want to explore ways to train AI models to better understand grid systems and compositional rules, so the collaboration can extend even further into layout design.

References

Dorst, K. (2011). The core of "design thinking" and its application. *Design Studies*, 32(6), 521–532. https://doi.org/10.1016/j.destud.2011.07.006

Verganti, R. (2009). Design-driven innovation: Changing the rules of competition by radically innovating what things mean. *Harvard Business Press*.

7

Empathize & Define: AID Tools and Use Cases

The Empathize and Define activities of design thinking serve as the foundational bedrock for human-centered innovation, requiring designers and innovators to develop deep understanding of users, contexts, and problems, as detailed by Brown's authoritative article in 2008. Today, AI is fundamentally transforming these research activities from manual, time-intensive processes into efficient, insight-rich approaches that enhance rather than replace human empathy and understanding.

The integration of AI into Empathize and Define activities represents a significant evolution in qualitative and quantitative methodology. Recent comprehensive research indicates that AI deployment in UX research shows remarkable efficiency gains, with 90% of professionals using AI during analysis and synthesis phases, particularly for summarizing notes, transcripts, and identifying trends and themes. However, this transformation requires careful consideration of AI's limitations, as 29% of professionals report that AI lacks nuance and context, while 27% cite accuracy concerns, necessitating substantial human review and validation, according to Wiedmaier in 2024.

The evolution of design thinking research tools reflects decades of human-centered design development. Building on foundational frameworks, contemporary AI-enhanced approaches leverage pattern recognition, sentiment analysis, and automation capabilities while preserving the empathetic core of user research. Recent systematic literature reviews have explored the synergies between design thinking and AI, highlighting the complementary nature of these approaches, as discussed by Sreenivasan & Suresh in 2024.

© The Author(s), under exclusive license to Springer Nature Switzerland AG 2026

D. Graff et al., *Design Thinking with Artificial Intelligence*, Palgrave Executive Essentials,
https://doi.org/10.1007/978-3-032-10543-1_7

AI's impact on Empathize and Define extends across multiple methodologies and applications. Current implementations show strength in data processing and analysis, where AI can "sift, scan, sort, and sum up open-ended data—including voice, video, and text," according to authors Moran and Rosala in 2024. This capability proves especially valuable for mixed-methods research approaches that combine qualitative insights with quantitative analysis. Advanced AI systems can now process and summarize video clips, opening possibilities for automated analysis of usability studies, though current technology still requires significant human oversight for meaningful interpretation, as stated by Oberoi in 2024.

The democratization of research capabilities through AI tools represents another significant development. AI-powered platforms enable broader organizational participation in research activities, reducing traditional barriers and allowing design thinking teams to conduct more frequent, iterative studies. However, this accessibility requires careful consideration of research quality and methodological rigor, as AI outputs must be validated by experienced researchers to ensure accuracy and relevance.

Looking toward practical implementation, successful AI integration in Empathize and Define requires strategic consideration of several critical factors. Organizations must assess their current research processes and data infrastructure before selecting appropriate AI tools. The most effective approaches begin with pilot projects that allow teams to understand AI capabilities and limitations in their specific context. Investment in team training for AI-enhanced methodologies proves essential, along with gradual integration that preserves existing workflow strengths while adding new capabilities.

Critical success factors for AI-enhanced design thinking research include ensuring high-quality input data for all AI applications while maintaining careful balance between AI insights and human judgment. Regular updates to AI models with new data and feedback help improve accuracy over time, while cross-functional stakeholder support facilitates broader organizational adoption. Proactive attention to privacy, bias, and transparency concerns throughout implementation helps maintain ethical research standards and user trust.

The preservation of human-centered design principles remains paramount in AI-enhanced research, as discussed in an article by Saeidnia and Ausloos in 2024. The most effective implementations use AI to amplify human capabilities rather than replacing empathetic understanding and strategic thinking. This synthesis combines AI automation for data processing and pattern recognition with human expertise for interpretation, validation, and strategic decision-making. Such approaches preserve design thinking's human-centered foundation while unlocking unprecedented research efficiency and depth of insight.

This chapter examines ten essential AID tools (7.1, AI Support for Empathy Interviews; 7.2, Explorative AI-to-AI Interviews; 7.3, Ask 5x Why; 7.4, 5W+ H with AI; 7.5, AI Lead User; 7.6, AI Generated User Profile; 7.7, Empathy Map with AI; 7.8, Customer Journey Map; 7.9, AI Storytelling; 7.10, Context Mapping with AI) and two use cases (7.11, Co-Creating University Chairs & Tables with AI; 7.12, AI-Driven Empathy in Shanghai Metro Carriages), demonstrating how each maintains its empathetic core while gaining new capabilities through intelligent augmentation. These AID tools span the complete research lifecycle, from initial user discovery through insight synthesis and strategic application. Each tool includes practical implementation guidance, current AI capabilities, and considerations for maintaining research quality and ethical standards.

Interviews occupy a central place in Empathize and Define, serving as both a means of generating empathy and a tool for exploration. With the rise of AI, interviewing can now take two complementary forms. On one side, AI supporting human interviews enhances traditional empathy-building conversations by lightening the researcher's cognitive load and amplifying insight, while keeping the focus squarely on the lived experiences of participants. We explore this option in AI support for Empathy Interview (7.1). On the other side, in Explorative AI-to-AI Interviews (7.2) we shift the stage to dialogues conducted entirely between AI agents, generating speculative insights and surfacing hypotheses that can inspire new research directions. Taken together, these approaches illustrate how AI can act both as an assistant in deepening human connection and as a generator of novel ideas, offering design researchers a spectrum of tools that balance empathetic depth with creative breadth.

The future of design thinking research lies not in replacing human intuition and empathy with AI, but in orchestrating their collaboration to create more comprehensive, efficient, and impactful user understanding than either approach could achieve independently. This collaborative model preserves the essential human elements of design research while leveraging AI's computational strengths to process larger datasets, identify subtle patterns, and accelerate insight development in service of better human-centered design outcomes.

Figure 7.1   AI Support for Empathy Interviews. An AI-supported empathy interview, where a digital agent augments human discussion by facilitating shared understanding, emotional insight, and reflective sense-making during user research. AI generated image created with Ideogram, Inc., Ideogram.ai, 3.0, 2025.

7.1   AI Support for Empathy Interviews

Description of Tool

Interviews for empathy are the backbone of design thinking, enabling researchers to understand users beyond surface behaviors. They emphasize the act of listening deeply and encouraging participants to share their lived experiences, emotions, and motivations. This method requires the interviewer to maintain full presence, allowing space for the participant's story to unfold naturally rather than rigidly following a script.

Traditionally, empathy interviews rely heavily on the researcher's ability to manage the conversation, record responses, and interpret subtle cues simultaneously, which can be mentally demanding. With AI support, many of these logistical burdens can be reduced, freeing the interviewer to focus entirely on cultivating trust and empathy. In this sense, AI functions as a quiet partner in the background, helping to document, organize, and analyze without taking away from the essential human-to-human dynamic.

Why Use AI in Interviews

AI can enhance the empathy interview process by amplifying the researcher's ability to observe and interpret. Instead of splitting attention between note-taking and active listening, the interviewer can remain fully engaged with the participant while AI handles transcription and preliminary coding. For example, real-time transcription reduces the stress of missing important quotes, and automatic detection of emotional tones can serve as a gentle prompt to deepen the conversation when a participant expresses hesitation, excitement, or discomfort. Over time, automated theme extraction across multiple interviews allows patterns to emerge that may not be immediately visible to a single researcher. Language barriers are also minimized since AI programs can transcribe and translate in multiple languages, enabling design thinking teams to include diverse voices. The overall result is a more humane, empathetic experience for participants and a more efficient workflow for researchers, who gain both immediacy of presence and depth of post-interview insight.

Suggested AI Programs

- Insight7: Useful for extracting emotional tones and recurring themes across interview transcripts, especially in multilingual contexts.
- Looppanel: Provides transcription with automatic sentiment detection, useful for fast thematic clustering and speaker recognition.
- Otter.ai: A lightweight transcription tool that integrates with online meetings and provides quick speaker identification.
- Rev.com: Provides AI transcription with a secure environment and additional AI-based insight tools.
- ChatGPT 5 (or other LLM powered tools): Can be used to summarize transcripts, identify emerging themes, or generate interview debriefs that highlight contradictions, tensions, or opportunities in participants' narratives.

Work Instructions

1. Pre-interview setup:
   (a) Begin by selecting your AI programs and clarifying research objectives. For example, you might load your discussion guide into ChatGPT 5 and ask it to suggest possible follow-up questions or to refine wording

for clarity and cultural sensitivity. At the same time, configure transcription tools like Otter.ai or Looppanel to record the session.

(b) Before beginning, always explain to participants that AI will be used to transcribe and analyze responses, and ask if they are comfortable with this approach.

2. During interviews:

(a) Once the conversation begins, let AI take care of the documentation. For instance, with Looppanel, you can monitor sentiment flags in real time that may suggest when to probe deeper, such as when a participant sounds uncertain or emotional.

(b) Meanwhile, remain focused on body language, tone, and the flow of conversation. If the participant mentions something surprising, you can jot a quick note and later ask ChatGPT 5 to help generate probing questions for follow-up sessions.

3. Post-interview analysis:

(a) After the interview, export the transcript and run it through Insight7 to identify themes and emotional drivers.

(b) Next, bring the transcript into ChatGPT 5 and ask for a thematic summary that includes representative quotes.

(c) For example, write prompts like "*Summarize the top three pain points expressed in this transcript and highlight one direct quote for each.*" The AI-generated synthesis can then be compared with your own field notes to validate accuracy and enrich interpretation. This step produces stakeholder-ready reports with both narrative depth and analytical structure.

Limitations and Tips

The heart of an empathy interview is still human connection. Always prioritize the participant's story, letting them speak in concrete terms about their experiences rather than over-focusing on AI-generated prompts. Some participants may prefer not to have their words processed by AI, so offering them a choice builds trust.

Most importantly, do not let technology replace human active listening. Empathy is learned through presence, not automation. AI outputs are only as reliable as the context provided; cultural nuances, humor, or irony may escape the algorithm. Think of AI insights as drafts that need human judgment to reach meaningful conclusions.

Figure 7.2 Explorative AI-to-AI Interviews. Human–AI–mediated dialogue, illustrating how AI agents support, structure, and augment communication among multiple participants to enable shared understanding, coordination, and collaborative decision-making. AI generated image created with Ideogram, Inc., Ideogram.ai, 3.0, 2025.

7.2 Explorative AI-to-AI Interviews

Description of Tool

Explorative AI-to-AI interviews represent a more experimental use of AI within design thinking, where the entire interaction takes place between artificial agents rather than between humans. These sessions are structured as conversations between two or more AI models, with one playing the role of interviewer and the other as respondent. The intent is not to capture personal experience, as in empathy interviews, but to generate ideas, hypotheses, or conceptual frames that might illuminate poorly understood problems. Because AI can ask adaptive follow-up questions based on prior responses, these interviews unfold in unexpected directions, surfacing possibilities that researchers may not have initially anticipated. In this way, AI-to-AI interviews serve as a form of generative exploration: a rapid, low-cost, and iterative method for probing new design spaces before human-centered testing.

Why Use AI

AI transforms explorative interviews through *adaptive questioning capabilities* that suggest follow-up questions based on response analysis. Early pattern discovery identifies emerging themes across interviews, while hypothesis development is supported by AI in building theory from qualitative data. *Efficiency gains* emerge through faster processing of unstructured, complex data, combined with consistent application of analytical frameworks and multi-perspective analysis from different theoretical lenses.

Suggested AI Programs

- MAXQDA with AI Assist: Maps conceptual relationships and supports early theory-building from AI-generated dialogues.
- ATLAS.ti: Enables coding of transcripts, visualization of concept networks, and testing of multiple thematic hypotheses.
- NVivo: Provides advanced query capabilities to cluster large batches of AI-to-AI transcripts and identify emergent trends.
- Atypica.ai: Generates realistic AI personas and conducts simulated interviews to surface emotional triggers, cognitive biases, and decision-making logic in high-fidelity user models.
- ChatGPT 5 (or equivalent LLMs): Plays both interviewer and interviewee, generates exploratory dialogue, and synthesizes patterns or contradictions across sessions.

Work Instructions

1. Research design phase:
   (a) Define broad questions or areas of interest. For example, if exploring "sustainable packaging," you might instruct ChatGPT 5 to play the role of an interviewer asking probing questions to another GPT or LLM model acting as an expert in material science.
   (b) At the same time, set up MAXQDA or NVivo to capture and organize the resulting transcripts for analysis.
2. Interview execution:
   (a) Start the dialogue by prompting ChatGPT 5 with a script such as: "*You are an interviewer exploring future trends in sustainable design.*

Ask follow-up questions until the respondent provides detailed reasoning and examples." The respondent model can then generate answers that evolve with each new prompt.

   (b) Use ATLAS.ti to track emerging concept relationships across conversations.

3. Iterative analysis:

   (a) After each session, review AI-identified themes.

   (b) For instance, NVivo can cluster recurring ideas like "biodegradable materials," "user adoption," or "cost efficiency."

   (c) Based on these clusters, refine your next round of prompts in ChatGPT 5, gradually moving from broad speculation to more specific hypotheses.

4. Theory development:

   (a) Import transcripts into MAXQDA to build conceptual maps that visualize the connections between emerging ideas.

   (b) Use ChatGPT 5 to generate draft hypotheses, such as this prompt: "*What potential conflicts exist between cost efficiency and environmental sustainability in the interviews conducted?*" These AI-generated insights should then be validated through human expertise.

5. Continuous training: Over time, adapt your prompts and fine-tune the AI by feeding it successful question–answer exchanges. This iterative process strengthens the AI's ability to produce increasingly relevant and in-depth interviews, potentially approaching the richness of human-led empathy interviews, though always as a complement, not a replacement.

Limitations and Tips

AI-to-AI interviews are exploratory tools, not definitive sources of knowledge. They risk producing content that seems coherent but lacks grounding in lived human experience. Over-structuring the process can also undermine the serendipity that makes these dialogues valuable. Always validate emerging themes with human judgment and field research before drawing conclusions.

Moreover, while AI can process large amounts of unstructured data rapidly, it cannot detect cultural subtleties, humor, or unspoken social cues that are central to human life. For this reason, explorative AI-to-AI interviews are best

Figure 7.3   Ask 5x Why. A team applying the "Five Whys" technique, illustrating collaborative root-cause analysis through iterative questioning to uncover underlying problems in design and decision-making processes. AI generated image created with Ideogram, Inc., Ideogram.ai, 3.0, 2025.

viewed as a complement to, not a substitute for, empathy interviews. They function as an idea generator and hypothesis builder, laying the groundwork for deeper, human-centered inquiry.

7.3   Ask 5x Why

Description of Tool

The 5 Whys method is an iterative interrogative technique pioneered by Toyota Motor Corporation to explore cause-and-effect relationships underlying specific problems. By asking "why" up to five times consecutively, researchers move beyond surface symptoms to identify root causes. In design thinking, it uncovers user motivations, reveals hidden needs, and challenges assumptions about behavior. This sequential questioning technique builds each "why" directly on the previous answer, maintaining focus on evidence-based responses rather than assumptions. The method continues until reaching actionable, addressable causes through linear progression.

Why Use AI

AI enhances the 5 Whys through intelligent question formulation, suggesting more effective ways to phrase investigative questions. Logic validation offers automated checking of causal relationships for consistency, while assumption detection identifies when responses contain opinions rather than facts. Pattern learning recognizes common root cause patterns across problems, enabling multiple perspective analysis from user, business, and technical viewpoints simultaneously.

Suggested AI Programs

- ChatGPT 5: Guides the structured 5 Whys process, rewrites each "why" to reduce bias, keeps context across turns, and drafts a clean causal chain with evidence notes and open risks.
- Insight7 (Analysis Grids): Extracts cause/effect statements from transcripts and renders visual causal chains; helpful for comparing chains across participants.
- Claude (Anthropic): Useful as a logic and bias checker; challenges leaps and highlights hidden assumptions in the chain.
- Microsoft Azure AI (Language/Text Analytics): Performs real-time sentiment and key-phrase detection during sessions and aggregates emotion shifts over time.
- Looppanel or Rev.ai: Provides accurate live transcription with speaker labelling; creates a reliable record to analyze afterward.
- Miro (with AI features): Maps the 5 Why's chain visually; converts text outputs into tidy diagrams that teams can refine together.

Work Instructions

1. Problem definition:

    (a) Start by using AI to refine the problem statement so it is specific and user-centered. For example, the team's draft might be "users leave checkout often." When entered ChatGPT 5 with the prompt *"Rewrite this problem statement to be observable and user-centric,"* it produces: *"First-time mobile shoppers abandon checkout immediately after the shipping-cost screen."*

(b) Meanwhile, set up Looppanel or Rev.ai to record and transcribe the upcoming interview, ensuring there will be a reliable text record to analyze afterward.

2. Questioning process.

(a) Once the interview begins, use AI as a companion in refining each "why" prompt. ChatGPT 5 can generate multiple phrasings of the same question, allowing interviewers to avoid sounding repetitive or leading. The model can also suggest follow-ups based on the interviewee's previous answer.

(b) *Example*: If the participant answers, *"I don't trust the payment screen,"* the AI might generate alternatives such as: *"Why do you feel the payment process is untrustworthy?"* or *"What specific signals cause you to lose trust?"*

(c) This variation keeps the conversation fresh while deepening the causal probe. AI also flags assumptions hidden in answers, such as blaming "design" when the issue may stem from prior experience or external policies.

3. Analysis and validation.

(a) After the session, feed transcripts into analytic platforms. Rev.ai's structured outputs or Looppanel's tagged highlights can be connected to visualization tools.

(b) AI then generates a causal chain diagram, showing how one "why" connects to the next. In addition, historical data can be cross-referenced to test whether identified causes appear in other projects or industries.

(c) Example: An analysis of "why users don't trust payment screens" might link to a past dataset showing that *"lack of visible security logos"* caused similar mistrust in other e-commerce contexts. This comparison helps teams validate whether the identified root cause is unique or widespread.

4. Action planning.

(a) The final stage involves moving from understanding to solution. AI can suggest a menu of potential interventions derived from the identified root causes.

(b) For prioritization, tools like ChatGPT 5 or Notion AI can rank solutions against weighted criteria such as *impact, feasibility,* and *speed to implement.*

(c) Example: If the root cause is *"unexpected shipping costs,"* the AI might recommend: (1) redesigning the cost display to appear earlier in the

process, (2) offering transparent price breakdowns, or (3) running A/
B tests with alternative pricing screens.

(d) The AI then produces an implementation roadmap with clear milestones, ensuring the 5 Whys exercise culminates in actionable outcomes rather than abstract insight.

Limitations and Tips

One limitation is that AI-driven emotion recognition can surface contradictory signals: for example, an interviewee may smile while describing a frustrating checkout process. This inconsistency can confuse teams if taken at face value. The tip here is to treat such contradictions as valuable leads: use the next "why" to probe the mismatch, asking "Why do you say it was frustrating, even though you smiled?" This often reveals deeper layers such as social embarrassment or coping strategies.

Another limitation is that teams may stop too early when answers seem adequate. In AI-supported interviews, the system may flag that emotional intensity rises or falls abruptly, suggesting further probing is warranted. The tip is to follow the AI's signal and continue asking "why" even when the human interviewer feels the thread is complete. This persistence often uncovers systemic issues invisible at surface level.

A third limitation is that the 5 Whys can drift into philosophical or highly abstract territory, especially when participants reflect deeply. An interviewee might eventually respond with statements like "Because people don't trust systems anymore." Rather than dismissing these as unhelpful, the tip is to capture them verbatim. AI can then contextualize such philosophical insights by linking them back to design decisions (e.g., transparency features, social proof, or trust cues), turning abstract beliefs into concrete design requirements.

7.4   5W+H with AI

Description of Tool

The 5W+H framework (Who, What, When, Where, Why, How) provides a systematic sweep across a problem space, ensuring that essential dimensions are considered without leaving critical blind spots. Originally developed in journalism to guarantee comprehensive reporting, it has been adapted into design thinking as both a preparatory and synthesis tool.

Figure 7.4   5W+H with AI. The 5W+H framework augmented by an AI agent, illustrating how structured questioning (what, why, who, when, where, and how) is collaboratively explored to support problem framing, analysis, and design reasoning. AI generated image created with Ideogram, Inc., Ideogram.ai, 3.0, 2025.

In design thinking, 5W+H helps teams to frame inquiry before fieldwork and organize insights afterward, structuring raw observations into actionable categories. Each of the six questions directs attention to a vital aspect of context: actors and stakeholders (Who), actions and artifacts (What), temporal rhythms (When), spatial and contextual constraints (Where), underlying motivations (Why), and processes or mechanisms (How). Its true power lies not in depth but in breadth: by scanning all angles of a problem, teams avoid tunnel vision. When paired with tools such as empathy interviews or the 5 Whys, 5W+H can become a scaffold for discovery and definition, leading to more robust problem framing.

Why Use AI

AI strengthens 5W+H by augmenting both completeness and synthesis. LLMs such as ChatGPT 5 can quickly generate domain-specific questions for each category, ensuring coverage that a design thinking team might overlook. AI also accelerates the aggregation of responses, automatically detecting patterns, inconsistencies, or missing categories across large datasets. Visualization and clustering tools further enhance sense-making by transforming raw answers into maps and summaries. In effect, AI extends the reach of 5W+H, enabling teams to cover ground more quickly, maintain rigor, and surface insights that may remain hidden through manual analysis.

Suggested AI Programs

- ChatGPT 5: Generates tailored 5W+H question sets for specific domains, explains rationales behind questions, identifies blind spots, and drafts structured interview guides segmented by stakeholder group.
- Notion AI: Hosts a 5W+H workspace (six columns) and supports summarizing, cross-comparing entries, and flagging incomplete categories for teams.
- Miro (AI clustering): Clusters free-text responses into themes and automatically produces mind maps or affinity diagrams aligned to 5W+H categories.
- Microsoft Power Platform (Power Automate, AI Builder, Power BI): Automates data collection, extracts entities from responses, detects gaps, and visualizes distributions across categories.
- Visual Paradigm (5W1H tool): Converts tabular 5W+H data into diagrams for reporting, presentations, and hand-off to non-design stakeholders.

Work Instructions

1. Set up a structured workspace.
   (a) Begin by building a digital environment that mirrors the six categories of 5W+H. In Notion, create a database with columns labelled Who, What, When, Where, Why, and How, along with extra fields such as Evidence and Uncertainty. Then, use ChatGPT 5 to generate a tailored set of initial prompts.
   (b) Example: For a design brief on "Redesigning a campus clinic booking system," prompt ChatGPT 5 with:
   "Generate at least five 5W+H questions tailored to student health services, covering each category."

    (c) ChatGPT 5 may produce items such as: Who usually cancels appointments? What devices do students prefer when booking? When are peak booking times? Where are bottlenecks occurring? Why do no-shows happen? How do students currently reschedule?

2. Collect and input data systematically.

    (a) Deploy AI-supported forms via Power Automate to collect answers from users and staff. As responses arrive, AI Builder can extract entities (e.g., student type, device type, appointment time) and check which W+H categories remain underpopulated. This ensures balanced coverage.

    (b) Example: If "Where" questions (such as physical constraints of clinic layout) remain unanswered, Notion AI can flag the gap, prompting the team to revisit that dimension.

3. Analyze and cluster responses.

    (a) Feed collected responses into Miro's AI clustering tool. This will group free-text answers by themes and visualize them in real time. Teams can see, for instance, that "peak booking times" (When) overlaps heavily with "system crashes" (How), suggesting linked pain points.

    (b) Example: AI identifies that many "Why" responses—such as "students don't trust the booking confirmation"—intersect with "Who" (first-year students), surfacing hidden causal connections.

4. Synthesize insights into visual models.

    (a) Import your cleaned and clustered 5W+H dataset into Visual Paradigm to auto-generate diagrams. This helps translate raw tables into structured visuals suitable for team workshops or executive presentations.

    (b) Example: The diagram might show "Who: first-year students" mapped to "Why: lack of trust" and "How: no notification reminder," highlighting an actionable design opportunity.

5. Apply insights to design artifacts.

    (a) Use ChatGPT 5 and Notion AI to turn the synthesized findings into personas or journey maps. By weaving together categories, you can construct narratives such as: *"A first-year student attempts to book an appointment on a mobile phone at 10 a.m., but due to lack of confirmation (Why), cancels frequently (What), causing system backlog (How)."*

    (b) These outputs directly inform ideation, ensuring that subsequent brainstorming builds on systematically uncovered user realities.

Limitations and Tips

One limitation of using AI in 5W+H is that AI-generated questions may sometimes feel generic or overly broad, reducing their usefulness in context. To address this, always pair AI outputs with domain knowledge—ask ChatGPT 5 to regenerate prompts while specifying the design context in detail (e.g., "student health services in an urban Asian university").

Another challenge is that AI clustering tools may oversimplify nuanced responses, merging subtle differences into a single theme. A good workaround is to manually review the AI's clustering; re-splitting or refining categories that are important distinctions matter for design outcomes.

A further limitation is the risk of data overload: automated tools can generate or collect more responses than a team can meaningfully use. The tip here is to use AI summarization features—such as Notion AI's "generate executive summary" to condense responses into thematic briefs before team workshops.

Finally, AI cannot capture the emotional resonance behind some "Why" answers, such as user frustration or aspiration. To mitigate this, combine AI outputs with direct empathy interviews, ensuring that qualitative depth complements AI-driven breadth.

7.5 AI-Lead Users

Description of Tool

The AI Lead User method focuses on learning from individuals who live on the margins of a problem space. It includes extreme users whose circumstances, constraints, or behaviors amplify unmet needs: for example, students with disabilities navigating a campus, or senior citizens struggling with mobile banking. Their experiences often expose challenges overlooked by mainstream users.

It also includes lead users, a concept popularized by Eric von Hippel at MIT, represent a particular subset whose needs foreshadow mainstream demand. They encounter problems earlier than the general market and frequently create their own makeshift solutions. A well-known case is the development of advanced mountain bikes in the 1970s: recreational cyclists in Northern California, unable to find equipment strong enough for rough terrain, improvised solutions that later defined the mainstream mountain bike industry.

Figure 7.5   AI-Lead Users. Identification of AI-lead users, illustrating how early adopters and highly engaged users are recognized as key contributors to insight generation, validation, and innovation in human–AI system design. AI generated image created with Ideogram, Inc., Ideogram.ai, 3.0, 2025.

Traditionally, identifying such users is laborious. Researchers conduct pyramiding interviews: asking participants to recommend others who are "more extreme" than themselves: until a small set of extreme or lead users are found. This usually requires a large number of in-depth interviews (e.g., 12 to 20) combined with networking through associations, market research, and trend scanning. While powerful, the method is time-intensive and resource-heavy. AI radically streamlines this process, offering scale, speed, and new creative extensions through synthetic personas.

Why Use AI

AI expands the reach of the Lead User method by processing enormous volumes of behavioral data: from online forums, product reviews, or app usage: to detect unusual patterns at a scale no human researcher could manage. Instead of slowly "pyramiding" through referrals, AI can instantly surface thousands of candidates who display early-adopter traits or extreme pain points. AI also reduces bias, as algorithms scan across categories (age, disability, nationality, profession) rather than relying on a researcher's social network. Most importantly, AI tools can generate synthetic personas that either represent hard-to-reach extremes or imagine future-oriented "near impossible" users, allowing designers to explore radical design possibilities alongside real user insights.

Suggested AI Programs

- atypica.ai: Provides persona simulation and synthetic user dialogues. Designers can generate personas representing extreme demographics or lead users, then run structured interviews with them.
- Delve AI: Builds data-driven personas from analytics and behavioral data, identifying emerging lead user segments from actual digital traces.
- UX Pilot: AI-driven UX research platform that assists in user identification, clustering behaviors, and tracking patterns over time.
- Synthetic Users (general category of LLM-powered simulation): Allows researchers to create simulated users aligned with real-world feedback data; useful for experimenting with personas that are difficult or impossible to recruit in practice.
- ChatGPT 5 (or other LLMs): Generates tailored interview questions for different extreme or lead user categories, role-plays user perspectives, and can facilitate persona-to-persona dialogues that spark new design ideas.

Work Instructions

1. Integrate diverse data sources.

    (a) Begin by connecting customer databases, app usage logs, and social media streams into a platform like Delve AI. These integrations allow the AI to scan for anomalies or patterns that suggest extreme needs.

    (b) Example: For an online education startup, Delve AI may detect that a very small group of learners are attempting to complete courses entirely on smartphones with weak connectivity: an extreme use case that signals urgent design considerations.

2. Define trends and categories of extremes.

    (a) Use ChatGPT 5 to create prompts that specify categories such as age, disability, nationality, experience level, or lifestyle. This guides the AI in searching for meaningful extremes rather than random outliers.

(b) Example prompt: *"Identify potential extreme users of a telehealth platform focusing on elderly patients in rural areas, patients with language barriers, and patients with chronic conditions."*

(c) The AI then generates candidate personas and behaviors for each category.

3. Automated screening and flagging.

(a) With UX Pilot, set filters for behaviors associated with early adoption or high frustration: such as users creating workarounds, posting repeated complaints, or customizing systems in novel ways. The tool flags potential Extreme or Lead Users and prepares summary briefs.

(b) Example: UX Pilot might flag a cluster of parents modifying an education app to track children's sleep cycles, suggesting lead users who anticipate future integrations of learning and health data.

4. Enhance interviews with AI prompts.

(a) Once real or synthetic extreme users are identified, use ChatGPT 5 or atypica.ai to generate personalized interview guides. These guides go beyond generic questions and adapt to the persona's traits.

(b) Example: For an extreme user who is visually impaired, the AI might suggest: *"How do you navigate features when audio descriptions are missing? Can you describe a workaround you've invented?"* This ensures richer insights.

5. Experiment with synthetic personas.

(a) Advanced exploration involves creating "impossible" users with atypica.ai. For instance, simulate an *"alien diplomat using human educational software"* or *"the Pope using a VR prayer application."*

(b) Run dialogues between these personas and real lead users. This playful extension often produces novel ideas that spark mainstream innovations later.

6. Synthesize into actionable requirements.

(a) After interviews (real or synthetic), prompt ChatGPT 5 to extract concrete design requirements per category.

(b) Example: For elderly rural telehealth users, the system may summarize: *"Design must prioritize low-bandwidth connections, multilingual audio interfaces, and simplified onboarding."* These outputs become design criteria for ideation.

Limitations and Tips

A common limitation in extreme user simulation is that AI-generated personas can drift into stereotypes if prompts are vague. The solution is to specify categories clearly: e.g., "a visually impaired college student in an urban Asian city" rather than just "a disabled student" and validate the persona's realism with domain experts.

Another limitation is that synthetic personas may lack authentic lived emotion, especially for categories involving trauma, disability, or cultural nuance. To mitigate this, always complement synthetic interviews with at least a few real user conversations, then let AI summarize the differences between simulated and actual voices.

For Lead Users, a challenge is that AI tends to describe adoption behavior without asking users how they actively solve problems. A tip is to prompt lead users: real or synthetic: to describe *their own design solutions* or to role-play as co-creators. This brings forward actionable design hacks that can inspire the team.

Finally, AI's creativity can overwhelm without structure, generating endless quirky personas or dialogues that distract from project goals. The solution is to run short AI-generated "dialogue workshops" (e.g., have atypica.ai simulate a lead user conversing with a synthetic extreme user) and then immediately ask the AI for a concise summary of design opportunities. This keeps the method playful yet focused on outcomes.

7.6   AI Generated User Profile

Description of Tool

User Profiles are structured descriptions of target users that capture demographic details, behaviors, goals, pain points, and motivations. They act as the foundation for persona creation, enabling design teams to empathize with users and align product decisions with real needs. Profiles can take several forms:

- Demographic profiles: highlighting age, gender, location, income, and education, useful for market segmentation.
- Mindset profiles: describing how users approach problems, their values, and decision-making styles.

Figure 7.6   AI Generated User Profile. A composite representation of diverse user personas, illustrating varied backgrounds, roles, and perspectives that inform inclusive design and human-centered decision-making. AI generated image created with Ideogram, Inc., Ideogram.ai, 3.0, 2025.

- Jobs-to-be-Done profiles: focusing on tasks users want to accomplish, regardless of demographic category.

Traditionally, compiling these profiles required weeks of effort, combining interviews, surveys, analytics, and observational studies to identify behavioral clusters. While robust, this process often limited teams to producing only a handful of profiles due to time and resource constraints.

Why Use AI

AI revolutionizes user profiling by generating detailed, structured outputs in seconds. Instead of extrapolating from a small interview pool, AI programs process large-scale behavioral data to surface reliable trends. This reduces human bias by grounding profiles in evidence rather than assumptions. Scalability enables multiple segment profiles to be built in parallel, so a single design sprint can consider dozens of user groups instead of just two or three. Furthermore, AI platforms provide real-time updates: profiles automatically evolve as new analytics, CRM (Customer Relationship Management) entries, or customer feedback streams in. This responsiveness keeps teams aligned with shifting user behavior without restarting the research cycle from scratch.

Suggested AI Programs

- UserPersona.dev: Instantly generates user profiles from a short product or service description, offering exports in multiple formats (PDF, image, JSON) for easy integration.
- Delve AI: Creates dynamic personas by analyzing live analytics, CRM data, and social media signals; includes conversational "persona chats" for exploration.
- UXPressia AI Persona Generator: Provides customizable persona templates enriched with industry-specific datasets; allows easy visualization for stakeholder presentations.
- FounderPal AI User Persona Generator: Lightweight tool that generates user personas from minimal input; ideal for early-stage projects or quick exercises.
- atypica.ai: Persona-simulation platform that creates interactive, AI-driven personas for role-playing interviews, scenario testing, or team workshops.

Work Instructions

1. Select an AI platform.

    (a) Begin by choosing a persona generator based on your project's data availability. For example, if you have only a product description, UserPersona.dev may be sufficient. If you want to integrate CRM and analytics data, Delve AI or UXPressia provide richer pipelines.

    (b) Example: For a startup launching a wellness app, the team chooses Delve AI because they already have Google Analytics data from a beta website.

2. Connect and input data.

    (a) Integrate available sources: such as Google Analytics, HubSpot CRM, or customer survey exports: into the chosen platform. If you have limited data, provide a detailed product description and intended target market.

(b) Example: The wellness app team inputs: *"A mobile app for young professionals that tracks stress and offers quick relaxation routines."* Delve AI links this with web analytics showing high traffic from 25 to 34-year-old visitors in urban areas.

3. Generate initial user profiles.

(a) Run the AI to produce draft profiles. These will typically include demographics, goals, frustrations, motivations, and digital behaviors. Some platforms also predict likely "jobs-to-be-done" tasks.

(b) Example: Delve AI generates *"Urban Professional Paula"* (29, female, stressed due to workload, goal: find daily wellness routines; pain point: apps that take too long). It also creates *"Remote Worker Raj"* (34, male, struggles with isolation; goal: reduce anxiety; pain point: inconsistent engagement reminders).

4. Customize and validate outputs.

(a) Use ChatGPT 5 or atypica.ai to refine profiles with more context. For example, simulate a conversation with *Urban Professional Paula* to ask: *"What would make you trust a wellness app enough to use it daily?"* Incorporate these responses into the profile.

(b) Then validate by comparing AI-generated insights with actual user interviews or small surveys.

(c) Example: Simulated Paula emphasizes *"integration with calendar apps"*: a feature later confirmed by real beta testers.

5. Distribute profiles across teams.

(a) Export the finalized personas into visual templates using UXPressia or Canva for presentation. Share them across design, marketing, and product teams to ensure alignment.

(b) Example: The wellness app team circulates Paula and Raj's profiles to marketing for messaging tests, while designers use them to prioritize calendar integration and notification features.

6. Maintain and update regularly.

(a) Set review cycles (e.g., quarterly) where the AI regenerates profiles based on the newest data. This ensures the profiles evolve with market shifts.

(b) Example: Six months later, Delve AI reveals a new persona, *"Student Joe"* (22, heavy mobile use, stress from exams). The team adapts product strategy to include study-break routines.

Limitations and Tips

One limitation is that AI-generated profiles may overgeneralize behaviors, collapsing nuanced user differences into neat categories. The tip is to validate each profile with at least a handful of real interviews to ensure lived experiences match the AI's synthesis.

A further limitation is that AI tools sometimes introduce fictional details (hallucinations) when given sparse input. The recommendation is to clearly mark these speculative fields and replace them with verified data as soon as it becomes available.

Finally, profiles can become outdated quickly if treated as static. AI makes updating easier, but only if teams set regular review cycles. The tip is to embed "profile refresh" checkpoints into your design workflow (e.g., before every major sprint) so that personas remain living documents rather than artifacts.

7.7   Empathy Map with AI

Description of Tool

An empathy map is a collaborative visualization used to synthesize what a team knows about a user's thoughts, feelings, behaviors, and environment. Typically divided into quadrants: Says, Thinks, Does, Feels: the map highlights both direct user statements and deeper interpretations of behavior or emotion. It was popularized in design thinking as a quick, yet powerful tool to foster shared understanding across multidisciplinary teams. By externalizing user knowledge in one view, empathy maps reveal contradictions (for example, when users say one thing but do another) and highlight emotional drivers behind behaviors.

Traditionally, empathy maps are filled in during or after field interviews, with sticky notes representing fragments of data. The process is collaborative, but also time-consuming: synthesizing transcripts into quadrants often requires hours of manual clustering.

Why Use AI

AI enhances empathy mapping by transforming raw qualitative data into structured insights. Natural language processing can quickly categorize user quotes into the "Says" quadrant, while sentiment analysis tools detect the emotional undertones for "Feels." Behavior-tracking data or app logs enrich the "Does" quadrant, and AI clustering uncovers hidden themes that humans may overlook. Instead of relying solely on team interpretation, AI ensures consistency across maps while leaving room for human nuance. Most importantly, AI enables real-time updating: as new interviews are added, the empathy map evolves automatically, keeping the design team aligned with the latest user insights.

Suggested AI Programs

- Creately AI Empathy Map Generator: Automatically converts transcripts and notes into empathy map quadrants, producing clean visualizations within minutes.
- Miro Assist: Clusters sticky notes by keywords and sentiment directly on a collaborative canvas, ideal for live team workshops.
- Hume AI: Specializes in multimodal emotion recognition (voice tone, facial cues, text), enhancing the accuracy of the "Feels" quadrant.
- Dovetail AI: Automates sentiment analysis and theme identification from interview data, producing structured outputs aligned with empathy map sections.
- Lovable: An AI product design assistant that creates empathy maps, personas, and wireframes from a short prompt, allowing innovators to move quickly from raw data to early design artifacts.
- ChatGPT 5: Generates interview outlines, reformulates ambiguous quotes, and suggests empathy map categories for messy or incomplete notes.

Work Instructions

1. Initial setup of the template.

   (a) Start by selecting a digital empathy map template. Platforms like Creately or Miro provide AI-enabled templates with predefined quadrants (Says, Thinks, Does, Feels). If none are available, create a custom grid in Canva or Figma. Before interviews begin, use ChatGPT 5 to generate tailored interview questions aligned with the quadrants.

   (b) Example: For a project on improving urban bike-sharing, prompt ChatGPT 5: "*Generate 3: 4 empathy map interview questions for bike-sharing users across Says, Thinks, Does, Feels.*" The AI may produce: "*What do you usually say about bike availability?*" (Says), "*What thoughts run through your mind when the app shows no bikes nearby?*" (Thinks), and so on.

2. Data collection and transcription.

   (a) Record user interviews with tools like Rev.ai or Otter.ai for automatic transcription. Simultaneously, deploy Hume AI to capture emotional signals (tone of voice, hesitation, or stress).

   (b) Example: A participant says, "*I always get anxious when the app crashes.*" Rev.ai transcribes the text into Says, while Hume AI flags the emotion as *frustration,* adding it to Feels.

3. Populate quadrants in real time.

   (a) Import transcripts into Creately AI or Miro Assist. These tools cluster sentences into the appropriate quadrants, creating a draft empathy map within minutes. Designers can manually adjust misplacements.

   (b) Example: AI places "*I cycle to save time*" under Says, but the team may move it to *Thinks* to capture the underlying belief.

4. Add environmental context.

   (a) Expand beyond transcripts by asking ChatGPT 5 to infer *what the user sees and hears.*

   (b) *Example*: From logs of a student bike-sharing app, AI might generate: "*User sees a cluttered app screen and hears peers complaining about late arrivals.*" This contextual detail enriches the empathy map beyond interview quotes.

5. Identify pains and gains.

   (a) Once quadrants are filled, use Dovetail AI to extract pain points (frustrations, obstacles) and gains (opportunities, positive outcomes). These insights can be displayed as add-on sections at the bottom of the map.

   (b) Example: Dovetail AI highlights: *Pain: fear of unsafe parking spots at night; Gain: sense of independence and freedom in avoiding traffic.*

6. Visualize and share. Export the completed empathy map as a visual artifact. Creately AI or Canva can produce polished diagrams with color-coding for emotions, making it easy to share with stakeholders. A good practice is to generate one empathy map per user segment, then use Miro to compare them side-by-side.

Example

A student team redesigning the campus bike-sharing app used Creately AI to build three empathy maps (freshmen, graduate students, staff). The maps revealed that while all segments said the app was "convenient," graduate students felt constant anxiety about late returns due to tighter schedules. This led the team to prototype a priority-reservation feature: an insight directly surfaced from AI-enhanced empathy mapping.

Below is a text-based version you can later adapt into a diagram or include as a figure or table, such as Table 7.1. In a visual version (e.g., Creately AI or Miro), these entries could be color-coded.

- STEP 1: Ask ChatGPT 5 to collect the entries of "Says, Thinks, Does, Feels, Pains, Gains" into this text-based table.
- STEP 2: Open Creately's "AI Empathy Map Template" webpage, in this case: https://creately.com/diagram/example/6I5KbZUGpkf/ai-empathy-map-template.
- STEP 3: Paste the text-based table in Creately, you will get an interactive Empathy Map that can be shared with others for voting. Below are captured from the user interface in https://app.creately.com/

Limitations and Tips

A frequent limitation is that AI sometimes misclassifies ambiguous statements across quadrants: for instance, placing "I think it's dangerous" under Says instead of Thinks. The tip is to always conduct a quick team review, letting humans adjust quadrant placement to preserve nuance.

Another limitation is that emotion recognition may overgeneralize feelings (e.g., labelling all raised voices as "anger"). To avoid skewed results, pair Hume AI's output with team discussion: ask, "Does this sound more like stress than anger?" This balances AI's speed with human interpretation.

A third limitation is that AI-generated empathy maps can feel sterile if left unedited, missing the storytelling power of direct quotes. The tip here is to reinsert raw user phrases into the "Says" quadrant: even if AI already summarized them: to retain authenticity and human voice.

Table 7.1   AI-Generated Mockup for Empathy Map with AI

Quadrant	AI-Generated Entries for Mockup
Says	"The app is convenient when bikes are available." "I get anxious when the app crashes." "I always tell friends it's cheap but unreliable."
Thinks	Worries about being late to class if no bikes are nearby. Believes parking is unsafe at night. Wonders why there's no reservation system.
Does	Refreshes the app multiple times during peak hours. Walks extra blocks to find available bikes. Leaves bikes outside designated areas when in a rush.
Feels	Excited when rides save time. Frustrated by inconsistent availability. Stressed about safety in late hours. Relieved when confirmation messages appear quickly.
Pains	Uncertainty about bike availability, app crashes, unsafe parking.
Gains	Freedom to avoid traffic, affordable transportation, sense of independence.

7.8   Customer Journey Map

Description of Tool

Customer Journey Maps provide visual representations of customer experiences with organizations, offering 360-degree views of customer engagement over time and across channels. It helps design thinking teams to understand common customer experiences while uncovering needs and routes to improve products or services.

Core components include timescales, scenarios, channels, touchpoints, and emotional states. Traditional creation requires comprehensive research through interviews, surveys, social media listening, and competitive intelligence with cross-functional collaboration and iterative refinement.

Why Use AI

AI revolutionizes journey mapping by dramatically accelerating the process, reducing mapping time from weeks to hours or minutes while providing higher accuracy through data-driven insights rather than assumptions. Scalability enables handling large volumes of customer data automatically with real-time insights from continuous updates. Predictive capabilities anticipate future customer needs and behaviors while reducing costs and manual analysis time significantly.

Suggested AI Programs

- ChatGPT 5: Generates tailored journey scenarios, reformulates unclear touchpoints, and suggests emotional markers or icons for each stage.
- Lovable: AI design assistant that can generate customer journey maps, personas, and even wireframes from a short description. Especially useful for quickly turning journey insights into design concepts and prototypes.
- Browse AI (ethical web scraping): No-code web-scraping bot for pulling customer reviews or ratings from public sites (with respect for platform policies).
- MonkeyLearn AI Word Cloud: Transforms large sets of user comments into visual word clusters, highlighting frequent complaints or positive expressions.
- TheyDo Journey AI: Enterprise-grade journey mining with live updates, insight scoring, and graph-based retrieval to surface hidden relationships between touchpoints.
- UXPressia AI Customer Journey Mapping: Combines persona building with journey mapping, auto-detecting pain points and opportunities in multilingual data.

Work Instructions

1. Provide basic product/service information.

   (a) Start by giving AI a description of the product or service along with the target audience. ChatGPT-5 can generate an initial persona and journey outline.

   (b) Example: For a coffee chain, prompt: *"Create a draft customer journey for a young professional using our mobile ordering app, from ordering to pick up."*

2. Define specific tasks and scenarios.

   (a) Clarify the stages your customers go through. For a café, this might include entering the app, waiting for confirmation, ordering, paying, arriving at the store, receiving the order, and leaving. AI ensures these stages are broken down consistently across personas.

3. Collect user data ethically.

   (a) Use Browse AI or similar tools to scrape public customer reviews and ratings. Combine these with survey or interview transcripts. Always filter for ethical use and respect platform policies.

(b) Example: Collect 200 Google Play app reviews mentioning "coffee order app" and export them for analysis.

4. Analyze user experiences with NLP.

(a) Feed the collected data into Dovetail AI or MonkeyLearn to detect themes, sentiments, and recurring keywords. ChatGPT-5 can then map responses to journey stages.

(b) Example: Reviews mentioning "crash during payment" get placed under the *Paying* stage with a negative sentiment marker.

5. Visualize emotional states.

(a) Use UXPressia AI or MyMap.AI to generate a journey map where each stage is marked with emotional states (e.g., emojis or color-coded markers).

(b) *Example*: The map shows green (delight) during Ordering for its speed, but red (frustration) during *Pickup* due to long waiting times.

6. Identify opportunities for improvement.

(a) Ask ChatGPT-5 to summarize pain points into design opportunities.

(b) *Example*: From "long waits at pickup," AI suggests: "Introduce staggered pickup slots to spread customer arrivals."

7. Share and update regularly.

(a) Export the map for workshops and share it across teams. Set up TheyDo or UXPressia to refresh the journey map weekly as new reviews or analytics flow in.

(b) Outcome Example: For the coffee chain, the AI-enhanced journey map revealed that although customers *loved* the ordering interface, dissatisfaction spiked at the pickup counter. This insight prompted a redesign of store layout and the introduction of "express pickup shelves."

Example

Limitations and Tips

AI accuracy depends heavily on data quality. Scraped reviews may be biased or spammy. The tip is to clean and triangulate data: combine scraped reviews with in-store surveys and CRM records for balance.

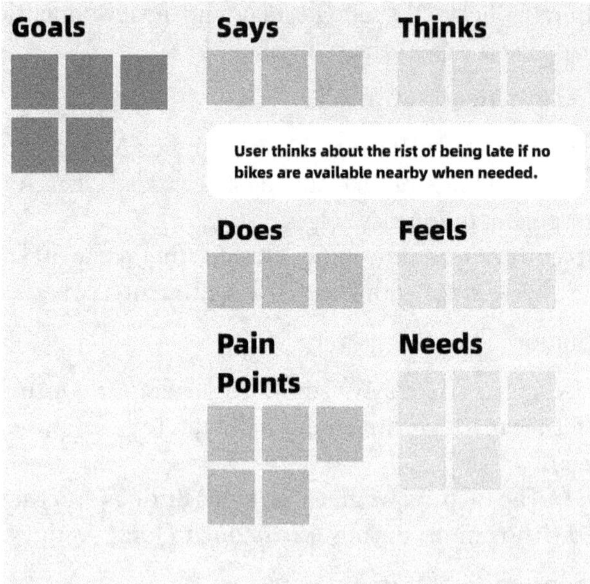

Figure 7.7   Empathy Map with AI. Book Author captured from the user interface in https://app.creately.com/

AI may miss cultural nuances in customer emotions, especially in multilingual contexts. The solution is to pair AI analysis with bilingual team members who can re-interpret idiomatic expressions (e.g., "so spicy it killed me" as positive humor, not a complaint).

A third limitation is the risk of privacy violations when integrating CRM or scraping user data. To address this, always anonymize personal identifiers and use only ethically permissible sources. Transparency with customers about data use builds trust.

7.9   AI Storytelling

Description of Tool

Storytelling is one of the most powerful ways to communicate user needs, motivations, and lived experiences. In design thinking, stories create a compelling thread that keeps teams emotionally engaged and aligned around the people they are designing for. They help transform abstract research data into human-centered narratives that drive empathy and innovation.

Traditionally, storytelling has been integrated into design processes through methods such as:

- Story sharing: Teams retell moments from interviews or observations, preserving the user's voice through direct quotes and anecdotes.
- Journey mapping through narratives: Instead of a static diagram, the customer journey is written as a story, with a beginning, middle, and end that highlight user struggles and triumphs.
- Multi-perspective storytelling: Different team members adopt the voices of various users or stakeholders, often enhanced with role-playing.
- Visual storyboards and sketches: Designers illustrate scenes that capture environments, interactions, and emotional turning points.

Why Use AI

AI enhances storytelling by expanding creative capacity and lowering technical barriers. Large language models like ChatGPT can propose story structures (e.g., Hero's Journey, Three-Act Structure) and generate dialogue in minutes. Text-to-image models allow anyone to turn prompts into compelling visuals, while image-to-image tools refine sketches into polished frames. These capabilities dramatically reduce the time required to build storyboards, enabling teams to focus on interpretation and alignment rather than execution. Most importantly, AI often introduces unexpected variations and angles, sparking creativity that may not emerge from human effort alone.

Suggested AI Programs

- ChatGPT 5: Generates narrative outlines, dialogue drafts, and alternative story structures; adapts user stories into the Hero's Journey or Three-Act framework.
- MidJourney: Text-to-image tool for creating visually rich storyboards with stylistic control (e.g., cinematic, sketch-like, or realistic).
- Stable Diffusion: Open-source text-to-image and image-to-image workflow; allows iterative refinement of visuals and consistency across multiple frames.
- Runway Gen-2: AI tool for generating video sequences from text or images, useful for bringing storyboards to life as short clips.

- Subtxt / Narrative First: AI-driven narrative framework using Dramatica theory; generates plotlines with predictive coherence and logical consistency.
- Squibler AI Story Generator: Rapid story ideation platform with customizable parameters and collaborative editing.
- Canva Magic Write: AI text generator integrated with Canva, enabling seamless pairing of narrative text with design-ready visual layouts.

Work Instructions

1. Develop a story outline.

   (a) Begin with the core narrative: Who is the user? What challenge do they face? What is the setting? Use ChatGPT-5 to generate alternative outlines, then refine with your design team.

   (b) Example: For an umbrella design project, you might prompt: "*Generate a Hero's Journey outline for a college student whose umbrella breaks during a storm.*"

   (c) ChatGPT-5 produces stages like: Ordinary world (commuting student), Call to adventure (unexpected rain), Crisis (umbrella breaks), Transformation (discovers a new foldable umbrella concept).

2. Create storyboard scripts.

   (a) Translate the outline into scene prompts, detailing characters, environments, and emotional cues.

   (b) Example: Script a scene as: "*A young woman looks frustrated as her umbrella collapses in heavy rain. A crowded city street with blurred car lights. Pedestrians rush past, ignoring her struggle.*" This text becomes the input for image generation.

3. Generate images with AI tools.

   (a) Use MidJourney or Stable Diffusion to create storyboard panels. For consistency across frames, include recurring descriptors at the beginning of each prompt (e.g., "*a young woman with long brown hair, wearing a red coat*"). You can generate scenes individually and assemble them later or attempt batch generation for faster results.

   (b) Example: MidJourney produces three frames: broken umbrella, frantic run to shelter, and discovery of a sleek, AI-inspired umbrella stand inside a shop.

4. Optimize and refine visuals.

(a) If character or setting consistency slips, use image-to-image features in Stable Diffusion or Runway to adjust details. Alternatively, manually edit with design software (e.g., Photoshop or Figma) to align with your vision.

(b) Example: Replace a background skyline that looks futuristic with a more grounded city street to match user reality.

5. Assemble the visual narrative.

(a) Combine story text and AI-generated visuals into a storyboard template in Canva or Figma. Share with your team for feedback, noting how emotional cues (fear, frustration, relief) align with user insights.

Limitations and Tips

Maintaining consistency across images. Always place recurring details at the start of prompts: e.g., "*long-haired girl in a red coat*": to ensure the same character appears across scenes. Use image-to-image functions to lock key visual traits.

Making details align with your vision. Treat AI outputs as frameworks, not final products. Refine perspectives (e.g., "*close-up of face with raindrops*") or splice together elements from multiple generations to create a coherent storyboard.

Balancing AI creativity with manual input. Don't hesitate to override AI outcomes that feel off-tone. Adjust manually or reframe prompts to shift emotional impact.

Learning tool strengths over time. Each tool has quirks: MidJourney excels at cinematic lighting, Stable Diffusion at iterative refinements, Runway at video sequences. Experiment and note which suits your workflow best. Over time, your fluency in prompt design will shape AI into a true creative partner.

7.10 Context Mapping with AI

Description of Tool

Context Mapping is a research method used to explore the broader environments: physical, emotional, social, and cultural: in which people live and interact with products or services. Unlike interviews or surveys that rely heavily on what users can articulate, context mapping often uncovers insights that remain unspoken: routines, tacit habits, social influences, or cultural values.

Stage	Customer Actions (Does)	Customer Thoughts (Thinks)	Customer Feelings (Feels)	AI-Identified Pain Points	Improvement Opportunities
Discover App	Browses app store; downloads app	"I hope this app saves me time."	Curious, slightly skeptical	Confusing app description	Simplify app store copy; add screenshots of fast ordering
Ordering	Selects coffee in app; customizes options	"It's fast, I can pick what I want."	Delighted, in control	Some users can't find seasonal drinks	Highlight seasonal menu upfront
Payment	Inputs card; confirms purchase	"Will this payment go through?"	Anxious if app lags	App crashes reported during payment	Add PayPal/Apple Pay; ensure confirmation within 2 seconds
Pickup	Arrives at store; waits for barista	"Why is the line so long if I ordered ahead?"	Frustrated, impatient	Long pickup times during peak hours	Introduce "express pickup shelves" and digital queue display
Post-Use	Drinks coffee; may leave app review	"It worked, but waiting was annoying."	Mixed: satisfied with product, annoyed at service	Negative reviews mention "pickup bottleneck"	Trigger push notification asking for feedback and offer coupons for off-peak pickup

Figure 7.8 Customer Journey Map. Sample AI-Generated Customer Journey Map. In UXPressia AI or MyMap.AI, each row becomes a step in a visual map (timeline with touchpoints) (table above). Teams can run workshops around the AI-generated map, editing the details collaboratively.

Traditionally, this method involves generative techniques such as cultural probes (kits with tasks or diaries), collages, and workshops where users express their lived experiences. Designers then analyze these artifacts in multi-dimensional ways, often co-creating with participants to map influences, environments, and needs. The result is a context map: a visual representation of the user's world that highlights opportunities for design innovation.

Figure 7.9   AI Storytelling. AI-supported storytelling illustrates how a digital system structures, visualizes, and mediates narrative flow to support collaborative sense-making, creativity, and shared meaning-making. AI generated image created with Ideogram, Inc., Ideogram.ai, 3.0, 2025.

Why Use AI

AI strengthens context mapping by organizing complexity into clarity. Natural language models can instantly categorize interview transcripts or diary notes into themes like "social influences," "economic concerns," or "daily routines." Image generation tools can turn abstract insights into icons or sketches, enriching visual maps without needing professional illustrators. More importantly, AI can surface contrasts across datasets: pointing out what has changed since last month's workshop or highlighting patterns that humans might miss. This makes the process faster, more comprehensive, and more collaborative.

Suggested AI Programs

* ChatGPT-5: Summarizes transcripts, identifies emerging patterns, and generates comparative insights across different datasets.
* Miro AI: Clusters sticky notes from workshops, organizes context mapping boards, and creates visual diagrams collaboratively.

- Expert.ai: Provides semantic analysis to detect contextual cues in user narratives, such as social relationships or emotional drivers.
- Canva + AI Elements: Generates icons, colors, and visual symbols to make maps clearer and more engaging.
- Runway Gen-2 / Stable Diffusion: Transforms text insights into illustrative images that can be placed on maps for emotional impact.

Work Instructions

1. Define the scope of context.

   (a) Begin by clarifying which environments matter most for the design project: physical (where), social (who influences), emotional (feelings), or cultural (beliefs, traditions). Use ChatGPT-5 to brainstorm prompts that capture these layers.

   (b) Example: For a project on redesigning community libraries, prompt: *"List questions to explore the physical, social, emotional, and cultural contexts of library users in a mid-sized city."* AI may suggest: *"Where do users usually read? Who do they go with? What emotions arise in crowded spaces? What role does tradition play in using physical books?"*

2. Collect authentic field data.

   (a) Record interviews, photos, and short video clips of users in their environments. Tools like Rev.ai can transcribe conversations in real time. Highlight surprising or "novel" insights with tags to ensure they are not overlooked later.

   (b) Example: A librarian says, *"I feel guilty when I can't help a child because the computers are too slow."* Tagging this comment ensures it enters the emotional context category.

3. Preliminary screening and clustering.

   (a) Feed the transcripts and diary entries into ChatGPT-5 or Expert.ai. Ask the AI to classify data into categories such as *location, routine, emotion, influence.* This reduces redundancy and creates a manageable dataset for the team.

   (b) Example: From 50 diary entries, AI clusters "library as safe space," "lack of digital access," and "family bonding."

4. Generate differentiated insights.

(a) Use prompts to explicitly highlight contrasts or changes.
Example: Ask: "Compare what today's library users say versus what last year's users said about digital access."

(b) AI may identify a shift: more complaints about slow Wi-Fi, fewer about book shortages. These contrasts enrich the context map.

5. Create the preliminary context map.

(a) Use Miro AI or Canva to lay out clusters on a shared board. Place physical environment on one side, emotions on another, and social/cultural factors around them. Use AI-generated icons (e.g., an open book, a Wi-Fi symbol, a frowning face) to improve clarity.

(b) Example: For the library case, icons for "family time" and "frustrated emoji for slow Wi-Fi" make patterns visible briefly.

6. Enhance in real time during workshops.

(a) In team discussions, let ChatGPT-5 generate live summaries such as: "*The strongest theme is frustration with technology, closely tied to emotional stress among librarians and students.*"

(b) AI helps align the team quickly, keeping conversations focused on emerging opportunities.

Limitations and Tips

A key limitation in AI-assisted context mapping is that generated user perspectives can easily slip into stereotypes or generic narratives, especially when prompts are vague. The best way to counter this is to ground the AI's input in real data: transcripts, diaries, or field notes: and use AI primarily for structuring and clustering, not for inventing user details.

A further limitation lies in the visual outputs of AI, such as icons or generated images, which can be mismatched or too generic for the design context. The solution is to use these images as placeholders, refining them with manual sketches, curated icon libraries, or co-created visuals once the team aligns on the concepts.

Finally, AI introduces risks around data privacy when transcripts, images, or recordings are uploaded to third-party platforms. Sensitive details may inadvertently be exposed, especially when tools are connected to cloud services. The tip here is to anonymize user data before analysis and to make sure consent procedures explicitly cover the use of AI tools. In practice, AI should

Figure 7.10   Context Mapping with AI. Collaborative context mapping, illustrating how teams externalize and organize relationships, factors, and dependencies to support shared understanding and informed problem framing in design processes. AI generated image created with Ideogram, Inc., Ideogram.ai, 3.0, 2025.

accelerate synthesis, but the responsibility for ethical handling of user data remains firmly with the design team.

7.11   Empathize & Define Use Case: Co-Creating University Chairs & Tables with AI

Our challenge: to redesign classroom furniture for students who shift modes and tasks during class.

Classrooms are changing. Group work, hybrid setups, and long solo sessions do not fit well with traditional fixed desks and stiff plastic chairs. Our team focused on students like us at Shanghai's Tongji University who move around a lot, sketch on paper, flip open laptops, shift between group discussions and quiet focus. This wasn't just about comfort; the furniture that looked modern and professional, matched the aesthetics of a newly renovated space, and could be mass-produced without blowing past cost or material limits. We had to design for function, form, and feasibility all at once.

As students, we believed that we could empathize well with the users of university chairs and table—it would essentially be ourselves, at least as the start of our use sample. The definition aspect was more challenging—we really didn't expect the hardest part to be our own inexperience. With little background in industrial design or manufacturing, our early sketches for adaptable chairs and tables felt uninspired and impractical. We knew what we wanted to achieve flexible, ergonomic furniture for dynamic learning environments, but we didn't know how to get there. Instead of guessing our way through it, we turned to AI.

Using **Tiangong AI**, a generative design tool, we began feeding in prompts based on use cases: collaborative group work, long solo study sessions, hybrid classrooms with digital tools. To our surprise, AI didn't just give us furniture mockups, it pointed out things we had missed entirely. For example, it proposed features like detachable storage compartments, posture-correcting backrests, and lightweight modular materials that could be rearranged quickly in class.

At first, we took these AI outputs at face value, but when we showed them to classmates, the feedback was mixed. Some designs were beautiful but uncomfortable. Others were clever but unrealistic to build. That's when we realized AI couldn't work alone.

We split into two teams. One focused on gathering real-world insights: interviewing students, observing classroom behavior, and testing prototypes. The other team refined AI prompts using that feedback. When students said they needed more storage, we added that. When someone pointed out that chairs without footrests were tiring, we modified our prompt to address it. AI became less of a design machine and more of a sparring partner and quick to respond, but only as good as the questions we asked.

Over time, we learned to design the prompts, not just the products. Better input meant better suggestions. Eventually, we had a set of furniture concepts that blended AI's expansive ideation with real human needs including modular tables for group brainstorming, chairs with storage built into the frame, and materials optimized for sustainability and comfort.

Key Learnings

- AI can rapidly expand your design vocabulary but only if grounded in human insight.
- Prompting is a design skill in itself. Iteration is everything.

- AI works best when paired with real feedback. Our best designs emerged only after multiple feedback loops.

Final Reflection

We didn't just design better chairs; we designed a better process. AI gave us speed and scale. Human users gave us purpose and grounding. The intersection made our ideas real.

7.12 Empathize & Define Use Case: AI-Driven Empathy in Shanghai Metro Carriages

Our challenge: to gain deep insights into users, without direct access to a large, diverse user base, in order to design an optimal Shanghai Metro carriage.

Designing an improved passenger carriage for the Shanghai Metro is a difficult task, requiring empathetic understanding of populations of passengers and potential passengers, and how their needs can be accommodated within the world's longest and largest citywide passenger train system. Over 10 million passengers ride the Shanghai Metro each day, with a variety of purposes and needs as they navigate among the 500 stations. Without the resources to conduct extensive new passenger research, we leveraged AI tools for journey mapping and synthetic personas, creating scalable, user-centered solutions. Our goal was to test and refine carriage concepts with virtual users, enabling rapid feedback without the logistics of traditional research.

To define our challenge more specifically, we began using Chuangwuji, a multifunctional AI platform offering a user journey mapping template. Our inputs included descriptions of target audiences, design goals and pain points, and usage scenarios (e.g., parents with strollers during rush hour). Detailed prompts allowed the AI to map user behaviors, needs, and emotions across the passenger journey. For example, it highlighted stressors for parents navigating crowded carriages, such as narrow doorways and lack of child-friendly features—critical insights that shaped our concept for a parent-child carriage module.

To learn more about our passengers we used Synthetic Users, an AI program for persona generation and user interviews. Starting with simple descriptions, we iteratively refined them to produce realistic personas varying by age, lifestyle, and travel habits. The "concept testing" module produced simulated interviews with these virtual users. Their feedback helped us refine features such as emergency access, child seating, and storage. One persona, a mother who commutes with a stroller during peak times, emphasized the importance of safety grips and designated standing zones—ideas we later embraced.

Overall, AI-generated insights surfaced pain points we hadn't originally identified and enabled us to capture behavioral nuances across different user types—all without conventional fieldwork.

AI in team processes. We also integrated AI tools into our team workflow. We divided into two groups, each focusing on one AI tool. Collaboration between the groups allowed us to compare AI-generated insights and reach deeper conclusions. Using both tools in tandem created a richer understanding of passenger needs and validated critical design decisions quickly.

Key Learnings

- AI helped overcome logistical challenges in gathering user input.
- Good prompts—grounded in actual user behavior and future trends—tremendously boosted AI output quality.
- Virtual users were most effective when used selectively for concept testing and feedback collection.

Final Reflection

Introducing AI into the early design thinking stages let us empathize with users effectively, despite limited access to actual passengers. While not a complete replacement for human-centered research, AI empowered our small team to produce big insights—offering a scalable, insightful path for future transportation design projects. It is important to remember that because AI tools derived their insights from manually crafted prompts which attempted to simulate accurate personas, and thus could not predict future user behaviors with certainty. Human input remained key during early research.

References

Brown, T. (2008). Design thinking. *Harvard Business Review, 86*(6), 84–92.
Moran, K., & Rosala, M. (2024, September 27). Accelerating research with AI. Nielsen Norman Group. https://www.nngroup.com/articles/research-with-ai/

Oberoi, K. (2024, April 29). *How AI is transforming UX research in 2025 (+10 powerful AI tools)*. Looppanel. https://www.looppanel.com/blog/ai-uxresearch-10-powerful-tools

Saeidnia, H. R., & Ausloos, M. (2024). Integrating artificial intelligence into design thinking: A comprehensive examination of the principles and potentialities of AI for design thinking framework. *InfoScience Trends*, *1*(2), 1–9.

Sreenivasan, A., & Suresh, M. (2024). Design thinking and artificial intelligence: A systematic literature review exploring synergies. *International Journal of Innovation Studies*, *8*(3), 297–312. https://doi.org/10.1016/j.ijis.2024.05.001

Wiedmaier, B. (2024, October 31). *The 2024 AI in UX research report*. User Interviews. https://www.userinterviews.com/ai-in-ux-research-report

8

Ideate & Select: AID Tools and Use Cases

Creativity is the essential element of ideation and selection activities, as it thrives where associative thinking, divergent exploration, and collaborative synthesis meet. As design guru Tim Brown puts it in his 2009 book, design thinking integrates "the needs of people, the possibilities of technology, and the requirements for business success," a stance that remains instructive as AI joins the toolkit. Generative models extend this integration by accelerating search through possibility spaces while leaving human intuition, empathy, and context in charge.

Cognitively, ideation relies on making remote connections, reframing problems, and resisting premature convergence. Contemporary studies suggest AI can both help and hinder here: access to generative-AI ideas can raise judged creativity for individual outputs yet narrow collective novelty—an efficiency that must be balanced with diversity, according to Doshi and Hauser's article in 2024. In visual ideation, AI image support can increase fixation and reduce variety if not facilitated carefully, underscoring the need for prompts, guardrails, and human moderation, as cautioned by Wadinambiarachchi and his colleagues at a 2024 conference panel. Conversely, when novices steer model behavior with lightweight controls, co-creation can expand exploration without overwhelming users—evidence that interface design and workflow matter as much as model capability.

Practically, AI is also democratizing access to creative support. Teams increasingly pair language models, clustering assistants, and rapid visualization tools with standard practices—shortening the path from raw insight to testable concept while keeping decision criteria visible, as detailed in the

© The Author(s), under exclusive license to Springer Nature Switzerland AG 2026 **177**
D. Graff et al., *Design Thinking with Artificial Intelligence*, Palgrave Executive Essentials,
https://doi.org/10.1007/978-3-032-10543-1_8

ITONICS blog in 2024. The goal in this chapter is to treat AI as a creative partner, not a replacement: a breadth-first accelerator that reduces bias, documents reasoning, and opens new paths—while designers remain the curators, critics, and ethical guides.

We focus on seven tools common to ideation and select, showing exactly how AI augments each: 8.1 How Might AI (reframing), 8.2 BrAInstorming, and 8.3 Special BrAInstorming (divergence), 8.4 Analogies on AI Power (cross-domain transfer), 8.5 Dot Voting (collective prioritization), 8.6 3-3-10 (fast brainwriting with AI mates), and 8.7 2×2 Matrix (structuring tensions), and Special Brainstorming (reverse and stimulus-based methods). Across them, you'll see repeatable patterns: use AI to propose variations, expose trade-offs, surface patterns, and draft rationales—then use human judgment to select, adapt, and test. That division of labor is where the creative gains are most reliable.

In addition, we include two use cases illustrating how ideate and select with AI can work in practice, (8.8) Replacing the Plastic Bag: Sustainable Human– AI Collaboration, and (8.9) Designing an AI-Powered Café.

8.1 "How Might AI" Questions

Description of Tool

"How Might We" (HMW) reframes research insights into opportunity-seeking questions that spark ideation. Originating in 1970s consumer-goods practice and popularized by IDEO, HMW converts needs, pain points, and tensions into prompts that are specific enough to focus attention yet open enough to welcome diverse solutions.

In a typical flow, a team distils insights from research, drafts multiple HMW variants, iteratively tightens scope, then uses the final set to drive brainstorming and early concepting. The craft lies in balance: too broad yields vague ideas; too narrow yields incrementalism. Modern teams increasingly pair HMW with collaborative canvases and knowledge bases, so questions are traceable back to evidence (quotes, observations, metrics), making later selection and prioritization defensible.

Why Use AI

AI strengthens HMW by accelerating the reframing loop and broadening perspective while keeping evidence in the foreground. Large language models

Figure 8.1   "How Might AI" Questions. An AI-augmented ideation workflow, illustrating an iterative process that integrates observation, need identification, prompt refinement, and collaborative brainstorming to generate, evaluate, and refine design ideas. AI generated image created with Ideogram, Inc., Ideogram.ai, 3.0, 2025.

can condense long transcripts into themed insight bullets, propose multiple HMW framings at different scopes, and compare them against constraints, personas, and business goals. Workspace-native AI (in whiteboards and docs) keeps the questions tethered to source material, reducing drift and duplication. Critically, AI can generate purposeful variation "adjacent-possible" framings you might not naturally consider then score or tag each question for novelty, feasibility, and user impact to speed selection, without replacing human judgment about what truly matters.

Suggested AI Programs

- ChatGPT: turns insights into HMW drafts, varies scope, explains trade-offs.
- Claude: long-context HMW generation, rationale and critique.

- Kimi (Moonshot): LLM alternative (particularly for Chinese workflows).
- Miro AI: proposes/refines HMW directly on the team board and clusters them.
- Napkin AI: turns HMW insights and problem statements into quick diagrams/visual thumbnails to aid internal alignment and kick-off concepting.
- Notion AI: generates HMW from project docs and maintains a linked question bank.
- Julius AI: quickly mines structured data for patterns that inform HMW scope.

Work Instructions

Example: commuters choosing dinner

1. Anchor your HMWs in evidence.

   (a) Start by extracting themes from a few research artifacts (interview notes, survey crosstabs, logs). Use an LLM (Large Language Models) to keep you close to the data.

   (b) Example (ChatGPT-5 or Claude): *"Please extract 6–8 themes from the following notes and include one verbatim quote or stat under each theme. Keep themes grounded in the text; avoid speculation. Notes: [paste short interview excerpt about commuters choosing dinner]"*

2. Turn themes into HMW questions at three scope levels.

   (a) Ask the model to generate broad/medium/narrow variants so you can compare focus before choosing.

   (b) Example (ChatGPT-5 or other LLMs): *"Using these themes: [paste], give me 9 HMW questions: 3 broad, 3 medium, 3 narrow. For each, add a one-line rationale and tag it with the source theme."*

   (c) Beginner tip: If you're unsure what "broad vs. narrow" looks like, ask ChatGPT-5 or other LLMs: *"If any HMW is too broad or too narrow, please provide 2 broader and 2 narrower alternatives and explain each trade-off in one line."*

3. Bind questions to constraints and personas.

   (a) Keep questions practical by testing them against simple guardrails (budget, pilot size, tech limits) and a basic persona.

   (b) Example (Notion AI or ChatGPT-5): *"Please score each HMW on Feasibility (F), User Impact (U), and Novelty (N) from 1–5. Flag one* *risk in ≤12 words. Constraints: budget <$5k, 4-week pilot, mobile-only. Persona: Busy Commuter, chooses dinner on the bus, limited data plan."*

4. Cluster and de-duplicate to find the strongest angles.

   (a) Move the list into your whiteboard and let AI group similar questions, then keep the best from each group.

   (b) Example (Miro AI): *"Cluster these HMW stickies by semantic similarity into 3–6 groups. Name each cluster with a short noun phrase and surface the strongest 2 HMWs per cluster."*

5. Select with a lightweight matrix and commit.

   (a) Ask the model to create a simple selection table (Impact × Feasibility) and propose measurable success criteria.

   (b) Example (ChatGPT-5): *"Build a table from the F/U/N scores and recommend 3 HMWs in High Impact–High Feasibility. For each, propose a one-sentence success metric (e.g., "decision time ≤ 30s")."*

6. Produce quick concept seeds for internal communication.

   (a) Turn 1–2 selected HMWs into a one-page brief and a few visual thumbnails to align the team.

   (b) Example (ChatGPT-5 → Adobe Firefly). Prompt ChatGPT-5: *"For this HMW: "How might we make dinner choice take ≤ 30s on the bus?", draft a one-page concept brief (problem, promise, key interactions, success metric). Then give 4 short image prompts for low-fidelity mobile UI thumbnails."*

   (c) Then, Use Firefly (or a similar tool) to render the thumbnails and paste them back into your doc/board.

Outputs/Artifacts for "commuters choosing dinner" example: an evidence-linked HMW bank with quotes, a clustered map, a scored selection matrix with 2–3 finalists, and a one-page concept brief plus 3–4 thumbnail visuals—ready to launch brainstorming and early prototyping.

Limitations and Tips

AI can overgeneralize from fragmentary inputs, producing vague or generic HMWs. Counter this by anchoring prompts in verbatim quotes and concrete constraints; require the model to cite which excerpt or metric each HMW reflects so you can trace it back to research.

Scope drift is common: models may create questions that are too broad ("reduce stress") or too narrow ("add a blue button"). Add guardrails in the prompt ("stay within mobile pre-order flow," "avoid UI-colour-only tweaks") and explicitly request three scope levels so you can compare before choosing.

Data sensitivity matters when pasting transcripts or logs. Redact personally identifiable information and competitive details; if needed, summarize locally first, then share only the abstractions with cloud-hosted tools. Maintain a private log noting what sources informed each HMW, such as outlined by McCallister and colleagues in the standards published in 2010 by the National Institute of Standards and Technology.

8.2   BrAInstorming

Description of Tool

Brainstorming is the classic divergent technique for producing many ideas quickly under a few simple guardrails: suspend judgment, go for quantity, welcome wild ideas, and build on others. Traditionally, a facilitator frames a clear challenge, participants speak ideas aloud, and a scribe captures them on sticky notes or a whiteboard. Quantity first enables novelty later; combination and improvement turn raw sparks into stronger directions. Modern teams extend the room with digital boards, short "micro-rounds," and quick synthesis passes that cluster, name, and shortlist ideas before moving to concepting.

Why Use AI

AI strengthens brainstorming by broadening the search space while reducing facilitation overhead. Language models can propose diverse "adjacent possibilities," remix partial ideas into combinations, or shift perspective (user, market, technology) on demand all without breaking momentum. In the background, AI can transcribe, de-duplicate, and cluster notes so humans stay in creative mode. When teams stall, AI can inject counter examples, constraints, or domain analogies to restart flow. Crucially, the value isn't "more ideas" alone; it's faster movement from raw quantity to shaped opportunity sets clean clusters,

Figure 8.2   BrAInstorming. A team of colleagues gathers around a whiteboard during a brainstorming session, mapping out connected ideas to solve a problem. AI generated image created with Ideogram, Inc., Ideogram.ai, 3.0, 2025.

named territories, and a shortlist with early success criteria—so the next phase (selecting and concepting) is grounded and faster.

Suggested AI Programs

- ChatGPT: fast prompts, variations, combinations for ideas.
- Claude: long-context brainstorming with rationale and critique.
- HyperWrite Brainstorming Tool: guided, back-and-forth ideation.
- Team-GPT: shared workspaces and prompt libraries for team ideation.
- Miro AI Assist: cluster stickies, suggest groupings, generate summaries on the board.
- Ideamap: visual mind-mapping with AI-assisted idea expansion and grouping.
- Adobe Firefly / Midjourney / Ideogram / Stable Diffusion: rapid visual riffs to turn text ideas into concept thumbnails.

Work Instructions

(A)   AI as Assistant (Documentation, Nudging, Organizing)

1. Frame a crisp challenge.

   (a) Open your board with a one-sentence prompt and 2–3 constraints.

   (b) Example (ChatGPT): *"Please list 10 alternative framings of: 'How might we make weekday dinners easier for commuters?' Keep within: mobile-only, 4-week pilot, <$5k."*

2. Capture and clean in real time.

   (a) While people speak ideas, route them to the AI to normalize phrasing and remove duplicates.

   (b) Example (Team-GPT → Miro AI): *"Please rewrite these 20 notes as one-line idea statements, remove duplicates, and number them 1–20. If two ideas are 80% similar, keep the clearer one."*

3. Cluster and name territories.

   (a) Create meaningful groups to reduce cognitive load and reveal patterns.

   (b) Example (Miro AI): *"Cluster these 20 ideas into 4–6 groups. Name each cluster with a short noun phrase (≤ 3 words) and list the top-3 ideas per cluster."*

4. Surface blind spots.

   (a) Ask the AI to compare clusters to the original challenge/persona and propose obvious gaps.

   (b) Example (ChatGPT): *"Check our clusters against: Persona = Busy Commuter (low data plan). What 3 gaps do you see? Give one prompt to explore each gap."*

5. Produce a quick digest for the team.

   (a) End with a tidy artifact to support selection.

   (b) Example (ChatGPT): *"Please summarize each cluster in one sentence and provide a shortlist of 6 ideas with a one-sentence 'why it could work.' Format as a table with columns: Idea, Cluster, Why."*

Outputs/artifacts: a de-duplicated idea list, 4–6 named clusters, 3 gap prompts, and a shortlist with rationales—ready for the selection matrix.

(B)   AI as Participant (Provocation, Variation, Mashup)

1. Seed the AI with room tone and rules.

   (a) Describe your brainstorming norms and ask for short, punchy contributions.

   (b) Example (Claude): *"Join as a participant. Speak in ≤ 12-word ideas. Follow: no judgment, build on others, welcome wild ideas."*

2. Run timed micro-rounds.

   (a) Alternate humans and AI to sustain momentum and avoid dominance effects.

   (b) Example (HyperWrite Brainstorming Tool): *"Given idea #3 'preset dinner packs,' please generate 5 wild variations and 5 practical variations. Tag each as Wild/Practical."*

3. Force combinations on demand.

   (a) Ask the AI to combine one "wild" with one "practical" and state a value hypothesis.

   (b) Example (ChatGPT): *"Combine Wild #2 with Practical #4 into a single idea; add a one-sentence value hypothesis and a 10-word user benefit."*

4. Visualize 2–3 frontrunners.

   (a) Turn text into quick thumbnails to align understanding before selection.

   (b) Example (Firefly/Ideogram/Midjourney): *"Generate 3 low-fidelity thumbnail prompts of a mobile flow for '30-second dinner choice'—no branding, simple wireframe look."*

5. Recover from generic ideas.

   (a) If suggestions feel generic, add constraints or switch perspective.

   (b) Example (ChatGPT): *"These feel generic. Please rewrite 5 ideas for 'rural bus commuters with spotty data,' each ≤ 12 words, and state the constraint you used."*

Outputs/artifacts: a mixed human+AI idea bank, labeled variations, 2–3 mashups with value hypotheses, and thumbnail prompts for early communication.

Limitations and Tips

AI can flood the session with quantity but dilute originality if left unchecked. Keep a human facilitator in charge of pacing and explicitly cap AI turns (e.g., "AI only speaks every third turn") to preserve human serendipity while still harvesting breadth.

Clustering can conceal nuance when ideas are short. When an idea sits awkwardly between groups, ask the AI for a one-sentence elaboration before deciding where it belongs; this small clarification step often rescues promising directions from being discarded too early.

Text-to-image thumbnails can prematurely anchor style. To avoid converging too soon, instruct the model to output wireframe-like renders or monochrome sketches and forbid branding until after selection; this preserves conceptual diversity while still aiding communication, as outlined by Jansson and Smith in their 1991 article.

8.3   Special BrAInstorming

Description of Tool

Special Brainstorming refers to targeted ideation moves you bring in when classic free-form sessions stall or when you need a deliberate shift in perspective. In this tool we emphasize Reverse Brainstorming—asking "How could we cause the problem?" to surface root causes and countermeasures—and Random Word Association—injecting unrelated stimuli to force novel connections. Both are established creativity tactics that broaden search space by inverting or disrupting habitual framing; both maps well to AI assistance because models can generate contrarian prompts, provocative "failure modes," and cross-domain associations on demand.

Why Use AI

AI enhances special techniques by supplying structured provocation at speed. For reverse brainstorming, an LLM can enumerate "ways to make it worse," cluster root causes, and then flip each into a mitigative idea. For random word association, AI can source unexpected nouns from distant domains and walk

Figure 8.3   Special BrAInstorming. A diverse group of men in suits and one woman smile and point at each other around a central lightbulb, symbolizing a moment of collective brilliance and collaboration during a "Special Brainstorming" session. AI generated image created with Ideogram, Inc., Ideogram.ai, 3.0, 2025.

you through short association chains, explaining the leap from stimulus to concept. Across both, AI keeps momentum: it de-duplicates, labels clusters, and suggests "next experiment" blurbs so you don't lose flow to cleanup. The end result is not just more ideas, but better-organized provocation → insight → action loops that teams can replay and audit later.

Suggested AI Programs

- ChatGPT/Claude: contrarian prompts, association chains, rationale write-ups.
- Miro AI: clustering, naming themes, quick summaries on the board.
- Boardmix (AI Mind Map)/Ideamap: visual mind-maps from stimulus lists.
- Napkin AI: instant diagrams that turn "aha" moments into simple flows.
- Adobe Firefly/Midjourney: fast thumbnails for communicating oddball concepts.

Work Instructions

(A) Reverse Brainstorming (Cause → Countermeasure)

1. State the problem plainly and invert it.

   (a) Keep one sentence and a simple audience/context.
   (b) For example, prompt (ChatGPT/Claude): *"Problem: Commuters skip park events after work. Invert: How could we guarantee they skip? List 10 ways; keep each ≤ 12 words."*
   (c) Outcome: A sharp "make it worse" list that exposes barriers (e.g., poor timing, bad signage). (Reverse framing per method guidance.)

2. Cluster the "make it worse" list into causes.

   (a) Group to reduce duplicates and reveal patterns.
   (b) Prompt (Miro AI): *"Cluster these 10–20 items into 3–5 root-cause groups; name each ≤ 3 words; list two exemplars."*
   (c) Outcome: Labeled causes like Timing, Awareness, Effort, Relevance.

3. Flip causes into counter-ideas.

   (a) Translate each cause into "How might we. . . stop that from happening?"
   (b) Prompt (ChatGPT): *"For each cause, generate 3 counter-measures in 10-word idea lines + a 10-word user benefit. Return a table: Cause | Idea | Benefit."*

4. Pick quick experiments.

   (a) Move from ideas to tiny tests.
   (b) Prompt (ChatGPT): *"Recommend one 2-week experiment per cause with a success metric (≤1 sentence)."*
   (c) Artifacts: Cause map, counter-idea bank, and mini-experiments—ready for selection.

(B) Random Word Association (Stimulus → Bridge → Idea)

1. Generate distant stimuli.

   (a) Ask for unrelated nouns from far domains to avoid obvious links.
   (b) Prompt (Claude): *"Give 12 random nouns from art, biology, and logistics no tech or parks."*
   (c) Outcome: Stimuli like mycelium, semaphore, curator, tide, convoy (de Bono-style lateral prompts).

2. Make short association chains.

   (a) Force a three-step bridge from stimulus to context.
   (b) Prompt (ChatGPT): *"For each noun, produce a 3-step chain to after-work park events (Stimulus → Property → Analogy → Idea). Keep each chain to 25 words."*

3. Map and merge in a mind-map.

   (a) Visualize families of related ideas.
   (b) Action (Boardmix/Ideamap): Paste chains, auto-mind-map, and label branches by Mechanism (e.g., signaling, swarm, growth).
   (c) Outcome: A visible territory map and 6–10 merge-ideas per territory.

4. Communicate quickly with a sketch.

   (a) Prevent word soup—create one diagram or thumbnail per top idea.
   (b) Action (Napkin AI or Firefly): *"Diagram 4 nodes for 'Semaphore entry beacons for events"* or render a wireframe thumbnail.
   (c) Artifacts: Mind-map and 2–3 visual seeds.

Limitations and Tips

Reverse brainstorming can drift into generic "make it worse" lists. Counter this by adding a one-line rubric (e.g., timing, awareness, effort, relevance) and requiring each "worse" item to cite which factor it exploits; then flip systematically from each factor to a countermeasure.

Random stimuli can become too random to be useful. Use domain distance with constraints: ask for nouns from three far fields and force a 3-step bridge (stimulus → property → analogy → idea). This keeps novelty while maintaining a traceable reasoning path rooted in lateral thinking practice.

Early thumbnails can anchor style prematurely. Request wireframe-like renders or monochrome diagrams first; defer branding and color until after shortlisting to preserve conceptual diversity.

8.4 Analogies on AI Power

Description of Tool

Analogical thinking is the deliberate comparison of distinct domains to transfer structure—relations among elements—from a familiar "base" to a new

Figure 8.4   Analogies on AI Power. Collaborative analysis and synthesis, illustrating a team jointly interpreting data visualizations to compare perspectives, evaluate trade-offs, and support evidence-informed decision-making. AI generated image created with Ideogram, Inc., Ideogram.ai, 3.0, 2025.

"target," enabling insight and solution generation, according to Gentner in 1983. Key moves are: search for candidate sources, map structural similarities (not surface features), and adapt what works into the new context, according to an article by Gick and Holyoak in 1980.

In design thinking, this often pairs with benchmarking across industries and biomimicry, which abstracts principles from nature (e.g., self-healing, distributed sensing) and reinterprets them as design strategies.

Why Use AI

AI broadens the analogy search space and keeps the reasoning traceable. Large models surface far-field sources you might miss, draft the mapping ("what's like what and why"), and propose adaptations with short rationales. Semantic search tools pull cross-domain examples quickly; image tools build fast analogy boards so patterns are visible. Critically, AI also helps you structure the transfer—naming the property you're borrowing (e.g., "multi-point suspension") and the constraint you must keep (e.g., "no new hardware"). Humans still judge fit and ethics; AI accelerates breadth, mapping clarity, and documentation for later selection.

Suggested AI Programs

- ChatGPT/Claude: explore analogies, explain mappings, adapt to constraints.
- Perplexity/Felo: semantic search to find far-field sources.
- Miro AI/Idema: cluster sources and label principles on a canvas.
- ClipDrop/Pixian: quick image cleanup for analogy boards.
- Adobe Firefly/Midjourney/Ideogram: rough thumbnails to communicate transfers.
- Napkin AI: simple diagrams of the mapping and proposed mechanism.

Work Instructions

Example: "metro handrail redesign"

1. Frame pain points and extract transferable properties.

   (a) Keep pains focused (not hyper-specific) to allow wide search.
   (b) Prompt (ChatGPT/Claude): *"Here's the problem statement and pain points for metro handrails. List 3–5 transferable properties (e.g., multi-point support, anti-slip contact, dynamic stability) in one line each."*

2. Source far-field analogies with semantic search.

   (a) Cast wide across sports, nature, logistics, etc.
   (b) Action (Perplexity/Felo): Query "systems that stabilize humans in motion" and "hands-free balance aids." Save 8–12 candidates (e.g., aerial yoga fabric, sailing harness, airport moving-walkway rails, mycelial net).
   (c) Prompt (ChatGPT): *"For each candidate, name the property we might borrow and the constraint we must respect. Return a table: Source | Property | Constraint | 12-word note."*

3. Build an analogy inspiration board.

   (a) Make the mapping tangible.
   (b) Action (ClipDrop/Pixian): Remove backgrounds and compose a collage that pairs each Source image with a short Property label.

(c) Action (Miro AI/Ideamap): Auto-cluster by Property (e.g., Suspension, Grip Texture, Dynamic Damping). Rename clusters; keep top 2 exemplars per cluster.

4. Translate properties into solution seeds.

   (a) Move from "what it's like" to "what we'll try."
   (b) Prompt (ChatGPT/Claude): *"For each cluster, propose 2 solution seeds for metro handrails. Each seed = a 12-word idea + a 12-word user benefit + 1 risk."*
   (c) Optional visual (Firefly/Midjourney/Ideogram): "Create low-fidelity thumbnails (wireframe look) of two seeds from Suspension."

5. Commit with constraints and a quick test.

   (a) Keep it real and measurable.
   (b) Prompt (ChatGPT): *"Select 3 seeds that fit constraints: no new car structure, < $30k pilot. For each: 1-sentence 'why now,' a 2-week hallway test, and a success metric."*

Outputs/artifacts: property list; far-field source table; clustered analogy board; 6–8 solution seeds with risks; 3 shortlisted ideas with a quick experiment and metric.

Limitations and Tips

Push beyond obvious "look-alikes." When an analogy feels convincing because it resembles the target visually, pause and restate the relational property you're actually transferring (e.g., "multi-point suspension distributes load over time"). If you can't name the property in one line, you're likely doing surface mimicry rather than structural mapping, which weakens solutions, according to Gentner's 1983 work.

Force a structured bridge from stimulus to idea. To make far-field sources useful, require a short mapping chain—Stimulus → Property → Idea—for every candidate. This keeps leaps explainable and improves problem–solution fit. If a bridge collapses (e.g., property doesn't survive constraints), drop the source instead of stretching it.

Control fixation and premature convergence. Novel analogies can still trigger design fixation if the first "good" transfer anchors everyone's thinking. Counter this by generating at least two distinct property transfers before visualizing anything, and by time-boxing sketching to "wireframe-only" in the first pass.

8.5 Dot Voting - AI-Assisted Prioritization

Description of Tool

Dot voting serves as a democratic prioritization technique that enables teams to rapidly identify collective preferences from multiple options through visual voting mechanisms. The method involves each individual placing dots next to preferred options, creating a visual heat map that reveals group priorities without lengthy discussions. Core elements include silent voting, equal participation, visual results, and rapid consensus-building. Traditional approaches provide participants with limited dot stickers (typically 25% of total options) to allocate according to their preferences, with results immediately visible through dot concentration patterns. The technique promotes inclusive participation where everyone gets a voice while enabling quick decision-making without lengthy discussions.

Why Use AI

AI enhances dot voting through bias detection, identifying patterns that might indicate group think or uneven influence distribution, alerting facilitators to potential issues. Result analysis provides deeper insights beyond simple vote counting, suggesting why certain options succeeded and predicting implementation success. Optimization recommendations help teams structure voting sessions more effectively, suggesting vote allocation strategies and session timing. Pattern recognition identifies voting trends across multiple sessions, helping teams understand decision-making patterns and improve future prioritization processes. Automated facilitation guides teams through voting setup, rule establishment, and result interpretation for optimal outcomes.

Suggested AI Programs

- ChatGPT/Claude: option cleanup, vote-budget advice, bias checks, rationales.
- Miro (Dot Voting + AI): digital votes, clustering, summaries on the board.
- FigJam Voting: timed, anonymous voting with hidden totals until session end.
- Lucidspark Voting: templates and live visual tallies for consensus-building.

Figure 8.5   Dot Voting - AI-Assisted Prioritization. Dot Voting in a collaborative workshop, illustrating how teams cluster and interpret research artifacts to synthesize insights, identify patterns, and inform design decisions. AI generated image created with Ideogram, Inc., Ideogram.ai, 3.0, 2025.

- Retrium: private dot voting and agile-oriented follow-ups (ranked/tiebreakers).
- MURAL: guided voting sessions and quick "visualize the vote" templates.

Work Instructions

1. Prepare options and simple rules.

   (a) Keep items short, unique, and comparable; set a reasonable vote budget.

   (b) Prompt (ChatGPT): *"Please rewrite these options as single-line statements, remove duplicates, and recommend a vote budget for 14 options and 8 voters (give a formula and number)."*

   (c) Outcome: A numbered, de-duplicated list and a clear rule (e.g., "3 votes each").

2. Configure an anonymous, time-boxed vote.

   (a) Use your board's voting session with hidden totals to reduce influence.

    (b) Action (FigJam/Lucidspark/Miro): Start a 5-minute vote; set votes-per-person from Step 1; ensure results stay hidden until the session ends.

    (c) Outcome: Silent, equal participation and a clean reveal of totals.

3. Cluster the results into themes.

    (a) Reduce noise by grouping similar winners and labeling them.

    (b) Prompt (Miro AI / MURAL): *"Cluster the top-scoring options into 3–5 themes. Name each with ≤3 words and list the top 2 representatives per theme."*

    (c) Outcome: A tidy map of "what the room is really choosing."

4. Check for bias and stability.

    (a) Ask an LLM to test basic hypotheses (order effects, sub-group sway).

    (b) Prompt (ChatGPT / Claude): *"Here are the options, vote counts, and the order they were shown. Do you see signs of bandwagoning or order effects? Simulate a re-vote with the list shuffled and a +1/-1 vote budget change; report any rank flips with one-line reasons."*

    (c) Recovery if bias is suspected: Run a quick second vote with shuffled order or private ballots (Retrium supports this natively).

5. Turn the winners into a shortlist with next steps.

    (a) Translate dots into decisions, not just a chart.

    (b) Prompt (ChatGPT): *"From the top 5 items, recommend 3 priorities. For each: a one-sentence 'why now,' a 2-week experiment, one success metric, and risks in ≤ 12 words."*

    (c) Outcome: A defensible shortlist and a lightweight implementation plan.

Outputs/artifacts: de-duplicated option list, vote summary, clustered themes, a short bias/stability note, and a 3-item priority plan with experiments and metrics.

Limitations and Tips

Anonymous digital voting reduces social pressure but does not eliminate it if facilitators reveal interim totals or allow side-channel commentary. Keep totals hidden until the end, prohibit reactions during the vote, and remind participants of silent rules to avoid anchoring and bandwagon effects, according to Lorenz and colleagues in 2011.

Dot counts can over-favor popularity over practicality. Pair Smart Dot Voting with a quick criteria pass (e.g., a 2×2 or effort-impact score) before locking decisions; document assumptions in a one-page note so stakeholders see both preference and practicality.

If you paste sensitive research notes into AI tools for option cleanup, redact identities, and competitive details first. When in doubt, summarize locally, then share only abstractions with cloud tools; keep a brief trace of what source informed each winning option.

8.6   3-3-10 Method

Description of Tool

The 3-3-10 Method is a fast, AI-assisted brainwriting variant designed to maximize idea volume and variety with minimal facilitation. In each sprint, every participant works privately with a designated "AI mate" to produce 3 ideas in 3 minutes, then the table rotates inputs for a 10-minute exchange block (two quick sprints back-to-back). Teams repeat blocks as needed. The flow borrows from the classic 6-3-5 brainwriting format outlined by Rohrbach in 1969—six people, three ideas, five minutes—by preserving the silent, written exchange while adding AI to diversify styles, accelerate expansion, and auto-summarize outcomes.

Why Use AI

AI lifts the ceiling on divergence without increasing team size. First, it stays fast—models can keep proposing novel angles when human energy dips, so small teams still reach big-room breadth. Second, it shifts voice and lens "AI mates" with distinct roles (e.g., psychologist, gamer, operations lead) generate differently styled ideas that collide productively with human contributions. Third, it renders quickly—text-to-image tools create rough thumbnails that expose strengths/ risks early, helping selection later. Finally, it organizes on the fly—clustering and deduping keep sheets lean between sprints, so momentum isn't lost to cleanup. Humans keep editorial control; AI provides speed, variety, and structure.

Suggested AI Programs

- ChatGPT (LLM), Claude: fast ideation, role styles, rationales.

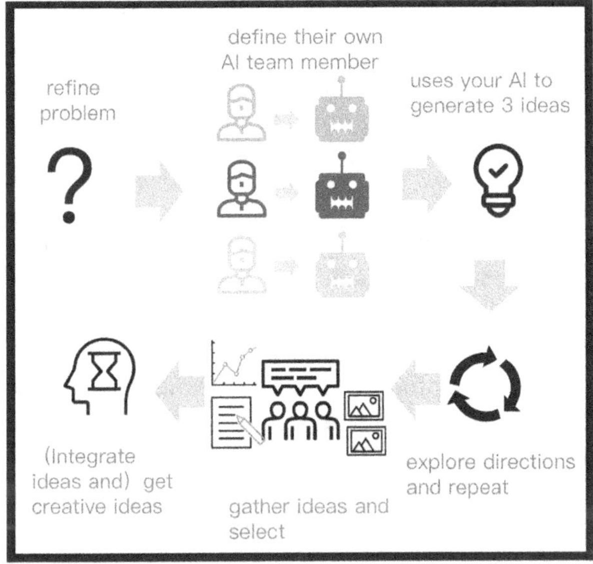

Figure 8.6   3-3-10 Method. A black and white flowchart illustrates an AI-assisted creative problem-solving process, detailing steps from refining a problem and generating ideas with AI to gathering, integrating, and iterating on solutions. AI generated image created with Ideogram, Inc., Ideogram.ai, 3.0, 2025.

- Team-GPT/Notion AI: shared spaces, light knowledge bases for prompts.
- Miro AI/Ideamap: clustering, summarizing, de-duplication between sprints.
- Adobe Firefly/Midjourney/Ideogram/Stable Diffusion: quick thumbnail images testing.
- Napkin AI: instant text-to-diagram to visualize flows.

Work Instructions

1. Refine the challenge and guardrails.

    (a) Keep the problem brief and scoped before you start sprinting. Prompt (ChatGPT/Claude): *"Please rewrite this challenge in one sentence and list 3 constraints (budget, time, tech). Return one line for the goal and three bullet constraints."*

    (b) Outcome: A crisp challenge + constraints that all participants copy atop their sheets.

2. Define your AI mate's persona.

(a) Each participant sets a distinct "AI mate" (tone, role, priorities).
Prompt (ChatGPT/Claude): *"Adopt the role of a [role: e.g., psychologist/ gamer/ops lead]. In this session, prioritize [2–3 values]. Confirm your role in one sentence and ask me one clarifying question."*

3. Sprint A (3 ideas in 3 minutes).

   (a) Work privately; don't read others yet.
   Prompt (your AI mate): "Generate 3 distinct ideas for [challenge] that respect [constraints]. For each: a 12-word idea line + a 10-word user benefit."

   (b) Optional visual (Firefly/Midjourney/Ideogram/SD): "Create 2 low-fidelity thumbnail prompts for Idea #2 (wireframe look, no branding)."

   (c) Outcome: 3 idea lines per person (+ optional thumbnails).

4. Pass and expand (3 ideas in 3 minutes).

   (a) Rotate sheets clockwise; skim what you received; push beyond the obvious.

   (b) Prompt (your AI mate): "Given these 3 ideas, suggest 3 non-obvious variations (new user, setting, or mechanism). Keep each ≤14 words. Mark 'Wild' or 'Practical'."

   (c) Outcome: Each sheet now has 6 ideas (original + expansions).

5. Quick clean-up and clustering (1–2 minutes).

   (a) Normalize text and group similar ideas before the next block.
   Prompt (Miro AI/Ideamap): "Deduplicate these 6 ideas and cluster into 2–3 groups. Name each cluster ≤ 3 words and list the top 2 representatives."

   (b) Outcome: Tidy clusters on each sheet; duplicates removed.

6. Selection mini-round (2 minutes) and share-out.

   (a) Each participant picks 1 favorite per sheet and notes why.
   Prompt (ChatGPT): "From this clustered set, recommend 1 idea that best fits [constraints]. Provide one-sentence 'why now' and one 2-week test with a success metric."

   (b) Optional diagram (Napkin AI): "Turn the chosen idea into a simple flow diagram (3–5 nodes)."

   (c) Artifacts: Per sheet—1 selected idea with a "why," a quick test, a metric, and (optionally) a thumbnail/diagram. Across the room an evidence-ready shortlist.

Limitations and Tips

Improve your problem. Vague prompts cause generic ideas. Ask AI to sharpen goals and constraints first; if ideas feel bland, add a perspective nudge (e.g., "rural teen user," "low-connectivity context") before the next block.

Think outside the box. Don't immediately riff from the last batch. Skim, then ask your AI mate for 2 "Wild" and 2 "Practical" pivots and only keep the ones that introduce a truly new mechanism or user behavior (helps mitigate early fixation).

Choose your mate. Assign contrasting AI personas aligned to the domain (e.g., psychologist for emotional design). Capture each persona's 1-line priority so their outputs stay distinct across blocks.

Guide the AI's direction. Request 5–8 options per prompt but enforce brevity and structure (idea line + user benefit). If you see convergence, switch roles or add a constraint ("offline only," "no new hardware") for the next block.

8.7   2x2 Matrix

Description of Tool

The 2×2 Matrix is a fast, visual way to compare options on two strategic dimensions so that trade-offs become obvious. Teams first define the axes (e.g., "Impact" vs. "Effort"), then place ideas into one of four quadrants to guide priorities—quick wins, strategic bets, filler, or avoid. The value comes from the tension between attributes and the discipline of agreeing what each axis really means before plotting anything.

Why Use AI

AI accelerates every decision loop without sidelining human judgment. First, it proposes axis candidates grounded in the project brief and prior evidence, helping teams avoid generic pairs like "Impact vs. Effort" when a sharper lens (e.g., "Community Interactivity vs. Environmental Impact") would reveal more. Next, it standardizes the option list, removes duplicates, and suggests initial quadrants from short rubrics, reducing facilitation overhead. Finally, it surfaces patterns (clusters inside quadrants), runs quick scenarios (swap axes or thresholds), and drafts short rationales and action lists. The team still decides—but gets to a defensible, documented shortlist faster, with clean visuals ready for stakeholders.

Figure 8.7   2x2 Matrix. A 2×2 matrix of user archetypes, illustrating comparative positioning across two key dimensions to support segmentation, prioritization, and strategic design decision-making. AI generated image created with Ideogram, Inc., Ideogram.ai, 3.0, 2025.

Suggested AI Programs

- ChatGPT (LLM): propose axis pairs, normalize options, draft rationales.
- Miro Templates + Miro AI: 2×2 canvas, clustering/summaries on stickies.
- MyMap AI: auto-generate matrices/decision grids from a short brief.
- Praxie 2×2: AI-assisted axis selection, plotting, and insights.

Work Instructions

Example: designing an urban green park

1. Choose axes that match your goal.

   (a) Ask an LLM (ChatGPT, Claude, Kimi, Deepseek, etc) for crisp, context-fit pairs, then pick one.

   (b) Prompt (ChatGPT): *"Please list 6 axis pairs for prioritizing features in a small urban green park. Include a one-line trade-off for each. Recommend the best pair for a 6-month pilot with < $50k."*

    (c) Likely outcome: You select Environmental Impact (low→high) × Community Interactivity (low→high).

2. Standardize the option list.

    (a) Keep ideas short, unique, and scorable.

    (b) Prompt (ChatGPT): *"Rewrite these 15 items as one-line options; remove duplicates; number them 1–15."*

    (c) Recovery if generic: "Please add a 6-word descriptor to each option that states its main benefit (e.g., 'reduces heat island')."

3. Create the matrix and place items.

    (a) Use a 2×2 template, then ask AI to suggest initial quadrants from simple rubrics; you still drag-drop.

    (b) Prompt (Miro Templates + Miro AI): *"Using this 2×2 (Environmental Impact × Community Interactivity), suggest a quadrant for each numbered option. Base decisions on: Impact = {biodiversity, shade, heat-island}, Interactivity = {co-creation, events, daily touchpoints}. Return a table: #, Quadrant, 12-word reason."*

    (c) Outcome: A populated grid plus a reasons table you can attach.

4. Cluster and name patterns inside quadrants.

    (a) Reduce cognitive load by grouping similar items.

    (b) Prompt (Miro AI): *"Cluster the stickies in each quadrant by similarity; name clusters with ≤ 3-word labels; list the top 2 ideas per cluster."*

    (c) Outcome: Clear territories like "Cooling Shade," "Community Food," "Play & Learn."

5. Test thresholds and run a what-if.

    (a) See how choices move when assumptions change.

    (b) Prompt (Praxie or ChatGPT): *"If Interactivity weights co-creation twice as much as events, which items shift quadrants? Summarize moves and explain in one line each."*

    (c) Optional (MyMap AI): *"Generate an alternative matrix using 'Maintenance Cost' × 'Interactivity'; export image."*

    (d) Outcome: A short scenario note and an alternate view you can compare.

6. Commit to next steps with rationale.

    (a) Turn the grid into a shortlist and first experiments.

    (b) Prompt (ChatGPT): *"Recommend 3 priorities from the High Impact–High Interactivity quadrant. For each: write a 1-sentence 'why now,' a 2-week experiment, and a simple success metric."*

Outputs/artifacts (designing an urban green park example): final 2×2 image, quadrant reasons table, in-quadrant clusters, a scenario note (what changed and why), and a 3-item priority list with experiments and metrics—ready for stakeholder review and resourcing.

Limitations and Tips

Axis ambiguity is the #1 failure mode—teams argue later because "Impact" meant different things. Avoid this by adding a one-line definition card under each axis before plotting (e.g., "Environmental Impact = shade, biodiversity, heat-island reduction"), and require every quadrant assignment to reference that definition.

AI placement can feel like a black box if rubrics are vague. Fix this by prompting for a short, explicit reason per placement and sampling two human checks per quadrant; if a reason reads generic, rewrite the rubric and re-score only that quadrant to keep momentum.

Matrices can over-simplify when options vary on a third hidden factor (e.g., maintenance cost). Counteract this by running one what-if with a different second axis or by annotating each sticky with a small secondary tag (e.g., "$" for high maintenance) so nuance isn't lost.

Pretty visuals can speed premature buy-in. Present the matrix with an accompanying assumption log (the definitions, rubrics, and weights used). That way, stakeholders agree not just on the picture but on the reasoning they're approving.

8.8 Ideate & Select Use Case: Replacing the Plastic Bag: Sustainable Human–AI Collaboration

Our challenge: design a sustainable alternative that could match the practicality of a plastic bag while encouraging consumers to change their behavior.

Single-use plastic bags are a global environmental problem. They are cheap, convenient, and deeply ingrained in supermarket shopping habits, but they create enormous waste. To meet our challenge, we wanted something affordable, functional, and capable of sparking awareness about overuse, without losing the ease that shoppers expect.

From the start, we decided to explore how AI could shape our ideas. To understand AI strengths and limitations, we split into two groups. One group, the "Machine Team," gave AI more control over decisions. The other, the

"Human Team," kept decision-making in human hands but still used AI for research and visualization. Both teams worked on the same brief, aiming to create an eco-friendly, practical alternative for supermarkets.

The Machine Team began by "training" a project manager AI with our design needs. This AI chose a focus area, such as user behavior, material innovation, or service models, and initiated brainstorming. Ideas were evaluated using graph-generating tools to compare solutions, followed by AI-driven market and user research plans. Visual analysis tools helped interpret the research data and guide discussions. Once the most promising idea emerged, the AI helped prepare it for prototyping.

The Human Team approached the task differently. They used AI search tools to gather targeted insights, such as shopping habits in different regions, and combined these with cultural and emotional perspectives. They created a rough human-centered design, refined it with ChatGPT, and used Midjourney to visualize the final look.

Across both groups, collaboration patterns evolved. We quickly saw that relying too heavily on large language models limited our creativity. AI was at its best when acting as a facilitator rather than a decision-maker. It could synthesize fragmented ideas, generate visual concepts, and rank solutions to streamline our discussions. But it could not replace the intuition, empathy, and context-specific reasoning that humans bring.

Prompt-writing became a design skill in itself. Vague instructions produced generic outputs, while clear, detailed prompts yielded more relevant results. We often worked from the same computer to keep information consistent, discussing each AI output together and deciding which elements to keep. If something felt off, we adjusted the prompt and tried again.

The final concept was a recycled plastic bag that retained the texture and appearance of the waste materials it came from. Sold at the same price as conventional bags, it would signal to consumers the environmental cost of plastic use, encouraging them to reduce their reliance. AI accelerated our research, visualized our ideas, and helped refine the logic of our solution. Human judgment ensured that the final design aligned with both environmental goals and user needs.

Key Learnings

- AI can speed up research, visualization, and idea refinement, but its outputs are only as good as the prompts.
- Human insight is essential for emotional resonance and cultural fit in the process and to facilitate achieving a quality outcome.

- Combining AI's data processing with human creativity creates more balanced and feasible solutions.

Final Reflection

This project showed us that AI is most effective as a facilitator. When paired with human empathy and decision-making, it becomes a powerful tool for turning a vague challenge into a clear, viable design. The experience not only gave us a solution for plastic bag replacement but also a method for working with AI that we can apply to future sustainability projects.

8.9   Ideate & Select Use Case: Designing an AI-Powered Café

Our challenge: to design a futuristic, AI-powered café.

The future is full of possibilities, and we found that AI can generate many starter ideas, as well as helping to narrowing down to a reasonable selection. We navigated the entire process using AI, from defining the design problem to brainstorming and creating prototypes. AI tools facilitated the exploration of various aspects of the café, including its theme, functionalities, and customer experiences. The future is full of possibilities, and we found that AI can help generate many starter ideas, as well as helping to narrowing down to a reasonable selection. We incorporated AI into our team's brainstorming process by using multiple large language models to propose café concepts. For instance, to start off we asked simple prompts such as, *"Do you have an idea for an AI café?"* The responses varied dramatically across different models, providing a broad set of starting points. When we instructed AI to "be more creative" and supplied whimsical examples, it went further—proposing recombined, unconventional concepts such as horror-themed cafés where atmosphere and emotion detection defined the experience, or fitness cafés that integrated movement with coffee consumption.

We found these "irregular" combinations fascinating: while humans may hesitate to link unrelated ideas, AI did so effortlessly. In further iterations, we gave AI contextualized prompts: *"How might you transform a dormitory into a smart café that solves nighttime accessibility for students?"* Here, AI's responses became more refined and targeted, outlining design workflows such as automated ordering for student schedules or menus aligned with localized tastes.

Through AI-supported defining and ideating, we produced a diverse portfolio of café concepts. AI elevated our brainstorming into realms we may not have reached independently, expanding ideas about space layout, decoration, personalization, smart menus, and user experience flows. For example, the dorm café idea crystallized from AI's ability to merge convenience with contextual specificity, directly addressing defined user pain points.

In summary, AI gave us a cycle of idea expansion, filtration, and workflow refinement. It provided unexpected suggestions when we were stuck, deepened rough ideas into structured proposals, and stimulated us to continuously push our brainstorm further.

Our group worked in a collaborative, reciprocal format: face-to-face discussion followed by joint use of AI. At first, we conducted a traditional roundtable, but when consensus was elusive, we shifted to AI-enabled brainstorming. Each member helped craft prompts, adding perspective while ensuring inclusivity of ideas. Members then used their preferred AI tools, generating parallel outputs which were collectively reviewed. This pooling of AI-generated content gave us a spectrum of starting points, after which we refined through consensus. AI thus acted like an external team member, passively waiting for our input yet instantly contributing when triggered. Whenever discussions reached a lull, AI re-energized brainstorming with fresh perspectives. However, we realized we occasionally leaned too heavily on AI outputs, sometimes at the expense of direct user validation. Striking a healthier balance between AI insights and real stakeholder perspectives emerged as an area for future improvement.

Key Learnings

* AI proved invaluable in helping us define the design challenge more holistically while ideating creative, even eccentric, possible futures for the café.
* AI tools were most useful during the brainstorming phase, playing a pivotal role in sparking creativity and generating ideas, with faster iteration cycles than humans alone.
* AI helped us to scaffold our ideas, adding breadth and depth, allowing selection of concepts favorable to our goals and to the next steps in a product design process.

Final Reflection

By integrating AI during the Ideate and Select activities, our team amplified creativity, refined ambiguous ideas, and enhanced collaboration. Surprising to us was that AI's creativity, while based more on re-combinations of existing ideas than novel invention, is nonetheless not bound by the social logic or experiential biases humans often carry, making it a powerful catalyst for expanding the design space. This makes AI a powerful partner to stretch imagination, while still requiring human judgment to filter ideas into feasible and meaningful café designs.

References

Brown, T. (2009). *Change by design: How design thinking transforms organizations and inspires innovation.* HarperBusiness.

Doshi, A. R., & Hauser, O. P. (2024). Generative AI enhances individual creativity but reduces the collective diversity of novel content. *Science Advances*, *10*(28), eadn5290. https://doi.org/10.1126/sciadv.adn5290

Gentner, D. (1983). Structure-mapping: A theoretical framework for analogy. *Cognitive Science*, *7*(2), 155–170. https://doi.org/10.1207/s15516709cog0702_3

Gick, M. L., & Holyoak, K. J. (1980). Analogical problem solving. *Cognitive Psychology*, *12*(3), 306–355. https://doi.org/10.1016/0010-0285(80)90013-4

ITONICS. (2024, July 11). *How AI is transforming design thinking.* ITONICS Innovation Blog. https://www.itonics-innovation.com/blog/design-thinking-transformation

Jansson, D. G., & Smith, S. M. (1991). Design fixation. *Design Studies*, *12*(1), 3–11. https://doi.org/10.1016/0142-694X(91)90003-F

Lorenz, J., Rauhut, H., Schweitzer, F., & Helbing, D. (2011). How social influence can undermine the wisdom of crowd effect. *Proceedings of the National Academy of Sciences*, *108*(22), 9020–9025. https://doi.org/10.1073/pnas.1008636108

McCallister, E., Grance, T., & Scarfone, K. (2010). *Guide to protecting the confidentiality of personally identifiable information (PII)* (NIST Special Publication 800-122). National Institute of Standards and Technology. https://doi.org/10.6028/NIST.SP.800-122

Rohrbach, B. (1969). Kreativ nach Regeln – Methode 635, eine neue Technik zum Lösen von Problemen. *Absatzwirtschaft*, *12*, 73–75.

Wadinambiarachchi, S., Kelly, R. M., Pareek, S., Zhou, Q., & Velloso, E. (2024). The effects of generative AI on design fixation and divergent thinking. In *Proceedings of the 2024 CHI Conference on Human Factors in Computing Systems* (pp. 1–18). Association for Computing Machinery. https://doi.org/10.1145/3613904.3642919

9

Prototype & Test: AID Tools and Use Cases

Prototyping and testing are the bridge between a promising idea and evidence that it works for real people. In design thinking, these activities turn abstract intent into observable interactions so teams can see what resonates, what breaks, and what to change next. That learning loop has long underpinned modern innovation, from design thinking's human-centered cycles to lean startup's emphasis on rapid, testable experiments (Brown, 2009; Ries, 2011).

AI speeds up and expands that loop without replacing judgment. AI systems help teams generate first-pass assets (screens, images, copy), analyze early user reactions, and suggest targeted next steps. Across software and product development, analysts report that AI is compressing build-measure-learn cycles and improving throughput when paired with clear goals and human oversight, as outlined in a report by McKinsey & Company in 2025.

Just as important, AI has broadened who can contribute meaningfully during prototyping. Tools such as Uizard's Autodesigner create multi-screen, editable prototypes from plain-language prompts—useful for product managers, researchers, and stakeholders who don't draw for a living. Whiteboard assistants in Figma (FigJam AI) and Miro cluster sticky notes, summarize themes, and turn messy boards into clearer maps of what to test next, as outlined in the Miro Microsoft help webpage in 2025. These capabilities make early prototypes faster to create and easier to discuss, while keeping humans in charge of decisions.

The operational impact is visible at the organization level. A 2024 OutSystems–KPMG survey of 555 software executives found 75% had experienced up to a 50% reduction in development time with increased use of AI and automation—gains concentrated in testing, QA, and code review

© The Author(s), under exclusive license to Springer Nature Switzerland AG 2026

D. Graff et al., *Design Thinking with Artificial Intelligence*, Palgrave Executive Essentials,
https://doi.org/10.1007/978-3-032-10543-1_9

that translate directly into more prototype cycles per quarter. These reductions don't simply reflect speed; they reflect learning density: more variations explored, more evidence attached to decisions, and more confidence in what to scale.

This chapter focuses on AI-enabled practices that preserve the soul of prototyping quick experiments in service of people—while widening the aperture of what you can test in a week. We included the following AID tools: 9.1, Concept Sketching, 9.2, Rapid AI Prototype, 9.3, Service Blueprint, 9.4, Exploration Map, 9.5, Powerful Questions with AI Experience Testing, 9.6, Concept Evaluation, 9.7, AI Assisted Feedback Grid, and 9.8, Foresight Scenario. None of these require a linear sequence; you can cycle among them as your project demands. The common thread is pragmatic: use AI to create clearer artifacts faster, connect them to real user evidence, and decide the next experiment with purpose, as discussed in Verganti's 2009 book. We also illustrate prototyping and testing through two use cases, (9.9) Next Generation AI-Design Alternatives to LEGO, and (9.10) Building a Website, Collaborating with AI.

You will also see recurring cautions. AI can over-confidently summarize noisy data; highly polished renders can bias participants; and automation can hide the trade-offs that make a product coherent. Effective teams counter these risks by labeling prototypes clearly, sampling raw data before final synthesis, and grounding every decision in a short rationale plus a link to evidence. Used this way, AI becomes a multiplier for the human skills that matter most in prototyping: framing good questions, noticing what users do, and choosing the next smallest test that reduces the most risk, similar to lean startup methods discussed by Ries in 2011.

9.1 Concept Sketching

Description of Tool

Concept Sketching is the foundational visual-thinking practice for exploring, communicating, and refining ideas at speed. Design thinkers externalize intent with quick hand or digital sketches, branch into alternatives, annotate trade-offs, and align stakeholders before heavier modeling. Precision is intentionally low; the goal is discovering the concept, not drafting finished art. Sketches can be thumbnails, callout sheets, exploded views, UI wireframes, or storyboard beats. The method's strength in Prototype and Test is its rapid

Figure 9.1   Concept Sketching. A co-creation sketching session, illustrating collaborative ideation through shared drawing, exploration of form and function, and early-stage concept development.A group of four designers sits around a circular table, each focused on a separate sketchbook. The individuals, bathed in sunlight from a nearby window, are engrossed in the creative process of sketching designs, with a shared set of drawing tools scattered across the table. AI generated image created with Ideogram, Inc., Ideogram.ai, 3.0, 2025.

iteration: you can move from fuzzy hunch → shared picture → concrete next step in minutes, keeping the team focused on the problem and decision at hand.

Why Use AI

AI expands sketching from a single drawing into a search through nearby possibilities. From a rough line sketch, diffusion models can propose materials, lighting, and forms; style-reference workflows keep results aligned to brand; and "sketch-to-UI" tools turn hand wireframes into editable screens. LLMs help with prompt craft, critique, and variant planning. Used well, AI doesn't replace gesture and judgment, it amplifies divergence (fast variations) and accelerates convergence (clearer next moves) while preserving the design thinker's authorship and intent.

Suggested AI Programs

- ChatGPT 5 (LLM): Drafts style prompts, critiques sketches, proposes variations and checklists for next iterations.
- StableDiffusion+ControlNet(Scribble/Lineart)inAUTOMATIC1111:"Sketch-to-image" with tight shape control from your lines.
- Adobe Firefly/Photoshop (Generative Fill + Style/Reference Image): Rapid renders and brand-consistent looks from a reference style.
- Uizard Wireframe Scanner: Converts hand UI wireframes into editable screens for quick flows.

Work Instructions

1. Sketch the core idea by hand (stay loose).

   (a) Pick a single use-case and storyboard 3 thumbnails. Keep lines chunky; annotate intent (e.g., "cap twists 90°; light ring = battery"). Ask ChatGPT 5 for a style deck prompt set (3 distinct moods) you can apply later: "industrial-minimal," "playful-eco," and "premium-tech."

   (b) Outputs: 3 thumbnails + a short prompt set.

2. Create first renders from your lines (structure-true).

   (a) Photograph or scan one thumbnail and run Stable Diffusion or ControlNet in AUTOMATIC1111. Use your sketch as the control image; paste the "industrial-minimal" prompt from Step 1.

   (b) Keep guidance high so geometry follows your lines; generate 6–8 candidates. Example prompt (shortened): *"sleek modular desk lamp, matte aluminum, soft area lighting, minimal joints, product render, studio lighting."*

   (c) Outputs: a contact sheet of faithful variations.

3. Align results to brand or art direction (style-true).

   (a) Choose the strongest candidate and apply Adobe Firefly/Photoshop with Style (Reference) Image: drop in a brand mood image (color/finish/material) to match tones and textures.

   (b) Use Generative Fill for small corrections (e.g., seam cleanup, base cable routing), keeping the silhouette from Step 2.

   (c) Outputs: 2–3 brand-consistent renders + a before/after note.

4. Branch into purposeful alternatives (diverge, then compare).

   (a) Ask ChatGPT 5 to propose three meaningful deltas: "magnetic joint," "touch slider on stem," "swappable base plate." For each delta, re-run ControlNet with quick line tweaks or over-draw on the render and run Photoshop Generative Fill for localized variations. Assemble a concept sheet with three labeled options and decision criteria (light spread, stability, part count).

   (b) Outputs: a 3-option concept sheet with callouts.

5. Wireframe companion UI (if relevant) and connect flows.

   (a) If your concept needs an app (e.g., lamp presets), sketch the UI on paper and run Uizard Wireframe Scanner to digitize screens; link into a 3-screen flow. Ask ChatGPT 5 to critique the flow for clarity and propose a usability micro-task (e.g., "Create a 30-min reading preset").

   (b) Outputs: clickable low-fi UI and a micro-task for the next test.

6. Package for test and archive prompts.

   (a) Make a one-pager: hero render + two alternates, UI snippet (if any), and a short hypothesis ("Touch slider reduces setting time ≤ 10s"). Include a prompt log (what worked/failed) so your team can reproduce results.

   (b) Outputs: test packet (PDF/board), prompt log, layered source files.

Example: Smart Refillable Bottle + Companion App

1. Sketch the core idea by hand (stay loose). Storyboard three thumbnails:

   (a) Bottle silhouette with a rotary cap (90° twist to lock), LED ring for hydration reminders, NFC tag for tap-to-log at refill stations.

   (b) "Travel sleeve" variant with a magnetic base that docks to a coaster-charger.

   (c) "Gym" variant with a thumb slider that sets a 30/60/90-minute reminder interval.Ask ChatGPT-5: *"Give me three style prompt sets (industrial-minimal, eco-playful, premium-tech) for a refillable bottle with LED ring + NFC refill."* Save the prompts for rendering.

2. Create first renders from your lines (structure-true).

   (a) Scan and use your sketch as the control image; paste the industrial-minimal prompt. Generate 6–8 candidates with higher control weight so the bottle proportions match your drawing. Select 2 that preserve the cap geometry and LED ring placement.

(b) Mini prompt (trim as needed): "*refillable water bottle, matte aluminum body, subtle LED ring under cap, clean seam, soft studio lighting, product render, minimal branding.*"

3. Align to brand direction (style-true) and fix small details.

(a) Open your chosen render in Photoshop/Firefly. Use Style (Reference) Image from your brand moodboard to match CMF (e.g., anodized aluminum + sage accent).

(b) Apply Generative Fill for small corrections: tuck the seam line, refine the LED ring gap, add a discreet NFC mark near the base. Export two options: A-1 cool gray, A-2 warm champagne. Capture before/after notes so changes are traceable.

4. Branch into purposeful product alternatives (diverge, then compare).

(a) Ask ChatGPT-5: "*Propose three meaningful variations that change function, not just style, for this bottle concept.*" Use the suggestions to create:
  (i) Mag-Dock Base (travel): small fillet at the base + pogo pin detail for charging.
  (ii) Slider-Cap (gym): add a low-profile capacitive slider on the cap shoulder.
  (iii) Grip-Groove (commute): add a helical micro-groove for grip + spill control.

(b) For each, over-draw your chosen render (or tweak the sketch) and re-run ControlNet for geometry-faithful variations; use Generative Fill for local edits. Assemble a 3-option concept sheet with callouts: LED visibility, charging stability, cleaning/part count, manufacturability notes.

5. Wireframe the companion app and connect flows.

(a) On paper, sketch a 3-screen flow:
  (i) S1 Home: current hydration %, next reminder time, quick "Refill logged" state.
  (ii) S2 Schedule: slider or presets (workday/gym/travel); NFC enable toggle.
  (iii) S3 History: daily bars with refill events; "streak" indicator.

(b) Run Uizard Wireframe Scanner to convert to editable screens; link a micro-task ("Set a 30-min reminder and log a refill"). Ask ChatGPT-5 to critique the flow for clarity and propose one usability micro-test (e.g., "Can a new user set a reminder in ≤10s without reading help?"). Export a lightweight clickable.

6. Package for test and archive prompts.

(a) Create a one-page test packet: hero render (A-1), two alternates (Mag-Dock, Slider-Cap), the 3-screen app flow, and a simple hypothesis:

    (i) H1 (hardware): "LED ring + 30-min cadence increases mid-day refills by ≥ 20% in unmoderated tests."

    (ii) H2 (app): "New users set a reminder in ≤10s with ≤1 error."

(b) Add a prompt/settings log (ControlNet model + weights, Firefly reference image, LLM prompts) so results are reproducible.

Limitations and Tips

Over-polished AI renders can shut down exploration. When early images look "finished," teams stop drawing. Keep the first two rounds obviously provisional: generate in grayscale, limit detail, and annotate *what's uncertain* alongside each render. Only escalate polish when you have a decision to validate.

Licensing and data provenance still matter. Firefly emphasizes training on licensed/public-domain content and offers reference-style workflows, but final usage is governed by tool terms. Keep a record of sources and check license notes before external release; when in doubt, replace style references with your own brand assets.

Models can homogenize style. Diffusion outputs often regress to common aesthetics. Counter this by feeding your *own* reference boards, sketching strong silhouettes first, and iterating with manual over-draw between AI passes. Use LLM critique to force variety on dimensions that matter (form language, affordances, CMF).

9.2 Rapid AI Prototype

Description of Tool

Prototype to Test turns prioritized ideas into minimum, testable representations that can be shown to real users quickly. The emphasis is on speed and learning over polish: build only what's necessary to validate assumptions, observe interaction, collect feedback, and iterate. Prototypes can range from paper sketches, storyboards, and simple mockups to clickable UI flows, 3D stubs, or short video enactments. Teams cycle rapidly—prototype → test → learn → refine—so weak concepts are discarded early, and promising ones are improved before any heavy build.

Why Use AI

AI shrinks the effort between idea and evidence. Generative tools can turn text or rough references into UI screens, images, and short

Figure 9.2   Rapid AI Prototype. Human–AI co-creation in a collaborative workspace, illustrating an AI agent embedded within team workflows to support coordination, ideation, and shared problem-solving across multiple design artifacts and tools. AI generated image created with Ideogram, Inc., Ideogram.ai, 3.0, 2025.

explainer visuals, so you can test multiple directions in the same week. During testing, LLMs draft neutral questionnaires and later summarize patterns across responses; creative models generate controlled variations for A/B-style comparisons without recoding. The result: more iterations, clearer signals, and fewer cycles wasted on guesswork (Adobe Firefly enables rapid text-to-image/video assets; Ideogram focuses on typography-reliable brand visuals; ChatGPT/Gemini handle prompts, scripts, and synthesis).

Suggested AI Programs

- ChatGPT 5 (LLM): Drafts hypotheses, test scripts, and decision rules; rewrites tasks for clarity; synthesizes feedback into next-step options.
- Uizard Autodesigner: Generates multi-screen UI prototypes from text prompts; editable screens for fast iteration.
- Figma + FigJam AI: Prototyping plus AI that sorts and summarizes sticky-note feedback to speed synthesis.

- Maze: One-click Figma import for unmoderated tests; collects success/time metrics and open-ended feedback.
- Adobe Firefly: Fast text-to-image (and short text-to-video/Image-to-Video) assets for mockups, storyboards, and concept clips.
- Ideogram.ai: Image generator strong at logos/typography and brand compositions for visual prototype options.
- Optimizely Feature Experimentation: Runs A/B tests on higher-fidelity or staged builds with feature flags and experiment workflows.

Work Instructions

1. Preparation: select what to test and define learning goals.

   (a) From your option set, pick 1–2 high-priority ideas (plus an optional low-stakes variant). Write what insight you need (e.g., Do users understand the value prop in 10 seconds?).

   (b) Ask ChatGPT 5 or Gemini to rewrite it as a falsifiable hypothesis with a success metric and decision rule (e.g., " *≥ 70% of users complete the core task in ≤ 45s; else, change flow*").

2. Initial prototype: build the lightest artifact that shows the idea clearly.

   (a) Choose the form that best communicates intent (mockups, video snippet, storyboard, 3D stills, UI wireframes).

   (b) Use Ideogram to generate two brand-consistent visual directions (e.g., logo/label variants), and Adobe Firefly to create a storyboard panel set or UI hero images that illustrate the core interaction.

   (c) Keep fidelity low enough to avoid misleading users, but clear enough to prevent confusion about purpose and next action.

3. Questionnaire & fielding window: collect fast feedback.

   (a) Embed the prototype artifacts (images, short video, or clickable frames) in your survey or unmoderated test. With ChatGPT 5/Gemini, draft a short questionnaire: overall impression, task clarity, perceived value, top confusion point, and "what would you change first?"

   (b) Keep the study open 2–3 days (adjust by scope and audience availability). The goal is quick directional signal, not statistical certainty.

4. Aggregate responses into a spreadsheet and analyze.

   (a) Export to a sheet with respondent meta (age/role, if collected), task outcomes, and open-ended answers. Use ChatGPT 5/Gemini on the spreadsheet content to summarize themes, patterns, and contradictions, and to propose priority fixes.

(b) If you need deeper analysis (e.g., segmentation or visualization), generate an analysis plan via the LLM, then execute in your preferred analytics stack.

5. Plan the next iteration and act.

(a) Translate findings into an action list: what to change now, what to test next, and what to drop. Use Ideogram to render two revised visual directions and Firefly to regenerate storyboard frames or UI hero shots reflecting the change.

(b) Re-run Step 3. Repeat until users can understand, navigate, and endorse the concept—or until evidence says it's time to pivot.

6. Optional visual-prototype workflow:

(a) Select a reference image (existing product or style cues).
(b) Use it as structure or style reference in Ideogram or Firefly.
(c) Draft a concise prompt with ChatGPT 5/Gemini; edit for specificity.
(d) Repeat until the image communicates the idea unambiguously.

Outputs/Artifacts: hypothesis + decision rule, low-fidelity prototype assets (image/video/UI), questionnaire link, a responses spreadsheet, and a one-page synthesis with prioritized next steps.

Limitations and Tips

Choosing the wrong prototype form leads to muddy feedback. Start by asking: Will this form communicate the idea efficiently? What value will this test reveal? Can users interact with it easily? If not, switch forms (e.g., from stills to a 15-second clip) before recruiting.

Generative polish can inflate perceived maturity. Highly finished visuals can bias users toward aesthetics over concept. Label prototypes clearly (concept only), constrain tasks, and keep fidelity intentionally modest until you're testing look-and-feel on purpose.

Tool fit and prompt craft vary by task; experimentation is required. Try multiple AIGC tools on the same prompt, note what you changed, and compare outputs. After each round, ask: Did the prompt/tool choice meaningfully improve clarity or testability? Keep a small prompt log so improvements compound.

Figure 9.3 Service Blueprint. Collaborative service blueprinting, illustrating how teams map frontstage and backstage interactions, roles, and information flows to align stakeholders and design cohesive service experiences. AI generated image created with Ideogram, Inc., Ideogram.ai, 3.0, 2025.

9.3 Service Blueprint

Description of Tool

A Service Blueprint is a structured visualization of how a service is delivered over time, aligning what customers see (frontstage) with the supporting operations they don't (backstage) and the enabling systems behind them. Typical lanes include customer actions, frontstage employee or channel actions, backstage processes, supporting systems, and physical/digital evidence. Lines of interaction and visibility separate these layers so teams can diagnose failure points, handoff risks, and evidence gaps. The technique originates in service-design and service-marketing scholarship and remains a cornerstone for designing, prototyping, and testing complex services because it ties user moments to operational reality, as explained in articles by Shostack in 1984 and Bitner and colleagues in 2008.

Why Use AI

AI accelerates blueprinting by turning messy descriptions and research artifacts into a coherent draft, then helping teams cluster signals, spot redundancies, and simulate "what-ifs." Diagramming tools can generate a first-pass blueprint directly from natural-language inputs; AI whiteboards cluster sticky notes into stages and lanes; and survey tools now summarize open-text feedback, letting you loop new evidence into the map within hours, not days, as explained on the Creately, Miro, and Google Forms-Gemini websites accessed in 2025. The human work—choosing boundaries, defining decision points, and judging feasibility—stays central; AI simply compresses the path from raw inputs to an actionable blueprint.

Suggested AI Programs

- Miro + Miro AI (Service Blueprint template): Collaborative board; AI clusters sticky notes and organizes cards to speed synthesis.
- Creately AI (Service Blueprint generator): Generates a structured blueprint from text; refine lanes and swim-lanes collaboratively.
- Boardmix (Service Blueprint template + AI assist): Quick templated layout and formatting for lanes, icons, and evidence.
- ChatGPT 5 (LLM) with service-design prompts: Drafts lane definitions, failure-point checklists, and improvement options; turns notes into decision rules.
- Google Forms + Gemini: Collects stakeholder or user feedback on pain points and summarizes open-text responses directly in Forms.

Work Instructions

1. Frame scope and success.

    (a) Define the service slice (e.g., "first-time onboarding") and the user goal. Ask ChatGPT 5 to draft explicit lane definitions, success metrics (e.g., completion, time, CSAT), and a short checklist of "must-capture evidence" (emails, screens, receipts).

    (b) Output: a one-paragraph scope notes plus lane definitions.

2. Draft a baseline blueprint from text.

    (a) Paste your scope, key touchpoints, and known steps into Creately AI and generate an initial blueprint with lanes for customer actions, frontstage, backstage, and systems. If you're facilitating live, start from Miro's Service Blueprint (with AI) or Boardmix template and let the tool place the core swim-lanes and headers automatically.

(b) Output: a machine-generated V1 map with basic flow.

3. Enrich with evidence and failure points.

   (a) Invite cross-functional partners to add artifacts (emails, IVR scripts, UI captures). Use Miro AI to cluster sticky notes by stage and to surface duplicates; ask ChatGPT 5 to propose likely fail points, backlog items, and SLA decision gates for each critical step.

   (b) Output: annotated V2 map with evidence tiles and a numbered fail-point list.

4. Structure lanes and handoffs clearly.

   (a) Use Boardmix (or Creately) to tighten labeling, arrows, and the lines of interaction/visibility; apply a unified color scheme (e.g., red for fail points, blue for system calls). Where ambiguity remains ("Who triggers KYC?"), have ChatGPT 5 draft options and trade-offs to review with owners.

   (b) Output: a readable V3 blueprint with clean lanes, handoffs, and unresolved questions flagged.

5. Prioritize improvements and define trials.

   (a) Run a quick synthesis: in Miro AI, generate a summary of top pain clusters; then ask ChatGPT 5 to convert them into ranked countermeasures with assumptions, effort, and expected impact. Attach 1–2 prototype tests to each (e.g., "callback promise within 10 min" service tweak).

   (b) Output: a prioritized improvement list + mini test plans pinned to the blueprint.

6. Validate with users/staff and iterate.

   (a) Publish a short Google Form that shows the relevant slices (images from the board) and asks open-ended questions ("Where did you feel stuck?"). Use Gemini's "Summarize responses" to extract themes, then paste key takeaways back onto the blueprint. Repeat steps 4–5 until decision criteria are met.

   (b) Outputs: a responses spreadsheet, Gemini summary, and an updated V4 blueprint ready for pilot.

Final artifacts: scoped blueprint (V4), evidence tiles, fail-point list, prioritized improvement backlog, and linked pilot test cards.

Limitations and Tips

AI-generated maps can oversimplify backstage reality. Because generators infer structure from text, they may miss exceptions and non-linear flows. Counter this by anchoring each lane to real artifacts (tickets, SOPs, logs) and by scheduling a 30-minute "exception storm" with operational owners before locking the map.

Automated clustering may hide minority but critical signals. Miro/LLM summaries favor frequent patterns; rare accessibility failures or compliance risks can get smoothed out. Sample raw notes each round and elevate low-frequency/high-impact issues to a visible "must-fix" lane before prioritization.

Sensitive process data requires care. Blueprints often include PII and system details. Redact exports, restrict permissions on boards, and keep a short retention policy for uploads and survey responses.

9.4   AI Exploration Map

Description of Tool

The Exploration Map is a visual system for planning, tracking, and communicating experiments during prototyping and testing. Rooted in the Lean Startup cycle: build → measure → learn—it makes hypotheses explicit, ties experiments to measurable outcomes, and captures results and learnings so teams can decide whether to iterate, pivot, or persevere (Ries, 2011). A typical map includes four columns: Hypotheses (what you expect to be true), Experiments (how you will test it), Results (what happened), and Learnings (what to change next). In workshop practice, teams co-create the map on a shared canvas, time-box experiments, and review patterns across multiple cycles. The tool's value in design thinking is its tight coupling to rapid prototyping: every sketch, clickable mock, or service pilot becomes an evidence-producing experiment with a clear decision rule.

Why Use AI

AI elevates exploration mapping from bookkeeping to decision intelligence. Models trained on your artifacts and prior experiments can surface recurring patterns, propose test ideas you may overlook, and flag weak hypotheses before time is wasted. During a sprint, AI can auto-cluster qualitative notes,

Figure 9.4   AI Exploration Map. Collaborative exploration and sense-making, depicting a multidisciplinary team jointly examining a shared map to navigate complexity, align perspectives, and uncover insights through collective inquiry. AI generated image created with Ideogram, Inc., Ideogram.ai, 3.0, 2025.

summarize user sessions, and forecast which experiments are most likely to reduce risk given current evidence. After each run, AI-generated syntheses help teams converge faster on "what we learned" and "what to try next," keeping the loop tight without replacing the human judgment required to weigh ethics, brand, and context.

Suggested AI Programs

- ChatGPT (GPT-5 Thinking): Drafts sharp falsifiable hypotheses, proposes experiment designs, generates success metrics, and explains trade-offs for next steps.
- Miro AI: Auto-clusters sticky notes, organizes experiment cards, and visualizes themes across cycles to reveal learning patterns.
- FigJam AI: Summarizes and sorts research stickies from prototype tests to speed synthesis between rounds.
- Maze AI: Runs rapid, remote prototype tests; AI-moderated interviews produce structured insights and usability metrics.

- Optimizely Experimentation: Manages A/B and multivariate tests for higher-fidelity prototypes or live features; includes hypothesis workflows.
- Dovetail: Transcribes and analyzes research data; AI turns sessions and surveys into tagged insights you can pin directly onto the map.
- Google NotebookLM: "Source-grounded briefings" from your own materials; ingest PDFs/links, then generate summaries, Q&A, outlines, and audio/video overviews that stay tied to your sources.

Work Instructions

1. Frame the riskiest assumption.

   (a) State a single, testable hypothesis linked to your prototype's goal.

   (b) Example: *"Reducing checkout steps from 4 to 2 will increase completed orders on a food-delivery prototype by ≥ 12%."*

   (c) Then use ChatGPT (GPT-5 Thinking) to tighten language ("falsifiable," "time-bounded," "metric-anchored") and propose alternative success metrics (e.g., time-to-complete, error rate).

2. Design the smallest useful experiment.

   (a) Pick the lightest prototype that can invalidate the hypothesis.

   (b) Example: Ask ChatGPT to outline three experiment options (unmoderated click-through, think-aloud task, A/B of two flows) with effort vs. confidence trade-offs. Select one and generate a task script and consent text. Log the experiment card on Miro with fields: cohort, task, metric, decision rule.

3. Run a fast user test and capture signals.

   (a) Ship the smallest test, collect human and AI feedback together.

   (b) Example: Connect your Figma prototype to Maze for an unmoderated task ("Order a veggie pizza for 7pm").

   (c) Maze records task success, time, and path; enable AI-moderated interviews to probe confusion moments.

   (d) Export notes to Dovetail, where AI auto-tags pain points and clusters verbatims by step.

4. Synthesize and update the Exploration Map.

   (a) Turn raw outputs into learnings, then decide next moves.

   (b) Example: Use FigJam AI to summarize 40 stickies from Dovetail into 5 themes (e.g., "address field confusion," "promo code placement").

(c) Paste key metrics from Maze.

(d) In Miro AI, auto-cluster experiment cards across cohorts to see pattern stability. Record a learning: *"Two-step flow improved time-to-order (–18%) but increased promo-code confusion (+26% errors)."*

(e) Add a Next Experiment card: *"Move promo to review screen; re-test error rate ≤ 5%."*

5. Escalate fidelity when evidence warrants it.

(a) If low-fidelity results are promising, test at higher fidelity.

(b) Example: Spin up an A/B in Optimizely for a staged environment: Variation A (baseline 4-step) vs. B (2-step with promo at review). Use ChatGPT to predefine the hypothesis and stopping criteria (sample size, MDE).

(c) Attach the Optimizely link to the map's experiment card and set a calendar date for the decision checkpoint.

6. Archive learnings and close the loop.

(a) Codify what changed and why; ensure findability for future sprints.

(b) Example: Ask ChatGPT to draft a one-page "Experiment Brief & Outcome" from the cards and Dovetail highlights. Store it in the project wiki. The Exploration Map now shows a traceable chain from prototype tweak → experiment → result → decision, supporting the next ideate-build-test cycle.

Outputs/Artifacts: An up-to-date Exploration Map (board or doc), experiment cards with decision rules, a synthesized learning report, and a prioritized backlog of next experiments tied to the prototype roadmap.

Background note: Google's Project Tailwind was renamed NotebookLM; if you want a "source-grounded briefings" helper attached to your Exploration Map, NotebookLM can ingest your docs and produce summaries you can paste into the map.

Limitations and Tips

AI can over-suggest tests that optimize easy metrics rather than learning the right thing. Guard against "metric myopia" by pre-committing to decision rules that reflect the true user/job outcome (e.g., repeat ordering), not just quick wins (e.g., first-session clicks). Use AI to propose metrics, then consciously elevate the ones aligned to user value.

Automated summaries may hide minority signals. When FigJam or Dovetail clusters notes, rare but critical insights (e.g., accessibility blockers) can be smoothed out. Counter this by sampling a handful of raw sessions each cycle and adding a "must-address" tag for low-frequency/high-impact findings before closing synthesis.

Privacy and compliance risks arise when piping real user data through AI tools. Anonymize transcripts, restrict PII fields in exports, and store links (not files) on the map where possible. Prefer tools with documented data handling; keep a short data-retention policy attached to the board.

9.5 Powerful Questions with AI

Description of Tool

Powerful Questions are prompts that uncover motives, barriers, context, and trade-offs—not just surface preferences. They turn user comments into testable learning: Why did this feel easy? What almost stopped you? What would you give up keeping X? Traditionally, teams build question banks, train interviewers, and capture notes on boards or forms. In Prototype & Test, powerful questions matter most at three moments: before sessions (to set intent), during sessions (to probe at the right depth), and after sessions (to synthesize what answers mean for the next iteration).

Traditional approaches involve developing question banks, training facilitators in effective questioning techniques, and using structured inquiry methods to guide user interviews and testing sessions toward meaningful discoveries.

Why Use AI

AI shortens the journey from raw observations to sharp, unbiased follow-ups. Language models draft question banks tied to hypotheses, propose neutral wording, and suggest "laddering" paths as the session unfolds. Research tools transcribe and summarize interviews; text-analysis tools group answers by themes and sentiment so you can ask better second-round questions. Session-replay tools add behavioral evidence (where testers hesitated or errored) that you can convert into targeted probes.

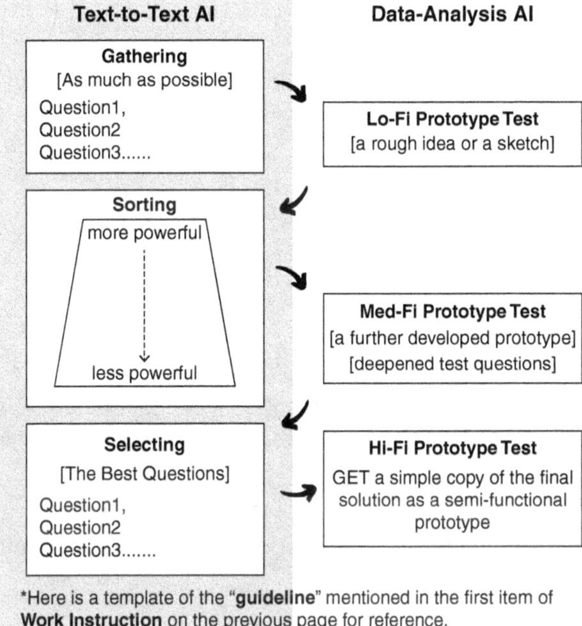

Figure 9.5   Powerful Questions with AI. An AI-supported prototyping workflow, illustrating how text-based AI aids in gathering, sorting, and selecting powerful questions, while data-analysis AI supports iterative lo-fi to hi-fi prototype testing and refinement. AI generated image created with Ideogram, Inc., Ideogram.ai, 3.0, 2025.

Suggested AI Programs

- ChatGPT 5 (LLM): drafts neutral, hypothesis-tied questions; suggests laddering and follow-ups in real time.
- Maze (AI features): unmoderated tests with transcripts, AI summaries, and themes to refine next-round questions.
- Dovetail: stores transcripts and auto-tags quotes; great for pulling evidence to justify questions.
- MonkeyLearn: quick sentiment/topic classification on open-ended answers to spot patterns and outliers.
- Insight7 Interview Analysis: Analyzes recordings to surface patterns and candidate follow-ups.
- Google NotbookLM: Summarize and enumerate terminology grounded in your sources. Great for source-grounded synthesis. However, It won't "extract keywords" in the strict NLP sense.

- IBM Watson Discovery/Watson NLP: Does true NLP extraction (keywords, entities, concepts) at scale. If you need a more formal pass (ranked terms, entity types, consistency checks across many files), run the same corpus through Discovery/NLU and pull the keywords/entities it identifies.

Work Instructions

1. Gathering: draft a question bank tied to learning goals.

   (a) Start with one hypothesis for your prototype (e.g., Users can set a 30-minute reminder via the slider-cap in ≤ 10s). Ask ChatGPT 5 to generate 12 open questions grouped by understanding, emotion, constraint, trade-off, plus 6 laddering prompts ("What makes that important?").

   (b) Use Perplexity (AI powered search engine) to pull quick context with citations (prior studies, regulations) that may shape your probes. Save everything in your guide.

2. Sorting: cluster and de-bias the list.

   (a) Paste the questions into MonkeyLearn to label by topic and sentiment; remove overlaps and reword anything leading ("easy," "obvious").

   (b) Run long background materials (e.g., policy PDFs, support logs) through Google NotebookLM/IBM Watson Discovery to extract terms you should use in neutral phrasing (e.g., "notification cadence" vs. "nagging"). Output a trimmed bank of 15—clear, open, non-leading.

3. Selecting: prioritize high-value probes.

   (a) Record 3–5 pilot sessions in Maze. Let the platform transcribe and summarize. Send audio/video to Insight7 to surface recurring pain points and suggested follow-ups.

   (b) From your bank, pick the top 6 questions that map to the biggest uncertainties. Mark two "branch" follow-ups for each so you can deepen.

4. Testing: link questions to real behavior.

   (a) Run a focused test round. In web/app flows, use Hotjar heatmaps and FullStory session replay to spot hesitation, rage-clicks, or dead ends; immediately convert those moments into targeted probes: "I saw you pause at the LED ring—what were you trying to do?"

(b) Keep ChatGPT 5 open to suggest two neutral follow-ups after each notable quote you paste in. Capture timecodes in your notes so answers are anchored to evidence.

5. Synthesis: turn answers into next-round questions.

(a) Export open-text answers and transcripts to MonkeyLearn for quick clustering; copy key quotes into your research hub (e.g., Dovetail) and tag them to the hypothesis they inform.

(b) Ask ChatGPT 5 to propose a next-round question set and a one-page "What we'll change/What we'll test" brief. Ship the smallest design change and repeat.

Limitations and Tips

AI can produce generic or leading wording. Always perform a "neutrality pass": strip adjectives, test questions aloud, and avoid implying a correct answer. When in doubt, ask the LLM to rewrite for neutrality and then edit again yourself.

Automated summaries can bury rare but critical signals. Before finalizing your next guide, sample 2–3 raw clips where users struggled; if a low-frequency, high-impact issue appears (e.g., accessibility), elevate it into your top questions for the next round. Tools like Maze and Dovetail help, but human review is decisive.

Behavior tools require clear consent and privacy controls. Session replay and heatmaps are powerful but sensitive. Get explicit consent, avoid capturing PII, and set retention windows. Link to evidence (timecodes, clips) instead of copying raw files into notes.

9.6 Concept Evaluation

Description of Tool

Concept Evaluation provides systematic frameworks for assessing and comparing design concepts against established criteria, user needs, and business objectives. This methodology helps teams make informed decisions about which concepts to pursue, combining quantitative assessment with qualitative judgment. Core elements include evaluation criteria definition, systematic

Figure 9.6   Concept Evaluation. Concept evaluation in a collaborative review setting, illustrating how teams collectively assess, critique, and refine design concepts against shared criteria and decision goals. AI generated image created with Ideogram, Inc., Ideogram.ai, 3.0, 2025.

scoring, comparative analysis, and decision-making support through structured assessment processes.

Traditional approaches involve developing evaluation matrices, conducting expert reviews, gathering stakeholder input, and using techniques like weighted scoring or SWOT (internal Strengths and Weaknesses, along with external Opportunities and Threats) analysis to assess concept viability and potential.

Why Use AI

AI transforms concept evaluation by automating assessment processes, predicting concept success probability, and providing data-driven insights that complement human judgment. Machine learning algorithms can analyze concept characteristics against successful design patterns, predict user acceptance rates, and identify potential implementation challenges. AI-powered evaluation can process multiple assessment criteria simultaneously, weight factors according to project priorities, and suggest optimization opportunities for concept improvement.

Suggested AI Programs

- ChatGPT 5 (LLM): drafts criteria, plain-language decision rules, and a short rationale for why one concept wins.
- Google Sheets + Gemini: creates the table, adds formulas/conditional formatting, and makes a quick chart.
- Dovetail (AI insights): pulls themes/quotes from research to justify scores.
- Miro (Dot Voting/2×2 templates): quick first-cut signal when you have many concepts.
- Notion AI: turns your table and notes into a one-page decision memo.

Work Instructions

1. Fix the goal, options, and criteria.

   (a) Write one sentence for the decision (e.g., *Pick a bottle concept to pilot in Q4). List 3–4 options. Ask ChatGPT(latest update): "Suggest 6 clear criteria and a simple decision rule for this choice."*

   (b) Keep the list short: User value, Feasibility, Cost, Risk, Brand fit, Time to pilot. Have it also drafted one-line definitions so everyone scores the same way.

2. Build a simple scoring table.

   (a) Open Google Sheets and let Gemini create a table with columns for the criteria and your concepts. Add a Weight row (e.g., User value 35%, Feasibility 25%, Cost 20%, Risk 10%, Brand fit 10).

   (b) Ask Gemini(LLM) to add data validation (1–5 scale) and a weighted score formula per concept. Add conditional formatting so high scores turn green

3. Attach evidence before scoring.
   (a) For each criterion, paste a link or quote: usability results, a cost note, or a risk comment. Use Dovetail to grab a key verbatim per concept (e.g., *"I couldn't find the promo code field"*), then drop the link under User value. This keeps scores honest and prevents hand-waving.

4. Score together, then sanity-check.

   (a) Each evaluator enters 1–5 per criterion (5 = strong).

   (b) Gemini (LLM) totals the weighted score and draws a quick bar chart. If you started with many options, run a 10-minute dot vote in Miro to narrow to a top three first, then score those in Sheets.

5. Do one small sensitivity test.

   (a) Ask ChatGPT 5: *"If we change Feasibility weight by ±10%, does the winner change?"* Adjust the Weight row and watch totals.
   (b) If rank flips, note the risk and agree on the weight set that truly reflects your priorities right now (e.g., speed to pilot over pure novelty).

6. Decide and log the next test.

   (a) Confirm the decision rule (e.g., *Advance if total ≥ 75/100 and no criterion < 3*).
   (b) Use Notion AI to generate a one-page memo: Winner, why it won, key risks, next experiment, owner, date. Link the Sheet and Dovetail items so the choice is auditable later.

Limitations and Tips

Numbers can look more certain than they are. A high total with thin evidence is still a guess. Always include at least one quote/metric per criterion and mark weakly supported scores as provisional. Use the decision to fund the next test, not a full build. (air focus has a clear primer on the strengths and limits of weighted scoring.)

Weights reflect values. Even "neutral" weights are a choice. Publish your weights and keep a screenshot in the file; revisit them when context shifts (e.g., a tighter deadline increases "Time to pilot").

Groupthink happens. Use dot voting or private scoring first, then discuss. If two concepts tie, run one more micro-test aimed at the criterion with the biggest disagreement (e.g., quick cost spike, 24-hour usability).

9.7   AI-Assisted Feedback Grid

Description of Tool

The Feedback Capture Grid structures prototype feedback into four quadrants: I Like, I Wish, Questions, and Ideas, so teams can turn raw reactions into actionable next steps. It's widely used in design-thinking practice and closely related to the "I Like / I Wish / What If" method common in d.school materials and industry guides. Digital boards make it easy to capture input in real time, tag by user/task, and synthesize

Figure 9.7   AI-assisted Feedback Grid. An AI-assisted feedback grid, illustrating how structured facilitation and AI-supported analysis help teams collect, interpret, and refine user feedback through collaborative reflection and iterative evaluation. AI generated image created with Ideogram, Inc., Ideogram.ai, 3.0, 2025.

patterns across sessions. Many teams also pair the grid with a short survey so open-text comments and session notes flow into the same analysis. The approach shines in rapid prototyping, because evidence is categorized the moment it's collected, keeping iteration focused on what to change next.

Why Use AI

AI shortens the path from raw feedback → structured insight → next iteration. Transcription tools remove note-taking overhead; sentiment and topic models draft a first pass of the grid; whiteboard AIs cluster stickies into themes; and survey assistants summarize open responses so you can converge within hours, not days. Critically, AI augments rather than replaces judgment: humans still validate nuance (e.g., accessibility edge cases, brand tone) and decide which changes to ship. Used well, AI means more sessions, cleaner evidence, and tighter loops between test rounds.

Suggested AI Programs

- Otter.ai: Live transcription, summaries, and action items during test sessions.
- Looppanel: Research repository with AI notes, themes, and searchable clips.
- Figma FigJam AI: Auto-sort/summarize sticky notes into grid themes.
- Google Forms + Gemini: Summarize open-text feedback inside Forms.
- Dovetail: AI sentiment/topic tagging across interviews and surveys.

Work Instructions

1. Set up your digital grid and capture stack.

   (a) Create a 4-quadrant grid on a collaborative board (e.g., FigJam/Miro). Pre-label lanes by user task and add fields for tester metadata.

   (b) Open Otter.ai for live transcription and recording; create a short Google Form with 5–7 open questions to capture post-session reflections.

   (c) Outputs: grid board link, Otter recording, Form link.

2. Run sessions and collect raw signals.

   (a) Moderate a think-aloud task; let Otter capture verbatims so you can focus on observation. After each session, paste top quotes into the board as raw stickies (no judgment yet).

   (b) Send the Google Form for asynchronous follow-up (e.g., "What confused you most?").

   (c) Outputs: transcript, raw stickies, initial Form responses.

3. Draft the grid with AI assistance.

   (a) Copy the transcript (or key quotes) into Dovetail or Looppanel to generate sentiment/topics. Map positive snippets to I Like and improvement-oriented snippets to I Wish; route questions/ideas accordingly.

   (b) Use FigJam AI to Summarize and Organize stickies into themes, then skim two raw clips/quotes per theme to verify nuance.

   (c) Outputs: first-pass grid with clustered themes and representative quotes.

4. Merge survey insights and prioritize.

   (a) In Google Forms, click Summarize responses with Gemini for open-text questions; paste key themes into the grid and tag them (S = survey).

(b) Ask an LLM to propose decision rules (e.g., "If ≥ 60% mention navigation confusion, redesign IA before next test"). Mark each theme with Impact×Effort and select 1–3 changes for the next build.

(c) Outputs: enriched grid, ranked change list, decision rules.

5. Close the loop with a change brief.

(a) Have the LLM generate a one-page brief from the grid: What we learned → What we'll change → What we'll test next. Attach example quotes, before/after frames, and owners/dates. Archive transcripts and boards in Looppanel or Dovetail so future teams can search by theme.

(b) Outputs: change brief, linked evidence, updated backlog.

6. Optional (video/voice affect): If you captured participant video or audio emphasis and have explicit consent, tools like Hume AI or Affectiva/Smart Eye can estimate vocal prosody or facial-expression signals. Treat these as supporting signals only; always validate with human judgment.

Limitations and Tips

AI sentiment can misclassify nuanced or culturally specific feedback. Don't ship changes based on color-coded sentiment alone. Always sample raw clips and re-tag where needed; elevate low-frequency but high-impact issues (e.g., accessibility blockers) into a "must-fix" row before prioritizing.

Emotion/affect detection is error-prone and sensitive. Prosody/facial inferences can be biased or context blind. If you use them, obtain explicit consent, restrict to opt-in studies, and treat outputs as exploratory—not definitive—evidence. Prefer observable task data (errors, time-to-complete) for decisions.

Grids can drift into unstructured idea dumps. Keep the quadrants tight by anchoring each theme to a quote + task + evidence. Re-run FigJam's Summarize after every two sessions and regenerate your ranked change list so iteration stays focused.

9.8 Foresight Scenario

Description of Tool

Foresight scenarios help you think about several plausible futures and what each future would mean for today's design choices. Instead of predicting one outcome, you write short, believable stories of different worlds, then ask: If

Figure 9.8   Foresight Scenario. A foresight scenario workshop, illustrating how teams collaboratively explore interconnected futures by mapping relationships, uncertainties, and emerging signals to inform strategic design thinking. AI generated image created with Ideogram, Inc., Ideogram.ai, 3.0, 2025.

this happened, how would our product or service need to change? A common way to structure the set is a 2×2 matrix (two important uncertainties on the axes → four different futures). The goal is to reveal blind spots, stress-test ideas, and choose actions that stay useful across multiple futures, as outlined by Schoemaker in 1995.

Why Use AI

AI speeds up the heavy parts: scanning lots of articles to find drivers (forces that push change), grouping related signals, and drafting first-pass scenario stories you can edit. Language models also turn scenarios into concrete design prompts, check whether your stories are internally consistent, and help you list signposts (observable indicators you can watch to see which future is emerging). You still make the judgment calls; AI just helps you cover more ground faster.

Suggested AI Programs

- ChatGPT 5 (LLM: Large Language Model): Drafts drivers, scenario narratives, implications, and signposts; rewrites for clarity.
- Futures Platform/Portage/Quid: Tools that help with horizon scanning, clustering trends, and organizing scenarios. Use any one your school or team can access.
- Google Sheets (or Notion/Docs): Keep the scenario grid, scoring table, signpost list, and next steps tidy and shareable.

Work Instructions

Example: a smart refillable bottle + companion app.

1. Frame the scope and time window.
   (a) Write a single sentence, like: *"How should our bottle + app evolve for 2028–2032?"* Add the near-term decision you face (e.g., Choose what to prototype this semester).
   (b) Ask ChatGPT-5 to list 10 possible drivers: city policies on refill stations, privacy laws, sensor costs, campus infrastructure, etc.

2. Pick two big uncertainties and build a 2×2.
   (a) From your driver list, choose two factors that are both high-impact and uncertain. Example axes:
       (i) Refill network adoption: slow ↔ fast
       (ii) Data rules for consumer devices: strict ↔ permissive
   (b) Put them as X and Y axes to form a 2×2 matrix (four quadrants = four futures).

3. Write four short scenarios (one per quadrant).
   (a) Name each world and draft ~150–180 words: a headline, what everyday life looks like, and what it means for your product/service. In practice, ChatGPT-5 is often used to generate a first draft that designers subsequently review, edit, and contextualize.
   (b) Examples:
       (i) Public Rails (fast network + strict data): Cities fund many refill stations, but PII (Personally Identifiable Information) rules are tight.

> (ii) Open Mesh (fast + permissive): Stations everywhere; data sharing is easy but raises ethical questions.
> (iii) Patchwork (slow + strict): Inconsistent access to stations and tough privacy enforcement.
> (iv) Walled Streams (slow + permissive): Few stations; companies collect a lot of behavioral data.

4. Pressure-test today's concepts against the futures.

   (a) Make a simple table (concepts down, scenarios across). For each cell, rate User value, Feasibility, and Risk from 1–5, with a one-line reason. Keep evidence nearby (class readings, quick desk research, prior test results).

   (b) Use ChatGPT-5 to suggest design moves that improve robustness in weak cells (e.g., an offline mode for Patchwork).

5. Define signposts and low-regret actions.

   (a) *"Signposts" = specific, observable indicators you can check monthly (e.g., "# of cities offering refill incentives," "new campus privacy policy on wearable sensors").*

   (b) "Low-regret actions" = steps that help in most futures (e.g., better modularity, simpler privacy settings, small pilots with refill partners). Ask the LLM to propose 3–5 signposts and 3–5 low-regret actions per scenario.

6. Backcast into a near-term plan.

   (a) Pick the most likely and the most challenging scenario.

   (b) "Backcasting" = start from that future and work backward to decide what to do this semester and next. Turn low-regret actions into a 6–9 month mini-roadmap: what to test, who to email, which policy to read, a quick supplier call, etc.

Limitations and Tips

AI can amplify noisy data and fashionable narratives. Trend scrapers can overweight what's over-reported. Counter this by mixing expert-curated libraries (e.g., Futures Platform's trend analyses) with your own domain sources and by forcing a counter-narrative pass ("Write the opposite story; what must be true?"). Document sources beside each driver so later teams can audit.

Scenarios without signposts become wall art. Teams often stop at stories. Avoid that by naming specific indicators you'll track and a review cadence (monthly/quarterly). If a signpost moves, trigger a pre-agreed action (e.g., re-weight privacy features, re-sequence supplier bets).

9.9 Prototype & Test Use Case: Next Generation AI-Design Alternatives to LEGO

Our challenge: create a competitive product alternative to LEGO minifigures. LEGO's minifigures are iconic—small, colorful characters that have brought joy to children for decades. They are also heavily protected by patents, which meant that to create a competitive alternative, we had to design a figure similar enough in its modular appeal, but differing in form and function. We wanted something that preserved the joy of building and personalization, while introducing new aesthetics, materials, and features that could resonate with today's users.

We began with group brainstorming, augmented by AI. The ideas came quickly but our first AI prompt, "Weird LEGO," was far too vague and the outputs reflected that. Some ideas were visually interesting but felt random. We realized that if we wanted AI to be a truly creative partner, we needed to learn how to communicate with it more effectively.

ChatGPT became our starting point to develop richer, more descriptive prompts from our loose ideas. It responded with expanded versions that included specific shapes, materials, and functional elements. This process revealed something important: the quality of AI's output depended entirely on the precision of our input. Once we understood that, the conversation with AI became more productive.

With better prompts in hand, we turned to Ideogram.ai to create visuals. The first renders were a mix of promises and problems. One design might have a great silhouette but awkward proportions. Another might have clever articulation but an unappealing color scheme. As a team, we examined each image, kept the strongest elements, and fed them back into new prompts. We repeated this cycle six to seven times, gradually moving from vague possibilities to concrete, viable designs.

In parallel, we used Ideamap.ai to explore broader concept directions. The tool generated mind maps filled with potential features and themes. We discussed each branch together, choosing ideas that matched our vision and setting aside those that did not. Organic shapes, sustainable materials, and modular accessories became recurring themes. Over time, we noticed that certain idea branches stopped producing anything new, even with different phrasing. This limitation reminded us that AI is best used alongside, not in place of human creativity.

Our decision-making remained entirely human. We ran informal surveys with classmates to test which features resonated most. Feedback influenced several changes, such as adding interchangeable accessories and integrating modular joints for smoother playability. AI could propose countless options, but it was our conversations and human insights that gave the design its final form.

The end result was a concept that balanced modular play, fresh visual identity, and sustainability. The figures featured smooth, organic contours, interchangeable parts, and eco-friendly materials, while steering clear of LEGO's protected design space. AI gave us speed, variety, and a broader creative range, but the human touch shaped the outcome into something that felt authentic and well-grounded.

Key Learnings

- Writing clear, detailed prompts is as much a design skill as sketching graphics.
- AI can expand creative possibilities, but human feedback provides direction.
- Iteration through AI and real-world input are essential for turning good ideas into great ones.

Final Reflection

This project showed us that AI works best as a tool not only for rapid ideation, as we expected, but also for creating viable, detailed graphic prototypes to help us decide. The limitation is that AI was not equipped to be a final decision-maker. By combining AI's imagination with our judgment and user insights, we created not just a new product concept, but a repeatable design process. One that can transform a vague idea into something tangible, functional, and ready for the real world.

9.10   Prototype & Test Use Case: Building a Website, Collaborating with AI

Our challenge: to create a website for this book using AI and design principles.

Website design is important for creating a user-friendly, informative online presence. We set out to see how AI could help in many aspects of the design process, including developing ideas and workable prototypes that can be tested on actual or simulated users. For us, AI served as a knowledgeable partner, workflow planner, and a decision-making assistant. AI helped us to facilitating collaboration as we investigated unfamiliar areas. Tools like PromptPerfect can refine prompts for optimal AI responses, while platforms like FeiShu enable seamless online meetings and collaborative conclusions with team members.

AI use in the task process: AI served as a strategic planner for our team, offering foundational knowledge and guiding the website's direction and structure. It proposed innovative design layouts, identified key content elements, and suggested aesthetic and functional ideas tailored to enhance user experience. A key contribution was AI's ability to clarify unfamiliar design principles, such as optimizing visual hierarchy for intuitive navigation. By providing examples, rationale, and alternatives, it improved the cohesiveness and accessibility of the design. Additionally, AI facilitated collaboration by generating ideas for interactive elements, making complex concepts more engaging. This support streamlined the process, ensuring the final design aligned with the book's mission of demystifying AI's role in design.

Surprisingly, achieving creative outcomes with AI did not always require highly specific prompts. For instance, relatively abstract inputs like "black white black" or even "[0,0,0,0]" yielded unexpectedly innovative results, adding originality and intrigue to the process. We also found that we received high quality responses by assigning AI a defined role, such as a "world-class website designer," which often led to more refined and impactful outputs.

We utilized ChatGPT AI to generate a table of AI applications, compared options, and selected tools based on our project goals. For website design, we employed B12 and MidJourney, both of which significantly shaped the process and final product. B12 streamlined website creation with intuitive design suggestions and automated routine tasks, enabling us to focus on high-level creativity and user experience. Its AI-driven insights into layout and content structure provided a strong foundation, helping us meet deadlines effectively while accelerating task completion.

MidJourney played a key role in generating visually striking elements, allowing for experimentation with AI-powered visual designs that aligned with the project's theme. Its rapid prototyping capabilities contributed directly to the website's aesthetic appeal and uniqueness. The combined use of B12 and MidJourney resulted in a polished, cohesive website while offering valuable learning experiences. We gained practical insights into integrating AI into workflows, achieving an effective balance of efficiency, collaboration, and artistic expression.

In our team, AI initially outlined the primary workflow, providing a structured framework that clarified each project stage. Tasks were divided among members, allowing individuals to focus on specific aspects of the process while independently using AI tools to develop their creative contributions. This approach combined personal styles with AI-driven insights, enriching the project with diverse perspectives.

Once individual tasks were completed, we reconvened to review and discuss each AI-assisted output. A voting system was employed to select the best ideas, ensuring the final product reflected the team's collective vision. This workflow struck a balance between structure and creative freedom, with AI acting as a versatile tool that facilitated both individual innovation and collaborative decision-making. The method enhanced efficiency and empowered meaningful contributions from all team members.

Key Learnings

- AI can suggest innovative website layouts, identify essential content elements, providing tailored aesthetic and functional ideas to enhance user experience.
- In some cases, relatively vague prompts on simple topics (which likely have many sources for AI to be trained on) can be effective in yielding innovation.
- Assigning a specific role to AI, such as "world-class website designer," can enhance the responses it gives.

Final Reflection

Through our design process, we discovered that AI is a valuable partner that can play many roles in addition to idea generation and testing, including as acting as a workflow planner and decision-making assistant. We found some challenges in maintaining originality with the sample prototypes, due to the similarities in outputs from certain AI programs. To address this, we balanced the use of various AI applications, fostering collaboration and creative expression. While AI serves as an excellent collaborator, it cannot replace human creativity, emphasizing the need for a synergistic approach.

References

Bitner, M. J., Ostrom, A. L., & Morgan, F. N. (2008). Service blueprinting: A practical technique for service innovation. *California Management Review, 50*(3), 66–94. https://doi.org/10.2307/41166446

Brown, T. (2009). *Change by design: How design thinking transforms organizations and inspires innovation.* New York: HarperBusiness.

Google. (2025, June 10). *Summarize responses with Gemini in Google Forms.* Google Docs Editors Help. https://support.google.com/docs/answer/16231981

McKinsey & Company. (2025, February 10). *How an AI-enabled software product development life cycle will fuel innovation.* https://www.mckinsey.com/industries/technology-media-and-telecommunications/our-insights/how-an-ai-enabled-software-product-development-life-cycle-will-fuel-innovation

Miro. (n.d.). *Miro AI with sticky notes.* Miro Help Center. https://help.miro.com/hc/en-us/articles/28781881506834-Miro-AI-with-Sticky-notes

Ries, E. (2011). *The lean startup.* New York: Crown Business.

Schoemaker, P. J. H. (1995). Scenario planning: A tool for strategic thinking. *Sloan Management Review, 36*(2), 25–40.

Shostack, G. L. (1984). Designing services that deliver. *Harvard Business Review, 62*(1), 133–139. https://hbr.org/1984/01/designing-services-that-deliver

Uizard. (2025). *Autodesigner 2.0: AI UI design generator.* https://uizard.io/autodesigner/

Verganti, R. (2009). *Design-driven innovation: Changing the rules of competition by radically innovating what things mean.* Boston: Harvard Business Press.

10

Implement & Learn: AID Tools and Use Cases

Implement and learn marks the point where ideas leave the whiteboard and confront real constraints, such as operations, compliance, budgets, and human habits. In design thinking, these activities are not a mechanical "hand-off," but a continuation of problem-solving in live settings, where solutions are exercised, adapted, and scaled, according to Brown's work in 2008. The work translates intent into outcomes: standing up pilots, measuring effects, addressing failure points, and strengthening the story that earns ongoing support. Done well, implementation becomes a learning engine that improves both the product and the organization's capacity to deliver.

AI now helps teams do this work faster and with better situational awareness. Project and portfolio tools use AI to surface risks, suggest priorities, and maintain a coherent picture across many moving parts; research platforms scan market signals so plan stay aligned with changing conditions; and generative systems draft the routine artifacts (e.g. briefs, status notes, FAQs) so teams can focus on judgment and relationships. These capabilities do not replace the human elements of design thinking (e.g. empathy, ethics, and trade-offs), but they compress time from input to insight and support more responsive execution.

Critically, "implement and learn" remains iterative. Evidence from after-action reviews shows that organizations improve when they capture lessons in context and apply them to the very next cycle, not just at project close, according to a Harvard article by Darling and colleagues in 2005. The same principle holds here: transcripts, tickets, and telemetry feed lightweight syntheses; AI helps theme the data and propose next moves; teams validate,

© The Author(s), under exclusive license to Springer Nature Switzerland AG 2026

D. Graff et al., *Design Thinking with Artificial Intelligence*, Palgrave Executive Essentials,
https://doi.org/10.1007/978-3-032-10543-1_10

adjust, and try again. Across the chapter's tools—from feedback rituals and pitch co-design to lean canvases, roadmaps, and strategy views—the through-line is simple: keep the human core of design, and use AI to speed collection, synthesis, prioritization, and communication, according to design thinking methods articles by Razzouk and Shute in 2012 and Martínez Casanovas in 2025.

This chapter assembles seven practical tools for Implement and Learn activities, 10.1, Lean Canvas; 10.2, Solution Roadmap; 10.3, Strategy Roadmap; 10.4, Communicating Vision; 10.5, Create a Pitch; 10.6, I like, I wish, I wonder; and 10.7, Reflect. Together they form a usable playbook for moving from a promising concept to measurable, durable impact—while building an organizational memory that makes the next implementation smarter. We also show how some concepts and AI tools can be implemented our two use cases, (10.8) Designing a Futuristic Poster with AI, and (10.9) Meituan Sustainable Community Pickup System.

10.1   Lean Canvas

Description of Tool

Lean Canvas is a one-page, nine-block framework (Problem, Solution, Unique Value Proposition, Unfair Advantage, Customer Segments, Channels, Key Metrics, Cost Structure, Revenue Streams) created by Ash Maurya to help teams turn ideas into testable business models quickly. It adapts Osterwalder's Business Model Canvas for early-stage innovation, emphasizing assumptions, risks, and fast learning cycles. In design thinking, it's ideal for "Implement and Learn" activities to align a concept with stakeholders, surface riskiest bets, and plan lightweight experiments before scale. Traditionally, teams run a workshop, fill sticky notes, then validate via interviews and pilots. Today's tools add living canvases, shared repositories, and analytics that update as evidence accumulates. (See Maurya/Leanstack for origins and intent; Miro/GroupMap for canonical blocks and facilitation guidance.)

Why Use AI

AI shortens the journey from hunch to evidence-backed canvas. It auto-clusters notes from workshops, drafts first-pass copy for each block, and turns vague claims into hypotheses with testable metrics. Market-intel tools surface

Figure 10.1   Lean Canvas. Collaborative lean canvas development, illustrating how teams jointly articulate problem statements, value propositions, assumptions, and key metrics to align strategy and guide early-stage concept validation. AI generated image created with Ideogram, Inc., Ideogram.ai, 3.0, 2025.

competitors, channel patterns, and audience behaviors; workspace AI scores assumptions by impact/risk and keeps a change log as new data arrives. As a result, teams spend less time formatting and more time running experiments. Crucially, AI augments, not replaces, human judgment: product sense, ethics, and feasibility still come from the team, while AI accelerates research, prioritization, and iteration.

Suggested AI Programs

- Miro AI: Cluster sticky notes, summarize themes, and speed board cleanup for workshops.
- Notion AI: Convert canvas notes to a database; autofill properties or summaries for each block.
- Airtable AI: Build a lightweight "assumption tracker" with AI fields for scoring and next steps.
- Similarweb (AI-powered): Market/audience insights to inform Channels and Customer Segments.

- Crayon: Competitive intelligence monitoring to inform UVP (unique value proposition)/Unfair Advantage.
- ChatGPT-5/Claude (LLMs): Draft block text, reframe assumptions as hypotheses, and propose lean tests.

Work Instructions

Example: "a campus meal-kit kiosk service for students"

1. Frame the objective and collect raw notes.

    (a) Kick off a 45-minute canvas session right after concept testing. In Miro, set up the nine blocks. Invite teammates to brain-dump stickies (e.g., "late classes → no time to cook"). Then use Miro AI: "*Deduplicate and cluster all stickies; output a table with Block, Cluster name (≤ 3 words), 2 example notes.*"

    (b) Outcome: a de-noised set of clusters mapped to each block.

2. Draft a first-pass canvas with hypotheses.

    (a) Paste each cluster into ChatGPT-5: "*Rewrite this cluster as a crisp Lean Canvas entry. For Problem, produce 3 user-language statements; for UVP, a 1-sentence 'only-ness' claim; for Metrics, 3 leading indicators; for Revenue, a simple formula.*"

    (b) Example UVP (unique value proposition): "Hot, balanced meals in < 3 minutes between classes." Capture results back on the board.

3. Ground Customer/Channels with external signals.

    (a) Open Similarweb to review digital behaviors of nearby food options and student services. Prompt example: "*Identify top referral channels and audience interests for [local competitor sites]; summarize in 5 bullets for 'Channels' and 'Customer Segments'.*"

    (b) Use Crayon to pull competitor positioning (meal price points, speed claims). Summarize example: "*For Unfair Advantage, propose 2 hard-to-copy assets based on monitored intel (e.g., exclusive campus card integration).*" Update blocks accordingly.

4. Prioritize assumptions and design tests.

    (a) In Airtable, create an "Assumptions" table with fields: Block, Statement, Impact (H/M/L), Evidence, Test, Owner, Due. Add an AI field to score Risk from text (Impact × Uncertainty) and to suggest a 2-week test.

    (b) Prompt example: *"For each assumption, propose the smallest test that yields directional evidence (survey, concierge prototype, price card A/B); include metric + success threshold."*

    (c) Example: Price acceptance: "If ≥ 60% of 100 students select the $8 meal over $10, proceed."

5. Create a living canvas and stakeholder brief.

    (a) Push the Airtable view into Notion and add a Canvas page. Use Notion AI to autofill a "Status" property from evidence ("Unproven/ Partially/Validated") and to draft a one-page brief: *"Summarize current Lean Canvas with top 3 risks, planned tests, and ask (kiosk hardware pilot in Library + $5k budget)."* Share the page with decision-makers; it updates as fields change.

6. Run tests, learn, and revise the canvas.

7. After two weeks, pull results into Airtable and ask ChatGPT-5/Claude: *"Compare each test against its threshold, decide 'pivot/persist/park,' and rewrite the affected blocks (Solution, Channels, Revenue) accordingly. Append a bullet 'What changed & why.'"*

    (a) Export a before/after canvas image for the appendix. This closes the loop for both the team and your AI copilot.

Outputs/artifacts: cleaned cluster table; first-pass Lean Canvas; competitor/ channel notes; an Airtable assumption tracker with AI risk scores and tests; a Notion one-pager for management; a before/after canvas snapshot for learning history.

Limitations and Tips

AI-generated market claims can be confidently wrong. Treat anything not linked to a source as a hypothesis, not a fact. Require citations for market sizes and competitor data, or label them "estimate—validate." Cross-check with primary research before locking the UVP or pricing.

Prioritization models may overweight what's easy to measure. AI tends to nudge tests toward digital signals; counterbalance with behavioral evidence (intercepts in the cafeteria line, kiosk mock-ups). Run a brief human review to re-rank "Impact" based on mission-critical risks (e.g., food safety, throughput at peak).

Tool sprawl can fragment the single source of truth. Decide early where the canonical canvas lives (e.g., Notion) and link out to Miro, Airtable, and intel sources. Use a weekly ritual to review status tags and archive stale assumptions.

Figure 10.2   Solution Roadmap. A solution roadmap, illustrating the staged progression from concept to implementation through shared milestones, decision points, and coordinated team action. AI generated image created with Ideogram, Inc., Ideogram.ai, 3.0, 2025.

Privacy and ethics still apply to student/consumer data. Do not paste personally identifiable or contractual data into external prompts unless your organization has approved the tool's terms. When in doubt, anonymize and aggregate.

10.2   Solution Roadmap

Description of Tool

Solution Roadmap is a structured way to map how a concept will be built, piloted, and scaled; what happens when, by whom, and with which dependencies, resources, and success criteria. In design thinking's implement & learn activities, the roadmap is both a planning artifact and a persuasion tool: it aligns stakeholders on milestones, makes trade-offs explicit, and sets measurable outcomes for each stage. Traditionally, teams run workshops, sketch timelines, and manually stitch together capacity, dependencies, and risks. Modern platforms add multi-team views, capacity planning, and "what-if" scenarios, while AI assists with first-pass sequencing, risk surfacing, and automatic updates as facts change (e.g., Jira Advanced Roadmaps; Asana Intelligence; Miro's AI timeline).

Why Use AI

AI compresses weeks of coordination into hours by converting goals and constraints into a draft, dependency-aware plan. Timeline generators visualize phases and propose milestone sequences; portfolio tools aggregate multiple teams' work and highlight capacity conflicts; AI assistants summarize risk registers and suggest mitigation owners. As new data arrives (estimates, lead-times, approvals), the roadmap can recalculate critical paths and ripple changes downstream. The team still decides trade-offs—AI accelerates the boring parts and keeps everyone working from a single, living plan.

Suggested AI Programs

* Jira Advanced Roadmaps: Multi-team plans, capacity, dependency views, scenario planning.
* Asana Intelligence: AI that surfaces risks/insights and supports Timeline/ Gantt plans.
* Miro AI Timeline: Drafts visual timelines and alternative milestone sequences.
* Productboard AI: Prioritizes initiatives and summarizes feedback for roadmap decisions.
* Smartsheet (GenAI + Resource Management): Allocations, workload balance, and AI analysis.
* Aha! Roadmaps AI Assistant: Assists with writing/planning artifacts linked to releases.

Work Instructions

Example: "rolling out a two-hour click-and-collect program[1] for a mid-sized retail chain "

---

[1] A two-hour click-and-collect program is a retail service promise: customers order online and can pick up the order at a nearby store within two hours of placing it. The program coordinates website/app, inventory, store staff, and customer notifications so the handoff is fast and reliable.

1. Set intent and constraints.

    (a) State the basics (value outcome + constraints).
        Example prompt (to your LLM):*"Create a one-paragraph scope statement for a two-hour click-and-collect launch. Value outcome: 90% of online orders ready in ≤2 hours. Constraints: budget $450k capex + $120k opex (6 months), 20 stores (4 regions), no work during 11/20–12/1 (peak), must reuse existing POS, security review required, legal review for curbside signage, accessibility compliance (WCAG 2.2 AA). Include 3 success metrics and 3 non-goals."*

    (b) Prompt ChatGPT-5: *"List milestones and dependencies for a two-hour click-and-collect launch across 20 stores; include legal, inventory API, store ops, comms, and CX. Return a table: Milestone, Inputs, Owner, Done-criterion."*

    (c) Possible output from ChatGPT-5:

2. Draft an initial timeline and dependencies.

    (a) In Miro AI Timeline, paste the milestone table and ask: *"Create a 24-week timeline; group by phases (Pilot Prep, 5-Store Pilot, Scale to 20); propose critical dependencies and a visual critical path."*

    (b) Export the board image for review.

    (c) Typical Miro AI additions: dependency lines from "Inventory API spec" → "Pilot store readiness," and from "Legal & safety review" → "Customer comms." Critical path highlighting Pilot Prep → Pilot → Scale.

3. Create a multi-team plan with capacity.

    (a) In Jira Advanced Roadmaps, connect fulfillment (engineering), store operations, and marketing projects. Use the plan view to spot overallocations and sequence conflicts (e.g., training before tooling).

    (b) Scenario: "If API integration slips 2 weeks, what shifts?" Save two versions: Baseline and Slip-2weeks.

    (c) Possible output from Jira (scenario diff):

        (i) Inventory API integration moves from Wk 8→Wk 10.
        (ii) 5-store pilot start shifts Wk 10→Wk 12 to keep dependency chain intact.
        (iii) Comms launch decoupled (keeps Wk 10) but adds banner "Limited Pilot (5 stores)."
        (iv) Scale to 20 stores compresses by adding 2 extra trainers (flagged risk on trainer availability).

Table 10.1   An Example of GPT Output Using a Solution Roadmap

Milestone	Inputs	Owner	Done-criterion
Define SLA & KPIs	Ops policy draft; historical pick/ pack data	Ops Lead	SLA doc signed; KPI tree (Ready-in-2h, NPS, Cancellations)
Inventory API spec	POS schema; store stock rules	Eng Lead	v1 OpenAPI spec approved by POS vendor
Legal & safety review	Curbside SOP; signage copy	Legal	Memo "approved with conditions"; risk register updated
Pilot store readiness (5)	Training kit; pick zones; scanners	Store Ops	5 stores pass readiness checklist
Customer comms	Brand guidelines; FAQ draft	Comms	Multi-channel plan approved; templates in CMS
5-store pilot	Staff roster; SLA dashboards	Ops + Eng	≥80% orders ≤2h for 3 consecutive weeks
Scale to 20 stores	Pilot learnings; training schedule	Program Mgr	20 stores live; ≥85% ≤2h in aggregate

(v) Roadmaps summary shows critical path +2 weeks; capacity heatmap turns red for Trainers in Wk 12–15 (over 85% load).

4. Prioritize initiatives with customer/ops signals.

   (a) Feed recent support tickets, comments, and store-manager notes into Productboard AI to summarize patterns (e.g., pickup signage confusion vs. stock accuracy).

   (b) Prompt: *"Rank roadmap items by expected impact on pickup customer satisfaction; suggest one quick win per phase."*

   (c) Typical Productboard output (condensed): Top drivers of dissatisfaction: unclear curbside signage; item substitution surprises; long handoff at peak.

5. Layer resources and budgets.

   (a) In Smartsheet Resource Management, import key roles (store trainers, drivers, CX writers). Ask LLM: *"Balance workload across 6 trainers; keep weekly hours < 32; propose an 8-week allocation plan with travel windows."*

   (b) Add a cost view and export a one-page resourcing summary for finance.

   (c) Possible output from LLM (trainer allocation excerpt):

Table 10.2 An Example of LLM Output for a Trainer Allocation Using a Solution Roadmap

Week	Trainer A	Trainer B	Trainer C	Trainer D	Trainer E	Trainer F
1	SOP build (16h); Travel buffer (8h)	Decks & job aids (24h)	Shadow store #1 (24h)	QA check-lists (24h)	—	—
2	Train store #1 (24h)	Train store #2 (24h)	Train store #3 (24h)	Train store #4 (24h)	Train store #5 (24h)	—
3	Sustain #1 (16h); Travel (8h)	Sustain #2 (16h)	Sustain #3 (16h)	Sustain #4 (16h)	Sustain #5 (16h)	SOP video edits (24h)
4–8	Rotate 5-store batches; keep each trainer ≤32h/week; Fri = travel/admin					

Cost summary (finance one-pager): Trainers 6 × \$85/h (avg 28h/wk × 8wk) ≈ \$114k; travel/lodging cap \$36k; scanners \$48k; signage \$22k; contingency \$25k → Total ≈ \$245k (within \$450k capex).

6. Publish the living roadmap and nudge decisions.

   (a) In Asana, build the master project using Timeline; enable Asana Intelligence to highlight risks ("Inventory feed dependency unresolved"). Prompt: "Draft weekly status: progress, emerging risks, asks."

   (b) Share a viewer link with leadership; when a date changes in Jira, update the Asana dates and attach the Miro timeline image so everyone sees the same story.

Outputs/artifacts: milestone/dependency table; Miro timeline image; Jira plan with Baseline vs. Slip scenarios; Productboard priority notes; Smartsheet resourcing plan and cost summary; Asana Timeline with weekly AI-assisted status—ready for approval and execution.

Limitations and Tips

Hidden dependencies are the silent killers. AI won't know about store security audits, union rules, or regional signage permits. Run a meeting session with store leaders to surface "unknown knowns," then encode them as blocking dependencies with owners.

Prioritization can overfit to text signals. If you feed only customer comments, Productboard may overweight CX (customer experiences) quick wins versus operational robustness. Balance with a small operational risk register (throughput, shrinkage, safety) and give those items explicit weight in prioritization.

Tool sprawl breaks the single source of truth. Decide where the canonical roadmap lives (e.g., Asana Timeline) and schedule a weekly sync job (or discipline) to update mirrored plans in Jira/Smartsheet. Export a PDF snapshot each Friday for audit and leadership continuity.

10.3   Strategy Roadmap

Description of Tool

A Strategy Roadmap is a high-level, multi-year map that shows how initiatives ladder up to company goals: where to play, how to win, and which capabilities you must build when. It connects strategy to execution by sequencing value streams, investments, and enabling platforms, and by defining the measurable outcomes that signal progress. Traditionally, leaders hold planning offsites, sketch horizons, and then hand work to portfolio tools for funding and delivery. Modern platforms extend this with AI: they surface competitive and market signals, transform qualitative plans into dependency-aware portfolios, and offer "what-if" scenarios to test pace, spend, and risk before you commit. Tools such as Jira Align and Planview Portfolios explicitly bridge strategy-to-execution with AI-assisted insights and multi-team roadmaps.

Why Use AI

AI compresses months of synthesis into days. Market-intel systems use large datasets to reveal category shifts and competitor moves; portfolio tools apply AI to prioritize initiatives by strategic fit, capacity, ROI, and risk, then simulate alternatives (e.g., "delay platform rebuild two quarters—what changes?"). Generative assistants draft narratives, align artifacts, and keep a single source of truth current as facts change. As signals update, such as traffic, funnel, support load, cost curves. Roadmaps can recall the critical path and recommend re-sequencing while preserving intent. Leaders still set direction; AI accelerates the evidence, the options, and the feedback loop.

Suggested AI Programs

* Jira Align/Advanced Roadmaps (Atlassian): Strategy-to-execution planning, multi-team roadmaps, scenario views.

Figure 10.3 Strategy Roadmap. Iterative pathways of solution development, illustrating how teams navigate decision points, feedback loops, and adaptive steps to progressively refine and operationalize complex design solutions. AI generated image created with Ideogram, Inc., Ideogram.ai, 3.0, 2025.

- Aha! Roadmaps (AI Assistant): Draft strategic narratives, objectives, and release plans inside a roadmap tool.
- Asana Intelligence: Risk/insight surfacing and status generation on timeline views.
- Similarweb (AI-powered): Digital-market and competitor signals to inform positioning and channel bets.
- Crayon: Competitive intelligence monitoring to track rivals' moves and messaging shifts.
- AlphaSense / CB Insights: AI-driven search and research to spot trends and adjacent opportunities.

Work Instructions

Example: a 24-month "AI-powered customer support" program: better help center, chat deflection, and agent-assist.

Recommendations for AI program choosing: Use one roadmap tool (Jira Align or Planview) and one LLM (ChatGPT/Claude) for wording.

1. Write the strategy in plain words.

   (a) A "north star" is a one-sentence aim that guides choices.

   (b) Use your LLM: Prompt example: *"Write a one-sentence north star and three measurable goals for a 24-month support transformation (e.g., ticket deflection, CSAT, handle time). Add top risks and a clear stop rule."*

   (c) Keep this text at the top of every document.

2. List the big pieces of work.

   (a) Think in simple chunks (we'll call each a "workstream"): knowledge base cleanup, AI chat, agent-assist, data access, training.

   (b) Use your LLM: Prompt example: *"Turn these workstreams into a checklist with outcomes and 'done' signs for each."*

   (c) Copy that list into Jira Align or Planview to start your roadmap.

3. Place the work on a timeline.

   (a) In the roadmap tool, create a basic timeline by quarter (Q1–Q8). Put earlier items that unlock others first (a "dependency" is something that must happen before something else).

   (b) Tip: show who owns each item and one measure you'll track (e.g., "deflection rate").

4. Check team capacity once.

   (a) Capacity simply means "how much each team can do this month." Use the tool's workload view to avoid overload.

   (b) If a team is packed, move one item to the next month. Keep it simple.

5. Sanity-check with outside signals. (Optional)

   (a) Pick one source (Similarweb, Crayon, or AlphaSense/CB Insights).

   (b) Use your LLM: Prompt example: *"Summarize three market signals (competitor moves, volume trends, cost notes) that might change our order. Suggest one small adjustment."*

   (c) Only change the plan if the signal is strong.

6. Create two options, then pick one.

   (a) In the roadmap tool, duplicate the plan:
       (i) Base: current staffing and dates.
       (ii) Faster: small extra help (e.g., short-term trainers) to pull one milestone earlier.

   (b) Make a tiny comparison box in the description: what date moves, rough extra cost, expected gain on the main metric. Choose one and archive the other.

7. Publish one "home" for the plan.

   (a) A "home" is the single place everyone checks.
   (b) In Aha! or Asana, paste the north star, the chosen timeline, owners, and measures.
   (c) Use your LLM to draft a one-page summary: Why now, What we'll do, When, Who, How we'll measure. Share a view-only link.

8. Review monthly with two simple rules.

   (a) Performance rule: If the key metric (e.g., deflection) stays below target for 2 months, bring the improvement item for that metric forward by one step.
   (b) Blocker rule: If something can't start because a dependency is stuck (e.g., data access), move only that item—not the whole plan—and note the reason on the roadmap.

Outputs: a one-sentence north star + 3 goals, a checklist of workstreams with "done" signs, a quarter-by-quarter roadmap with owners and measures, a short "option A vs. option B" note, one shared link as the plan's home, and a monthly change log ("what changed and why").

Limitations and Tips

AI can overweight what it can measure. If you feed mainly digital signals, the model may ignore cultural or regulatory hurdles. Add human reviews with legal, operations, and regional leaders before you lock the sequence.

Too many tools create version drift. Pick a single home for the roadmap (Jira Align or Planview or Aha!/Asana). Link out to intel docs but keep status and decisions in one place.

Privacy and compliance aren't optional. If your initiatives involve customer data, confirm data-handling rules before you paste content into AI features. Use enterprise settings and redact sensitive fields.

10.4 Communicating Vision

Description of Tool

Communicating Vision is the practice of shaping and sharing what you're building, why it matters, and how it changes people's lives. It translates complex solutions into stories, artifacts, and touchpoints tailored to executives, delivery teams, partners, and end users. In design thinking's implement & learn activities, a strong vision clarifies intent, binds evidence to aspiration, and sustains momentum through implementation. The craft draws on leadership storytelling, which uses concrete narratives to galvanize organizations around a goal, as Denning outlines in his 2004 *Harvard Business Review* article. Modern AI systems now help produce on-brand visuals, drafts for multiple audiences, and interactive formats with analytics so you can see what resonates and iterate quickly.

Why Use AI

AI shortens the path from intent to influence. Presentation generators turn a few lines of context into first-draft decks; writing assistants adapt the same core message for the CFO, engineering, and frontline teams; and interactive pages add scroll-depth and click analytics to show where the story lands. Copilot features in familiar office tools produce executive summaries and visuals directly where leaders work. This let's design leaders spend time on truth, tone, and trade-offs while AI handles format, brand alignment, and versioning.

Suggested AI Programs

- Microsoft Copilot for PowerPoint: Create/reshape slides and speaker notes inside PowerPoint.
- Canva: AI Presentation Maker (Magic Design): Prompt-to-deck with brand kits and quick visual polish.
- Google Slides + Gemini for Workspace: Draft/rewrite slides and generate images in Slides.
- Pitch (AI Presentation Maker): Prompt→deck with collaborative editing and on-brand templates.
- Beautiful.ai (DesignerBot): Fast prompt-based decks with smart slide layouts.
- Gamma: Lightweight AI deck generator with export to PPT/Slides.
- Storydoc: Interactive, scrollable "deck pages" with analytics for async reads.
- Copy.ai: Draft vision statements, exec summaries, FAQs. (Use alongside your deck tool.)
- Claude + Canva integration: Make/edit Canva decks directly from a Claude chat (like in-app assistants).

Figure 10.4   Communicating Vision. A collaborative design review of a proposed arti-fact, illustrating how teams collectively interpret, critique, and align around a shared concept to support informed decision-making and refinement. AI generated image created with Ideogram, Inc., Ideogram.ai, 3.0, 2025.

Work Instructions

Example: communicating the vision for "Design System 2.0."

Recommendation: For the following steps, pick one deck tool per step (e.g., PowerPoint+Copilot or Canva, etc.), and use one helper LLM (e.g., Copy.ai or Claude/ChatGPT).

1. Write the message spine.

   (a) Use your LLM (Copy.ai or Claude): *"Rewrite this brief into: (a) a 20-word vision sentence, (b) 3 proof bullets with numbers, (c) 1 honest risk + mitigation."*

   (b) Keep this text fixed across all versions. Hint: this will be the texts for the <spine> placeholder.

2. Generate a first draft deck.

   (a) PowerPoint + Copilot: "Create an 8-slide vision deck: problem, vi-sion, before/after, principles, roadmap, metrics, risks, ask. Use this text: <spine>." Hint: the <spine> a placeholder, which is the core message you'll paste into prompts.

  (b) Canva (Magic Design) or Pitch or Beautiful.ai or Tome/Gamma: start from prompt → select template → apply brand kit → drop in real screens.

3. Tailor titles and one FAQ, once.

  (a) Ask your LLM: "*Turn slide titles into short claims (≤8 words) that matter to executives.*"

  (b) Then: "Draft a 5-bullet Engineer FAQ (performance, tokens, theming, deprecations, support)." Paste into the deck. (If you prefer chat-driven creating inside Canva, use Claude + Canva.)

4. Collect signals and fix weak spots.

  (a) Scan Storydoc analytics (where people linger/bounce) or gather quick email replies.

  (b) Ask your LLM: "*Summarize top 3 objections and draft one slide that answers each with proof.*" Update the deck in the same tool you used in step 2.

Outputs: an 8-slide claim-driven deck, one FAQ slide, and (optionally) an interactive Storydoc link + a short "objections & next moves" slide.

Limitations and Tips

AI can sound generic. If the wording feels bland, add one real customer quote and one real number from your pilot. Keep those on the first two slides.

  AI may guess numbers. Never let the model invent metrics. Replace placeholders with verified figures or label them clearly as estimates until confirmed.

  Context gets lost across versions. Put the one-sentence vision and the two proof numbers on the cover and keep them unchanged. Let the details vary, not the core.

10.5 Create a Pitch

Description of Tool

Pitch with AI is the structured process of crafting a management-ready narrative, including problem, solution, value, plan, while using AI to accelerate content, design, and audience fit. The aim is to secure approval and resources for a final concept and to set up a learning loop after delivery. Classic pitching relies on storytelling, visual composition, and stakeholder alignment; teams typically spend hours arranging slides, polishing copy, and tailoring versions for finance, operations, or legal. AI now augments each of these moves: it can generate first-draft decks from a prompt, propose on-brand layouts and imagery, and adapt the story for multiple audiences without losing the core message. Crucially, the "co-design" mindset keeps humans in control of truth, tone, and trade-offs while AI accelerates iteration.

Why Use AI

AI strengthens pitching by compressing the distance between intent and a decision-ready artifact. Generators turn a few lines of context into an outline and slides; board-native design assistants clean layouts, maintain brand styles, and fill visual gaps so the team can focus on evidence and risk. LLMs clarify value propositions, convert features to benefits for each stakeholder, and draft alternative versions under constraints (e.g., "no new headcount"). Interactive formats add analytics (scroll depth, clicks), giving feedback to both the design team and the model for the next iteration. The result is faster alignment without sacrificing rigor.

Suggested AI Programs

- Pitch: AI Presentation Maker. Generate decks from prompts; on-brand templates; collaborative editing.
- Storydoc: AI Pitch Creator. Interactive, scrollable pitch pages with analytics and multimedia.
- Canva Magic Design for Presentations. Turn prompts into slide decks; Magic Studio assists copy, layout, and assets.
- Venngage AI Pitch Deck Generator. Prompt-based pitch decks with dataviz and export options.
- ChatGPT-5/Claude (LLMs). Reframe value stories, tailor copy per stakeholder, draft speaker notes; Claude also integrates with Canva for creation/editing.

Work Instructions

Example: "a modular reusable-packaging program for a beverage company"

Figure 10.5 Create a Pitch. Collaborative pitch development, illustrating how teams synthesize insights, refine narratives, and align around a compelling value proposition to communicate design concepts and solutions. AI generated image created with Ideogram, Inc., Ideogram.ai, 3.0, 2025.

1. Map the audience and their decisions.

   (a) Identify who must say "yes" and what they need (CFO: payback and risks; Ops: rollout complexity; Brand: customer impact).

   (b) Prompt ChatGPT-5: *"List likely objections and decision criteria for CFO, COO, and Brand VP about a reusable-packaging pilot in 10 cities; output a table with Role, Core win, Top risk, Evidence needed."* Use this as your guardrail for every slide.

2. Draft a first deck from a prompt.

   (a) In Pitch (AI presentation maker), enter a prompt such as: *"Create a 12-slide management deck for a 6-month reusable-packaging pilot: problem, solution concept, unit economics, capex/opex, ops plan, risk & mitigation, KPI tree, timeline, ask."*

   (b) Review the generated structure, then ask ChatGPT-5 to tighten slide titles: *"Rewrite each slide title as a persuasive claim (≤ 9 words) + proof cue in parentheses."*

3. Design for clarity and brand alignment.

(a) Open the outline in Canva Magic Design for Presentations to polish layout and brand elements. Prompt: *"Apply our brand kit and generate 3 visual alternatives for the KPI tree; include icons for return rate, breakage, logistics cost, and NPS."*

(b) If you use Claude, leverage its Canva integration to iterate on charts and layouts directly from chat.

4. Tailor versions by stakeholder.

(a) Export a "Finance" version and an "Operations" version. In Storydoc, convert the core story into an interactive page for asynchronous review.

(b) Prompt Storydoc's AI to "emphasize ROI and sensitivity analysis in the Finance version; add collapsible sections for assumptions; enable analytics."

(c) Then ask ChatGPT-5: *"Given CFO criteria, draft a one-slide 'Deal in numbers': baseline waste costs, pilot costs, breakeven month, three sensitivities."*

5. Add evidence and pre-empt objections.

(a) Feed the cost model and pilot benchmarks to ChatGPT-5/Claude: *"Generate a risk-mitigation table with owner and trigger thresholds (inventory, turnaround time, breakage rate)."*

(b) In Venngage AI Pitch Deck Generator, produce a clean, data-forward appendix (unit economics, routes, return logistics) that can be swapped into either version.

6. Rehearse, deliver, and learn.

(a) Draft speaker notes with ChatGPT-5: *"Write 120-word notes per slide, ending each with a 'management ask' in one sentence."* Deliver the live deck; share the Storydoc link for asynchronous readers.

(b) After the meeting, review Storydoc analytics (where did viewers linger or bounce?) and log questions. Prompt ChatGPT-5: *"Synthesize the Q&A and analytics into a one-page 'What to improve for v2' with prioritized edits to slides and model."* This closes the loop for both you and the AI.

Outputs/artifacts: a claim-driven slide deck (Pitch/Canva), stakeholder-specific versions (Finance/Operations), an interactive Storydoc with analytics, and a lessons-learned memo to refine the next pitch.

Limitations and Tips

Authenticity can flatten when AI over-generalizes voice. Counter this by adding two founder/field quotes and one customer vignette in your own words; keep AI to structure/clarity while the human story carries emotion.

Accuracy risks rise when AI drafts numbers or cites market data. Require human verification of every metric and assumption, store sources in a shared appendix. If an LLM suggests figures, mark them "estimates—validate" until confirmed.

Confidentiality and brand governance may be breached by default settings. Use enterprise or approved workspaces, disable public links, and lock brand kits. Keep sensitive data off external prompts unless your legal team has approved the tool's terms.

10.6   I Like, I Wish, I Wonder

Description of Tool

"I Like, I Wish, I Wonder" is a lightweight feedback ritual that channels critique into constructive, future-oriented language. Participants capture what worked ("I like…"), what could be improved ("I wish…"), and open questions or possibilities ("I wonder…"). The practice descends from the widely taught "I Like/I Wish/What if" method popularized by the Stanford d.school and widely adopted in design education and team retrospectives; "I Wonder" is a common variation used to invite inquiry and hypothesis generation. The method creates a psychologically safe frame for critique, reduces unproductive negativity, and yields structured input that can be themed and tracked across cycles.

In design thinking, it is especially useful right after concept pitches, pilots, or internal demos, where teams must both persuade management and capture learning for the next iteration. Its simplicity scales from five-minute stand-ups to company-wide town halls, and it pairs well with digital whiteboards and research repositories that turn sticky notes into durable, searchable evidence of progress. (On origins and diffusion of the "I Like/I Wish/What if" pattern, see practice write-ups by IxDF and IDEO; several guides attribute early classroom and d.school roots.)

Why Use AI

AI strengthens this method by transforming raw, often messy comments into themed, prioritized insights with traceability. Automatic transcription captures contributions verbatim; natural-language classifiers sort statements into Like/Wish/Wonder, tag sentiment, and surface duplicates. Large language models (LLMs) can draft synthesis notes, sharpen vague wishes into testable hypotheses, and propose "bridging" actions tailored to constraints (budget, timeline, compliance). Board-native AI speeds clustering and naming, while workspace AI converts notes into decision-ready tables linked to owners and deadlines. The result is a faster path from feedback to internal buy-in: evidence-backed summaries, clear asks for management, and a lightweight loop to learn across cycles.

Suggested AI Programs

- Otter.ai: Live meeting transcription, summaries, action items for workshops and reviews.
- Rev: Accurate speech-to-text (AI + human) for recorded sessions you need polished.
- Looppanel: Research-grade transcripts + AI analysis/repository for clustering feedback.
- Miro AI: Cluster stickies, suggest labels, tidy retro boards, and generate follow-ups.
- Notion AI: Turn text into tables/databases; draft synthesis and assign owners/dates.
- ChatGPT or Claude (LLM): Reframe wishes into experiments, propose metrics, and draft stakeholder briefs.

Work Instructions

Example: "redesigning the university course-registration page".

1. Open the session and capture every voice.

    (a) Begin a 30-minute retro immediately after student usability tests. Start Otter.ai to record so note-taking doesn't bottleneck.

    (b) Ask ChatGPT-5 for a short opener: "*Write 2 sentences inviting 'I Like, I Wish, I Wonder' feedback for a course-registration redesign. Emphasize*

Figure 10.6   I Like, I Wish, I Wonder. The "I Like, I Wish, I Wonder" reflection method in practice, illustrating how teams structure feedback to surface appreciation, aspirations, and open questions during collaborative design critique. AI generated image created with Ideogram, Inc., Ideogram.ai, 3.0, 2025.

psychological safety and concrete examples." Read it aloud to set tone and expectations.

2. Collect Like/Wish/Wonder quickly and cleanly.

   (a) Create three columns on a Miro board and give everyone 2 minutes per column. Then use Miro AI to tidy: "Deduplicate and cluster notes.

   (b) Output a table: Theme, Example notes (2), Type (Like/Wish/Wonder), ≤3-word label."

   (c) Outcome: crisp clusters such as "Clear Prereqs," "Search Pain," "Waitlist Confusion."

3. Turn vague wishes into testable changes.

   (a) Copy the "I Wish" notes into ChatGPT-5 and prompt: "Rewrite each 'I Wish' as a 2-week experiment we can run without engineering headcount; include: hypothesis, change, metric, and success threshold."

   (b) Example transformation: "I wish search was faster" can be translated to: "*If we surface top 5 popular courses as quick chips, time-to-first-result will drop from 18s to ≤ 8s for 70% of students.*" This produces a list of low-effort, measurable trials.

4. Create a trackable backlog for approval.

   (a) Paste clusters and experiments into Notion and ask Notion AI to build a database with fields: Type, Theme, Experiment, Owner, Priority, Metric, Due.

   (b) Prompt: "*Set Priority H/M/L using risk (students missing deadlines) × impact (task completion). Assign Owners from this list and stagger Due dates across 3 weeks.*"

   (c) Now you have a living, owner-assigned plan management can scan asynchronously.

5. Synthesize a one-page brief for stakeholders.

   (a) Feed the database to Claude: "*Draft a 1-page 'Apply & Learn' brief for the course-registration redesign: top 3 Likes as proof points, top 3 Wishes as risks with experiments, 2 'I Wonder' hypotheses for future research, and a 30-day timeline with KPIs (task success, time-to-register, help-desk tickets). End with a clear budget/time ask.*"

   (b) Optional: convert the brief into an interactive link in Storydoc for analytics on where leaders linger.

6. Run, review, and close the loop.

   (a) After two weeks, upload quick test readouts (recorded stand-ups or clips) to Rev or Looppanel. Use their AI summaries to tag outcomes (pass/fail/iterate).

   (b) Ask ChatGPT-5: "*Compare each experiment's metric against its threshold; produce a 'What changed & why' memo and recommend which changes ship to production.*"

   (c) Update the Notion database and schedule the next Like/Wish/Wonder—keeping both team and AI learning over time.

Outputs/artifacts: screenshot of clustered board; deduplicated themes table; Notion experiment backlog (owners, metrics, due dates); one-page executive brief (or Storydoc link with analytics); "What changed & why" memo tied to KPIs—ready for management approval and continuous improvement.

Limitations and Tips

A first limitation is context loss when AI paraphrases human nuance. Counter this by pinning two verbatim quotes per theme in your brief so decision-makers can "hear" the team's voice; use transcripts as linked evidence rather than replacing them with summaries.

A second limitation is over-automation of prioritization. LLMs can overweight sentiment and underweight feasibility or compliance. Always conduct a short human calibration pass where product, legal, and operations re-score the AI's priorities before approval.

A third limitation is privacy and consent in recorded sessions. Obtain consent up front, restrict access to transcripts, and configure workspace retention settings. When in doubt, anonymize contributors in exported artifacts before circulating widely.

10.7   Reflect

Description of Tool

Reflect is a structured, repeatable practice for capturing what worked, what failed, and what to change—and then turning those insights into living organizational memory. It draws on long-standing lessons-learned and after-action review (AAR) traditions, which emphasize extracting evidence from debriefs, documents, and outcomes, organizing it by theme, and linking each lesson to concrete follow-up actions.

Within Implement and Learn activities, this approach reduces repeat errors, speeds handoffs, and improves the quality of approval cycles by making rationale and risks explicit. While classic implementations relied on post-project workshops and write-ups, contemporary project-management guidance stresses building searchable repositories, standardizing capture steps (e.g., identify $\rightarrow$ document $\rightarrow$ analyze $\rightarrow$ store/retrieve), and applying lessons throughout the project—not only at closeout, as outlined in Rowe's work in 2007 and 2008. Today, AI tools extend that discipline with transcript capture, automated synthesis, and cross-project pattern detection so teams can retrieve the right lesson at the right moment.

Why Use AI

AI transforms lessons learned processes by automatically analyzing project data to identify patterns, extracting insights from unstructured feedback, and connecting current experiences to historical project outcomes. Natural language processing can analyze meeting transcripts, project documents, and team communications to automatically generate lessons learned summaries, categorize insights by theme, and identify recurring issues across multiple projects. AI compresses the path from scattered evidence to actionable learning. Transcription agents capture debriefs verbatim; board/workspace AI clusters notes, drafts summaries, and converts fuzzy takeaways into "if-then" rules tied to owners and dates. Human judgment still decides meaning; AI accelerates retrieval, synthesis, and follow-through.

Suggested AI Programs

- Otter.ai: Live transcription, summaries, action items for debriefs.
- Rev: AI + human transcription for polished postmortems.
- Looppanel: Research repository with AI search/summaries across transcripts, notes, and insights.
- Miro AI: Cluster sticky notes from retro boards; tidy themes fast.
- Notion AI: Database autofill/summaries for lesson logs and status.
- Confluence (Atlassian Intelligence): Summarize pages and recent changes; good for wiki-style knowledge bases.
- ChatGPT-5 / Claude (LLMs): Reframe raw notes into testable recommendations and owner/metric pairs.

Work Instructions

Example: "improving a campus health-clinic appointment flow".

1. Capture the debrief without losing nuance.

    (a) Schedule a 30-minute retro the day the pilot ends. Start Otter.ai to record and live-transcribe so facilitators can engage.

    (b) Open a Miro board with three lanes: Wins, Frictions, Surprises.

    (c) Prompt ChatGPT-5: *"Write a 2-sentence invitation to share concrete, evidence-backed notes (include metric or quote if possible)."*

    (d) Outcome: psychological safety + crisp inputs.

2. Cluster and name themes quickly.

    (a) Select all stickies and use Miro AI. Cluster (by keywords, then by sentiment) to group notes (e.g., "Insurance Eligibility," "No-Show Rate," "SMS Reminders").

Figure 10.7   Reflect. A collaborative discussion session, illustrating how diverse stakeholders exchange perspectives, negotiate ideas, and build shared understanding through structured dialogue and group deliberation. AI generated image created with Ideogram, Inc., Ideogram.ai, 3.0, 2025.

   (b) Ask: "*Output a table: Theme, Example notes (2), Sentiment, Suggested label (≤3 words).*"

   (c) Outcome: a de-duplicated map you can discuss.

3. Draft lessons and testable recommendations.

   (a) Paste one cluster at a time into ChatGPT-5/Claude: "Turn this into (a) Lesson (≤20 words, past-tense), (b) Recommendation (imperative), (c) If-then guardrail with metric + owner + due date." Example:
   (i) Lesson: "SMS reminders cut no-shows."
   (ii) Recommendation: "Ship two-step SMS with opt-out."
   (iii) If-then: "If no-show ≤8% for 2 weeks, expand to all clinics."

   (b) Outcome: action-ready entries.

4. Create the living log and status.

   (a) In Notion, create a Lessons database (fields: Theme, Lesson, Recommendation, Owner, Metric, Due, Status, Evidence link). Use Notion

AI to autofill Status from notes ("Unapplied / In progress / Verified") and to generate a one-paragraph Summary per theme.

(b) Outcome: a single source of truth that updates as work progresses.

5. Link evidence and cross-reference similar projects.

(a) Upload call clips or usability sessions to Rev or Looppanel; attach transcript links in the Evidence field.

(b) In Looppanel, search "no-show" or "eligibility" to find prior projects; paste the best match into a Related Work property so future teams land on it first.

(c) Outcome: traceable lessons with receipts and cross-project pointers.

6. Publish to the wiki and nudge follow-through.

(a) Use Confluence to publish a page "Clinic Pilot: Lessons & Actions." Ask Atlassian Intelligence to Summarize page and Summarize changes next week so stakeholders can skim what's new.

(b) Add a "30-day check" calendar task; at the check-in, prompt ChatGPT-5: "*Compare metrics to guardrails; propose keep/pivot/retire decisions and rewrite any stale recommendations.*"

(c) Outcome: a closed learning loop with visible ownership.

Outputs/artifacts: clustered retro board; Lessons database with owners/metrics/due dates; linked transcripts as evidence; a Confluence summary page for leadership; a 30-day update showing which recommendations worked.

Limitations and Tips

False generalization across projects. LLMs may merge superficially similar themes (e.g., "no-show" in clinics vs. counseling) and suggest one-size fixes. Require an Evidence link and Context tags (setting, audience, constraints) for every lesson; block promotion to "Verified" until metrics improve in the same context.

Stale lessons and drift. Without upkeep, recommendations survive long after conditions change. Add a Review date and use Notion AI to auto-flag items older than one release cycle; during the review, either refresh metrics or mark Retired with a reason.

Privacy/compliance in evidence. Store raw files in your approved drive; redact names in excerpts; use enterprise tiers of AI tools with data-handling assurances before attaching links or pasting content externally.

10.8   Implement & Learn Use Case: Designing a Futuristic Poster with AI

Our challenge: to create a fresh, futuristic, and visually striking poster to promote a publishing event for this book.

The poster must communicate our theme clearly while standing out in a crowded space. We wanted bold fonts, dynamic layouts, and imagery that hinted at technological creativity. None of us were professional graphic designers, and while we had ideas about the style, translating them into a polished design was another matter.

To begin, we tested different ways of working with AI. We set up four design pathways that varied the role of AI, ranging from completely AI-generated posters to designs created entirely by humans, and two mixed approaches in between. This structure allowed us to consider where AI excelled, where it fell short, and how human creativity could bridge the gaps.

The most surprising insight came early in the process. Using ChatGPT to refine our prompts drastically improved our efficiency. Instead of spending hours manually searching for typefaces or visual references, we could describe our vision and have GPT generate lists of futuristic font ideas, style suggestions, and pattern concepts in seconds. This meant we could move past vague ideas and quickly zero in on specific visual directions.

We then used Midjourney to turn these refined prompts into poster imagery. By specifying details such as color schemes, focal points, and even grid system requirements, we could push the visuals closer to our intended style. However, we discovered that AI struggled with certain design fundamentals, especially text layout. Specific words used in instructions matter! When we asked for a grid system, the AI often interpreted it literally, producing intersecting lines rather than balanced compositions.

Our team process was sequential but highly collaborative. Each member proposed initial ideas, which were then tested through AI-generated visuals. We reviewed every output together, voting on which elements worked best. In the pure AI pathway, the results were visually rich but often lacked logic in image arrangement and text placement. In the collaborative pathway, AI provided main images, logos, and fonts, while humans manually arranged them into a coherent layout. This hybrid approach proved the most successful, combining AI's speed and variety with human judgment in structure and readability.

The final poster used AI-generated patterns and typography suggestions but was assembled manually to ensure clarity and balance. It achieved our goal of a clean, modern, and futuristic look while still feeling approachable. AI had accelerated the ideation and asset creation stages, freeing us to focus our energy on refining the layout and ensuring the message came through clearly.

Key Learnings

* AI is a powerful tool for generating prompts, visual elements, and design inspiration, but it struggles with complex layout logic.
* Hybrid workflows, where AI produces components and humans assemble them, yield the best results.
* Effective prompting is critical; the more specific we were, the closer the outputs matched our vision.

Final Reflection

This project showed us that AI's value in design thinking lies not in replacing the designer or innovator, but in enhancing the designer's toolkit. By handling repetitive or time-consuming tasks like asset creation and style exploration, AI allowed us to experiment more and make better creative decisions. In future projects, we want to explore ways to train AI models to better understand grid systems and compositional rules, so the collaboration can extend even further into layout design.

10.9   Implement & Learn Use Case: Meituan Sustainable Community Pickup System

陈东,_王萱, 奇浩禄, 石瑞虹 (Tongji University)

Our challenge: to create a sustainable recycling pickup program for office buildings and university campuses, specifically targeting the use of recyclable packaging.

We knew that to successfully implement this sustainability program, we would have to understand the needs of our potential participants and design an operationally sound system, and communicate the process to both system operators and clients. We discovered that AI could help us in our process as well as our outcomes.

AI played the central role in translating our raw design research into structured, shareable diagrams. We began by inputting our interview findings, observations, and reflections from delivery riders, shop owners, and office workers into large language models (like ChatGPT and Tongyi Qianwen). These AI systems helped us process data, summarize recurring pain points, and propose draft workflows for reducing waste and optimizing pickup schedules. From there, instead of relying on generic diagrams or relying solely on hand-drawn sketches, we found it more efficient to use AI for text-to-code transformations. For example, by providing AI with structured prompts about recycling stations, collection schedules, and user interaction flows, Mermaid AI, a diagramming and charting tool, generated flowchart code that we could then edit for precision. Compared to text-to-image models, this method was significantly more accurate and adaptable. Through iterative refinement, we produced diagrams that communicated both the logic and sustainability principles of the recycling pickup system, supporting implementation and testing.

AI broadened our design perspective, helping us to clarify the creative and technical aspects of a operationally sound recycling pickup system. Mermaid allowed us to visualize and produce accurate, structured flowcharts that captured the recycling pickup process clearly and logically. These diagrams could be updated as needed when information was added, supporting quick iteration and communication with stakeholders. However, the diagrams often lacked visual appeal, appearing functional but uninspired.

Conversely, text-to-image outputs were engaging and creative but too imprecise for system mapping. This contrast highlighted one of the biggest insights of our implementation process: AI tools have strengths in different domains, and the best outcomes arise when we combine them strategically. For functional precision—especially in sustainability-focused implementation planning—code-driven outputs were superior. For storytelling or community engagement, the more expressive text-to-image tools have their place. This dual approach gave us a better foundation for both communicating and executing our recycling pickup proposal.

AI also reshaped how we collaborated as a team. Initially, we worked in separate sequences such that members explored different tools like **ChatGPT**, **Kimi**, and dedicated flowchart generators independently. Then, once a teammate discovered advantages of code-based visualization, our process shifted to a more collaborative and reciprocal approach. Together, we co-constructed prompts, experimented with different syntax outputs (e.g., **Mermaid** vs. Python programming language visualization libraries), and collectively reviewed the diagrams. AI outputs served as a shared reference point, reducing misunderstandings that often arose between text-heavy notes and design sketches. When reviewing visualizations, decisions were typically made through team consensus, since AI-generated diagrams were transparent and easy to modify in real time. This reciprocal back-and-forth with AI allowed us to quickly test and iterate on different system designs, helping to keep our implementation phase more efficient and aligned.

AI broadened our design perspective, helping us to clarify the creative and technical aspects of a operationally sound recycling pickup system. AI like **Mermaid** allowed us to visualize and produce accurate, structured flowcharts that captured the recycling pickup process clearly and logically. These diagrams could be updated as needed when information was added, supporting quick iteration and communication with stakeholders. However, they lacked visual appeal—appearing functional but uninspired.

Conversely, text-to-image outputs were engaging and creative but too imprecise for system mapping. This contrast highlighted one of the biggest insights of our implementation process: AI tools have strengths in different domains, and the best outcomes arise when we combine them strategically. For functional precision—especially in sustainability-focused implementation planning—code-driven outputs were superior. For storytelling or community engagement, the more expressive text-to-image tools have their place. This dual approach gave us a better foundation for both communicating and executing our recycling pickup proposal.

Key Learnings

- AI is helpful both in making sense of project information from multiple sources and in designing products that meet the users' technical and aesthetic requirements.
- Specific AI programs are written for specific purposes, and working with AI requires understanding of the relative strengths and shortcoming of these programs.
- Working with AI is a co-constructive process, where iteration among project team members and AI can lead to the best outcomes.

Final Reflection

AI supported us in converting research into actionable visualizations, reshaping our teamwork into a more reciprocal, prompt-co-construction process, and balancing accuracy against creativity in implementation planning. Our most surprising learning was that AI is not a monolithic solution but a collection of specialized tools, and selecting the right tool for each aspect of the task greatly impacts the quality of outcomes.

References

Brown, T. (2008, June). Design thinking. *Harvard Business Review*, *86*(6), 84–92. https://hbr.org/2008/06/design-thinking

Darling, M., Parry, C., & Moore, J. (2005, July). Learning in the thick of it. *Harvard Business Review*, *83*(7), 84–92. https://hbr.org/2005/07/learning-in-the-thick-of-it

Denning, S. (2004, May). Telling tales. *Harvard Business Review*, *82*(5), 122–129. https://hbr.org/2004/05/telling-tales

Martínez Casanovas, M. (2025). Exploring design thinking methodologies: A comprehensive analysis of the literature, outstanding practices, and their linkage to sustainable development goals. *Sustainability*, *17*(15), Article 7142. https://doi.org/10.3390/su17157142

Razzouk, R., & Shute, V. (2012). What is design thinking and why is it important? *Review of Educational Research*, *82*(3), 330–348. https://doi.org/10.3102/0034654312457429

Rowe, S. F. (2007). Lessons learned: Taking it to the next level. Paper presented at PMI® Global Congress 2007—EMEA, Budapest, Hungary. Newtown Square, PA: Project Management Institute.

Rowe, S. F. (2008). Applying lessons learned. Paper presented at PMI® Global Congress 2008—EMEA, St. Julian's, Malta. Newtown Square, PA: Project Management Institute.

11

Future of AI in Design Thinking

When used effectively, AI unlocks new opportunities to enhance innovation for design thinkers. Design thinkers can now innovate more quickly and cost effectively, developing high quality, human-centered products and services. In the first two chapters of this book, we have provided an introduction and overview of AI and design thinking. We first laid the foundation by introducing and elaborating on design thinking and AI, examining their connection. We defined design as a set of activities that contribute to the creation of physical artifacts or concepts independently if they were done by a human, AI, or other entity. Our starting point for understanding was largely based on the simplified design thinking process and tools developed by IDEO and others. However, we also went beyond the simplified version to enhance the readers understanding about the broader conceptualization of designing. We then explored the variety of AI systems, highlighting how AI is linked to design, particularly through generative AI.

In Chapter 3, we illustrated how the emergence of AI creates challenges while also offering opportunities for designers, innovators and their organizations. Unfortunately, there is a relatively large gap between the AI's actual use in organizations and its potential for enhancing competitiveness. While some part of this may be due to a lack of AI-related knowledge and skills, a significant remainder may be explained by the rejection of this new technology by many professionals. We identified and introduced three categories of designers and their relationship to AI: design traditionalists, technology futurist, and AI agnostics.

© The Author(s), under exclusive license to Springer Nature Switzerland AG 2026
D. Graff et al., *Design Thinking with Artificial Intelligence*, Palgrave Executive Essentials,
https://doi.org/10.1007/978-3-032-10543-1_11

While technology futurists drive the direction of AI in design thinking, design traditionalists present a roadblock, and AI agnostics remain uncertain about the role of AI in design thinking's future. These perspectives differ, but all seem to regard AI as a force or entity rather than a partner. We proposed viewing AI as a collaborator in design thinking, rather than seeing AI merely as another software tool, or as something which will replace humans. At this still-early stage of AI integration into society, collaborating with AI requires designers and innovators to take the role of a supervisor, managing AI throughout the design thinking process.

Chapter 4 proposes the future skill sets and goes into detail as to which future skills might be relevant to leveraging and partnering with AI. We highlighted the importance of continuous learning because AI is advancing quickly, requiring human collaborators to adjust as needed. Then, in Chapter 5, we provided some more direct and practical suggestion on how to work with the tools in this book. We went into detail what it means for humans to supervise AI in 2025. This chapter also introduces one of the latest trends in AI, termed AI agents or assistants. These AI assistants can help designers and innovators in various ways throughout the design thinking process. They can support administrative tasks and so free up time for the individual, or take part more directly in the design process, either as part of the design team, or by simulating users.

In Section 2 of the book, we introduced the various AID tools within the design thinking activities. These AID tools can be used, depending on the aim and demand of the designers and innovators. Each tool provides a short description, benefits and how to use AI within the tools. Some design thinking tools we have adapted remained quite similar, while others changed with the introduction of AI. It will be up to the individual designer and innovator to adapt these tools to their context and continuously update them. In the appendices, we elaborate on the creation and use of AI agents, then overview the AI programs we have used in the book as a handy reference for our readers.

We hope that this book can contribute to a better application of AI in design thinking, improving innovations for people and their organizations. Because AI is advancing quickly, we expect AI to continuously increase its contribution towards design thinking, necessitating frequent updates from human collaborators. We will populate our website, **ai-designthinking.com**, with developments in AI design thinking tools, including over 30 new AI process tools created since this book was first written. We hope that this book will remain a good initial foundation for those who want to enhance their design thinking processes and outcomes with AI.

Future Outlook

So, will AI augment or replace the role of designers and innovators in design thinking? While we cannot predict precisely what lies ahead, we can actively participate in defining this future. In Chapter 3, we briefly laid out how we see the short-term impact of AI on design thinking. In this chapter, we provide direction on what we can do to alleviate negative effects of AI, so supporting a more positive impact of AI in design thinking. We have three points to propose: (1) Re-framing the relationship of AI and design thinking, (2) Don't just save time and money, (3) The evolution of AI from a collaborator to a designer.

(1)   Re-Framing Our Relationship of AI and Design Thinking

Individuals vary highly in their acceptance of AI, including highly divergent views of AI's impact on design thinking. On one hand, optimistic perspectives state that AI will make designing easier, better, and more efficient, opening access to a wider world of design thinkers. These ideas aligning largely with the views of technology futurists. Alternately, a more negative view conceives of AI as a threat to good design, a view often held by design traditionalists. It may be that this polarization is due to AI's swift emergence, which upsets established practices while also running ahead of strong empirical evidence that might help us to better understand the consequences of AI in design thinking. As might be expected from our work in this book, integrating AI into design thinking tools as an avenue for human-AI collaboration, we believe successful use of AI in design thinking does not benefit from either extreme.

The Current Negative View

Critiques of AI often relate to its outcomes, sometimes judged to be inferior to human designs due to a lack of context, derivative ideas and bias due to AI being trained on existing human-created materials. In our view, this impression is flawed for at least two reasons: first, AI is not often used to its fullest capability in creating these inferior outcomes; and second, the standard for judging these outcomes is not comparable to that used for human design thinkers.

It seems that an AI outcome is often judged based on a very simple and shallow design process and AI use. This light design process starts with opening an AI system and entering a prompt, expecting a perfect response (i.e., a design outcome). Rarely depicted is a longer phase of iterations or interaction with AI, so as to enhance the outcome. In other words, AI is used as a traditional software tool. Would we have the same expectation from a human designer or innovator working under similar conditions? We do not believe that we would get a better outcome from a human designer or innovator who is working with a similar short description of a problem statement and about five minutes of sketching time. So, why do we have these expectations of AI?

Furthermore, in these negative opinions it is often argued that the outcome from AI is bad because it is biased or simply that it is un-imaginative. The underlying assumptions seems to be that human designers and innovators deliver continuously flawless designs that are contextual, impartial, and unique. In a way, and a bit ironically, the human designer and innovator assumed outcomes are descriptions of non-human, machine like outcomes (in other words, always flawless). Clearly, this is often not the case.

Let's assume that the assumptions are correct about the flawless nature of designers, so that we can discuss in more detail the two main reasons stated for why AI in design is bad; its biases and lack of creativity. Yes, AI programs have biases; however, these are due to human sources of their information, meaning that those biases are due to the humans in the trained data sets. The AI training will reflect human tendencies and preferences in decision-making, whether it is bias about fashion choices influencing clothing designs, preferences for open structures undergirding new buildings, or other areas. The evidence for human bias is clearly in the relative lack of variety in these designs and in the training data that AI uses. In other words, AI is only biased because we humans often are. The avenue for innovation would seem to be recognizing and addressing these biases, then proactively seeking new forms from other sources, such as natural formations.

Another myth is that human designs are always unique. However, many of the ideas from designers and innovators come from and build on other already existing ideas (e.g. through analogical thinking). Rarely, an idea arrives completely independent of existing things and ideas. Consider the design of Apple's iPod music player. The design was heavily influenced by Brauns transistor radio T3 from the 50s. Are we similarly critical to this human design as we are with the outcomes of AI? What about all mobile phones and televisions having similar looks? Most human designers and innovators are inspired by existing work. Further, it is often suggested that AI (or the companies that own the programs) should pay fees to those who created the inspiration for their work. This might be reasonable, if held to the standard that humans adhere to for copyright, trademarking, and so forth. To assert that AI should not be able to recombine ideas of others, as humans do, is not as reasonable in our view.

Why do we see so many negative depictions of AI in articles, social media, or conversations about the workplace? While some extreme opinions may be dismissed as bait for clicks, there also may be a belief among some that we must current of protect our jobs and the ability of humans to remain the dominant species. It may be that some designers and innovators are afraid of AI and its impact, seeing it as potentially taking away the "magic" of their contributions. While we cannot know this, we can say that this position is not in line with the more open-minded, future-oriented, and experimentally-focused mentality often associated with designers and innovators.

If a negative view of AI becomes dominant, it could lead to passive and uncommitted segments of the design thinking community, perhaps specifically among art-based designers who might feel more alienated by this new technology. The risk of ignoring or avoiding AI is that many designers might not adapt until it is perhaps too late. Leaving others to potentially influence the future of design thinking. We believe that we, as a community of designers and innovators, need to be more active and try to design the future of AI in design thinking together.

The Current Positive View

Much praise of AI's value to design thinking is related to its newness and relatively strong capabilities in areas that humans recently dominated, even if some activities (e.g., data gathering) and skills (e.g., thematic analysis) are not always enjoyable work. In our view, this impression is also flawed because this does not demonstrate understanding of what makes good design. Technologically driven design thinkers, for example, may be enamored of AI's capabilities of AI and, hence, view AI more as an exciting new partner than that a tool.

One basic challenge here is that AI's outcomes are often not assessed by professional designers, whether due to false confidence in AI, or to a more cost conscious, leaner workforce. In this case, AI's design outcomes may be judged to be higher quality than they merit. For example, a simple prompt may result in AI sketching a competent design, or even several design variants, that lead to onlooker amazement. However, the ease of the sketch production may mask flaws that a professional designer would be less likely to make, such as accounting for the surrounding context, the environmental impact, or perhaps operational viability. Thus, the question of whether the sketches are good enough may not be easily answered. More familiarity of AI's capabilities, as well as more skill-building by those who wish to employ AI, can result in a better design thinking process and outcome.

The challenge of adopting this view is that we are satisfied by a lower possible standard. We explore the consequences in more detail in the second point of this section (going beyond saving time and money). In short, the risk is that we develop much more products because the development of things is getting cheaper and easier, but not necessarily better. This could potentially extend already existing challenges for design, such as environmental concerns. We could theoretically produce many more things in much cheaper ways. The question is if we do want or need this.

Let's Take a Different View

Hence, neither the overly positive and negative perspectives on AI are helpful in design thinking. We suggest a middle ground. AI will have a prominent role to play in design thinking as time goes on (as we hope has been demonstrated in this book), but there is still an important place for the human design thinker. As we have suggested, this relationship could begin as a relationship similar to that of a supervisor and employee, and perhaps proceed to a true partnership. Rather than viewing AI versus people, we should value AI for its potential as a collaborator who can help us develop even better products and services.

Adopting this view will require changing minds, adding skills, and further developing our AI programs and tools. Designers and innovators who view AI as a negative force should consider possible ways that AI can support their design work. This will require them to experiment and learn to use AI in the design thinking process. So far, little structured guidance has been given to this group. This book may represent a starting point, showing how AI can support high quality design processes and product or service outcomes. Meanwhile, designers and innovators who are overly optimistic about AI's uses may need to remind themselves that AI currently has limitations. It is also critical for humans to sharpen their own design knowledge, so they can become good consumers of AI output, providing direction where needed.

Thinking in a positive and realistic way about AI in design thinking is essential not to its adoption (which may be inevitable), but in its most effectively leveraging it use in innovating better products and services. We hope this book can contribute to managing the expectation of AI and its adoption in design thinking. Further work is under way, with many organizations and universities developing courses and programs which teach students and managers how to design with AI. We have created accompanying website to this book called **ai-designthinking.com**, which we will update with new tools and further progress in AI.

(2) Don't Just Save Time and Money

It may be natural for many organizations to focus on the immediate, measurable cost effectiveness of AI solutions, whether time, money, or personnel. Indeed, AI has been noted to shrink costs related to process and labor efficiencies. However, such fast development cycles with lean workforces may negatively affect the quality of the designed product or service. Given the need to develop human competencies to effectively deploy AI in design, we cannot expect to achieve optimal innovation if our first tendency is to cut the people and processes necessary to fully leveraging AI. The obvious risk to such an approach is that, while the costs of new product development may decrease, so too with the quality of the products, reducing an organization's competitive advantage in the marketplace.

Further challenges relate to the leaner workforce associated with nonstrategic cost cutting. First and most obvious, the knowledge held by workers who leave the organization will likely be lost. Additionally, organizations that fail to hire more junior professionals, or to provide such employees with opportunities to engage in introductory work that may be subsumed by AI, may face critical gaps in their senior professional workforce of the future. Even the process of encouraging employees to utilize AI in their jobs may lead to unintended consequences. For instance, AI can substitute for basic skills and knowledge in design thinking, which allows less trained workers to develop new products and service. This could result in an increase of mediocre products, especially over time as these workers move to senior positions without necessarily understanding design principles.

We believe that investing in the development of employee AI management skills will pay great dividends for the future of organizations, and perhaps of society itself. While there are costs associated with this approach, both in labor and time, organizations following this path will realize higher quality products and a more talented, agile workforce, both of which lead to market competitiveness and societal good. Organizations should create systems that support such direction, such as internal AI champions to help focus training and support of all employees, outside experts who can help train the workforce, and product development process which allow time for learning as well as production. We also believe that academic institutions and scholars have a role to play, supporting both research and practice that move toward understanding of AI-related best practices.

(3)   The Evolution of AI from a Collaborator to a Designer

For most organizations and design thinking practices, the current best scenario for engaging AI is collaborative, with the supervisor-subordinate relationship we described. However, as AI continues its accelerated development, we could soon see AI gaining the skills, perspective, and autonomy to fill a role as partner or even independent designer.

What will be the consequence for design thinking? This will depend on large what type of design thinker AI will be. Will it be an independent, selfish individuum working alone from start to beginning with little to no human contributions? Or will AI act as a good colleague who works with us to develop great solutions to human problems? We will have a large role in determining how AI will perform in the near future, at least.

We suggest that it will be important, first, for an AI designer to have a good understanding of humans, including our skills and needs. AI must develop an understanding of people and situations that support effective design of specific solutions that fit the context. An important step toward this is through creating and training AI assistants to suit our needs and preferences. Over time and iterations of AI assistants, the training investment is likely to become less resource-intensive for organizations, even as the AI assistants increase in sophistication, because AI will help us with the creation and training. This means that AI will be less directly dependent on humans and their organizations, but also will be better equipped to add value to our work.

It is also essential, of course, for humans to develop a strong understanding of AI, its capabilities, challenges, and even where it may threaten human organizations or society. This increased understanding will come from in-depth interactions with AI in design thinking endeavors, particularly as new challenges are faced and overcome. AI itself will also advance, of course, with the likelihood of becoming more user-friendly for humans. For instance, AI developers are creating explanatory AI to mediate interactions among humans and more complex AI programs. Such efforts will in turn increase the knowledge of and trust in our digital counterparts, develop mental models that support relationships allowing AI to contribute significantly to human challenges, both large and small.

While our focus in this book is on offering tools and perspectives to improve the relationship between AI and humans to produce innovation, we recognize that there are other important considerations for people and societies as AI increasingly moves into our work and our lives. We remain cautiously optimistic that AI will be a great boon to our world, particularly if we invest the necessary time and resources into building a successful human-AI relationship.

Summary

In this book we have explored how innovators can successfully utilize AI as an integral part of the design thinking process. AI is not the holy grail, but it is able to help us design better products and services. It is up to the organizations and individuals to adapt to this new situation. We hope this book provides a first glimpse on how to use AI. AI is advancing as you read this book and some of the content might not be fully applicable. We will be running a website **ai-designthinking.com** to highlight the most recent developments and adjust to the changing environment. Best of luck in bringing the power of AI into your design processes - let's design together!

Appendix 1

AI Assistants in Design Thinking

In a world where creative work and technology increasingly intersect, AI assistants have emerged as powerful collaborators in design thinking. Designers and innovators are now partnering with chatbots, generative models, and intelligent tools to brainstorm ideas, create visuals, test concepts, and even write code. This appendix provides a comprehensive look at how AI assistants augment design thinking work. We'll begin with an overview of what AI assistants are, how they function (especially in creative contexts), and why they are valuable. Next, we'll explore specific applications across various design thinking activities, from UX research and prototyping to graphic design, mood boards, interior design, and collaborative workshops, highlighting AI tools like ChatGPT, Midjourney, Galileo AI, Synthetic Users, FigJam's AI, and more. Finally, we'll dive into how designers and innovators can extend these programs or build their own AI assistants, with accessible code examples (using platforms like OpenAI, Figma's plugin API, LangChain, and others) and guidance for those with limited programming background. Throughout, technical concepts will be explained clearly, with examples and best practices to ensure you can harness AI assistants effectively in your design practice. Let's get started!

Understanding AI Assistants in Design

At their core, AI assistants are software agents powered by AI that can perform tasks or provide support through natural language interactions. In everyday life, classic examples include Siri, Google Assistant, and Alexa—tools that respond to voice commands to set reminders or answer questions, as outlined on the Higher Logic website, as accessed in 2025. In the context of design and creative work, AI assistants take on more specialized roles: they might brainstorm concepts with you, generate a draft

© The Editor(s) (if applicable) and The Author(s), under exclusive license
to Springer Nature Switzerland AG 2026

D. Graff et al., *Design Thinking with Artificial Intelligence*, Palgrave Executive Essentials,
https://doi.org/10.1007/978-3-032-10543-1

layout or image, critique a design, or simulate a user's feedback. Unlike traditional software that follows fixed rules, modern AI assistants often use large neural network models to understand user requests and generate appropriate responses or outputs.

Most AI design assistants today are built on foundation models—very large machine learning models trained on enormous datasets. A prominent subset of these are LLMs, which specialize in understanding and generating text. LLMs like OpenAI's GPT-4 or Google's LaMDA have billions of parameters and have learned patterns from books, articles, and web content. For visual tasks, generative AI models come into play. Image-generating assistants (like Midjourney or DALL-E) are often based on diffusion models. Diffusion models create new images by essentially adding and removing noise in a learned manner—they start with random noise and gradually refine it into a coherent image that matches a text prompt (as on the SuperAnnotate website in 2023). Famous tools such as DALL-E 2, Midjourney, and Stable Diffusion use this approach to produce high-quality visuals from text descriptions. For instance, if a designer or innovator types "a surreal landscape in the style of Salvador Dalí", a diffusion-based AI will iteratively paint an image that fits that description. Some AI assistants are multimodal, meaning they can handle more than one type of input/output. A multimodal assistant might accept both images and text, for example, GPT-4's newer version can analyze an image you upload and discuss it with you. This opens new possibilities like feeding an AI assistant a design mockup image and asking for feedback or improvements.

Types of AI Assistants for Designers. Not all AI assistants are alike—they come in several flavors; each suited to different tasks:

Conversational Chatbots: These are AI assistants you interact with via text or voice in a dialogue format. ChatGPT is a prime example—designers can "chat" with it to brainstorm user personas, get writing help for UX copy, or troubleshoot a tricky design problem. Similarly, Microsoft's GitHub Copilot, though focused on code, acts as a conversational assistant within your editor, suggesting code snippets or answering technical questions. Conversational assistants rely on LLMs and excel at ideation, Q&A, and guidance in natural language.

Generative Design Tools: This category includes AI that directly generates design artifacts from images and illustrations to layouts and code. Image generators like Midjourney or Stable Diffusion-based tools fall here, as do UI-focused tools like Galileo AI or Uizard. They take creative prompts (text descriptions, sketches, etc.) and output a design proposal (an image, a UI mockup, a color palette, etc.). These assistants often use a combination of computer vision and language models to interpret input and produce visual output. They serve as on-demand creators, giving designers instant drafts to work with.

Feedback and Analysis Engines: Some AI assistants specialize in evaluating or simulating aspects of design. They might analyze a design and predict user reactions, check accessibility, or simulate a user research session. For example, the Synthetic Users tool generates artificial user personas and interview transcripts to mimic how real users might respond to a product idea. It uses LLMs to create these profiles and multi-agent simulations to have them "interact" and produce insights (such as seen on SyntheticUsers.com). Other analysis assistants include things like Attention Insight, which predicts where a user's gaze will go on a layout by outputting heatmaps (using computer vision models). There are also sentiment analysis tools (e.g., MonkeyLearn) that can read through user feedback text and quickly gauge overall sentiment or highlight common pain points. These AI act as tireless analysts, giving designers rapid feedback or preliminary research findings.

Autonomous Agents: A newer, more experimental breed of AI programs are agents like AutoGPT or design workflow "agents". Unlike standard assistants that act only when prompted, agents can take initiative and perform multi-step tasks autonomously. In design, an AI agent could hypothetically be told a goal—"Create a logo for X and get feedback"—and then it would generate options, critique them, refine, maybe even A/B test them with simulated users, all with minimal human input. This is still a nascent area; for the scope of this chapter, we focus on the assistive tools that work with design thinkers rather than entirely on their behalf. But it's worth noting the distinction: AI assistants are generally reactive (they do tasks when asked) whereas AI agents aim to be proactive (pursuing goals on their own).

Value of AI Assistants to Designers and Innovators

The appeal of AI assistants in design lies in augmentation—they extend a designer thinker's capabilities rather than replace them. Here are some key benefits these assistants offer to the creative process:

Idea Generation and Breaking Creative Blocks: Blank canvases can be daunting. AI assistants spark ideas by suggesting variations or generating quick sketches, offering fresh perspectives drawn from vast training data. A UX designer, for instance, can prompt ChatGPT for new user flows or edge cases, expanding exploration within seconds.

Speed and Efficiency: Work that once took hours can now take minutes. An image model can instantly generate poster thumbnails, while an NLP tool quickly summarizes survey responses. By automating rote tasks—slicing assets, writing code, resizing images—AI frees designers to focus on higher-level choices. As one UX blog noted in 2024, today's tools can even "generate polished UI designs in seconds." The workflow becomes leaner, with less drudge work and more creativity.

Augmenting Skillsets: Few designers excel across disciplines. AI fills gaps: a visual designer can turn mockups into HTML/CSS with a coding assistant, while a UX designer without illustration skills can generate icons or images with Midjourney or Canva. These tools function like a versatile team—covering writing, drawing, coding, and analysis—so individuals achieve results once needing larger groups.

Exploration of Alternatives: Good design relies on comparing options. AI makes this easy: request playful variations of hero text or new color palettes to iterate quickly. This process prevents teams from settling too soon and sparks stakeholder discussion with multiple AI-generated directions.

No-Code or Low-Code Creation: AI also increases accessibility with no-code interfaces. Galileo AI lets users generate UIs through text prompts, while FigJam's Jambot sorts sticky notes by theme. By turning natural language into tangible outputs, AI empowers nontechnical team members to contribute meaningfully without design or coding expertise.

Applications of AI Assistants in Design Thinking

AI assistants have permeated virtually every subfield of design thinking, acting as collaborators in tasks ranging from research to prototyping. In this section, we'll tour through specific applications in user research, ideation and mood boards, design and prototyping, and even design thinking facilitation. For each, we'll highlight real tools in use today, along with their strengths, limitations, and use cases. This will give you a panorama of what's currently possible when you pair AI assistants with human creativity.

AI Assistant in User Research and User Testing

Generating User Insights with "Synthetic" Participants: One of the more controversial yet intriguing applications of AI is the creation of synthetic users—AI-generated personas that can participate in faux interviews or tests. A platform aptly named Synthetic Users allows researchers to input a target user profile and research goal, and then it spins up multiple AI-driven "users" who produce interview transcripts and feedback as if they were real, as discussed by a Nielsen Norman Group article in 2023 about synthetic users. For example, if you're designing a new app, you could specify that user group and ask Synthetic Users to interview them about their daily challenges. Within seconds, you might get several simulated interview transcripts complete with the AI users' names, ages, backgrounds, and their responses to questions—essentially an instant focus group. These AI personas are powered by LLMs that have digested vast information about people's behaviors and attitudes, enabling them to mimic realistic responses. The cofounder of Synthetic Users noted it's useful when teams need very quick feedback to guide decisions and "absolute certainty isn't required." We captured explorative AI to AI interviews in our AID tool section (Chapter 7: Empathize & Define).

The obvious upside is speed and cost—AI users are available 24/7, and you don't have to recruit or incentivize them. They can be used for early-stage desk research to generate hypotheses. For instance, designers and innovators might use synthetic users to brainstorm potential pain points in a domain before conducting real user interviews, just to explore the landscape of possible answers. The limitations, however, are crucial to acknowledge. Research professionals warn that synthetic feedback often lacks the depth and unpredictability of real human responses. AI users may give shallow or overly positive feedback, since they lack genuine emotion and risk-aversion that real users have. Therefore, synthetic users can supplement user research but cannot replace it. They are best used in the initial stage of research to identify potential users and during initial testing, but not for final validation. When used responsibly (e.g. to supplement early research or fill gaps where doing some research is impossible), these AI assistants can "democratize access to qualitative research" according to SyntheticUsers.com, by lowering cost and skill barriers.

Another area wherein AI assists user research is making sense of large data. User research can involve surveys, open-ended feedback forms, usability session notes, and so on. NLP-based assistants can rapidly analyze these text corpora. For example, the program MonkeyLearn offers AI-powered sentiment analysis, if it is fed thousands of user feedback comments, it will tag each as positive, negative, or neutral, and even classify them by topic. This gives designers a quick pulse of what users like or dislike about a product. Similarly, one could use a general LLM like ChatGPT to summarize a long user interview or find key themes across multiple interviews by providing them as input (with caution on data privacy, of course). The benefit here is efficiency: what might take a researcher days of coding qualitative data, an AI might do in minutes, providing a draft summary or initial clustering of themes.

Some user researchers are also experimenting with AI to generate hypotheses or interpret analytics. For instance, feeding a web analytics report to a chatbot and asking, "What are possible reasons for the drop in conversion on page X?" might yield some sensible theories drawn from the AI's knowledge of user behavior patterns. There's even an AI tool called Neurons claims to predict user responses by analyzing visual stimuli—effectively using cognitive science models to foresee where users might be confused or engaged in a design. Neurons can simulate metrics like cognitive load or emotional impact of a design, providing "advanced behavior analytics" to guide designers on more user-centric paths.

An emerging use-case is employing AI as a stand-in for an expert to critique your design. Imagine you don't have another colleague ready to review your work—could an AI give you pointers? It turns out, yes, to some extent. Designers and Innovators can carefully describe a design to ChatGPT (or even uploading visuals to GPT-4 Vision) and receive valuable feedback. In one case, a designer named Guzman compared two versions of a webpage (old vs. redesign) by exporting them as PDF images and asking ChatGPT to evaluate the differences objectively, as he reported in a 2023 article. The AI responded with an analysis of each version's visual hierarchy, clarity, and emotional appeal, noting which design had a stronger call-to-action and more trustworthy look. It pointed out, for example, that the new design had a clearer visual rhythm and better focus on user needs compared to the older one. Essentially, it performed a heuristic review, referencing design principles it "knows." The designer already had A/B test data showing the new design performed better, and ChatGPT's evaluation aligned with those results; a validating moment. This kind of AI critique can be helpful to catch obvious issues or to get a fresh "pair of eyes," especially for solo designers. However, AI is not infallible in critique: it might miss context or overemphasize certain aesthetic rules (and of course, it has no real sense of users' emotional responses beyond learned patterns). So, treat AI feedback as you would a novice designer's opinion—useful, but to be weighed against your own judgment and, ideally, user feedback.

AI for Ideation and Mood Boards

When starting a new design thinking project or exploring a creative direction, brainstorming is key. AI chatbots like ChatGPT have proven to be excellent collaborators in brainstorming. You can fire off prompts like *"Give me 10 out-of-the-box ideas for a smartwatch app"* or *"What are some metaphors I can use in a campaign for eco-friendly packaging?"* and get a flurry of ideas in return. The value here is quantity and unpredictability—the AI might generate ideas that designers and innovators wouldn't think of, simply because it draws from a vast and eclectic knowledge base (everything from sci-fi novels to obscure Wikipedia pages could be lurking in its training data). For instance, a brand designer could ask an AI assistant for theme ideas around a concept (say, "imagine branding for a cafe that's also a bookstore") and receive suggestions like "Literary Lattes", "StoryBrew" with book-themed decor, etc., which might jump-start a concept board. Design thinking teams can integrate such AI programs into live workshops: programs like FigJam's Jambot allow everyone in a meeting to see AI-generated ideas pop up on sticky notes, which can then be discussed and refined. The AI essentially acts as an infinite idea generator in the room.

There is also a trend of custom-tailoring chatbots for specific creative tasks. OpenAI's ChatGPT (as of its 2024 update) introduced Custom GPTs, where you can train a bot with specific examples or instructions. Designers and innovators like Jacob Cass have used this to create bots specialized in branding and moodboarding. For example, Cass's team built a Brand Bot that is "an expert in branding, marketing strategies, and design" as reported by Designity in 2024. This bot not only answers questions but can also generate visual ideas using DALL-E.

They also made a Moodboard Maker GPT, designed to help create mood boards by generating ideas for logos, color palettes, typography, etc., all via chat prompts. Mood boards—those collages of images, textures, colors, and typography that convey a design direction—are a staple in early-phase design. Traditionally, making a mood board involves searching for inspiration images (on Pinterest, Behance, Google, etc.), curating and clipping them, and arranging them in a board to tell a visual story. It's enjoyable but time-consuming. AI is now turbocharging this process. You might type a request like *"Show me ideas for a vintage-looking logo and color scheme for a craft coffee brand"*, and Moodboard Maker will output descriptions and even AI-generated images via DALL-E 3 (Designity, 2024). Because it's a custom GPT, it has been primed with knowledge of branding elements and likely uses predefined prompt templates behind the scenes to give structured output (e.g., always providing a set of images plus a rationale for each). The result is a conversational tool that feels like a design thinking savvy colleague brainstorming with you, rather than a generic AI. This demonstrates how we can specialize AI assistants for creative ideation in particular niches.

Another approach in creating a mood board is using image generation models to directly produce concept images for a mood board. Instead of scouring the web for a "loft style interior with natural light and modern furniture," a designer or innovator can simply ask a tool like Midjourney or Stable Diffusion to create one. In seconds, you have a bespoke image that matches your vision, and you can generate variations of it with tweaks to the prompt (e.g., "now make it moodier with evening lighting"). Do this for a handful of aspects—one for color vibe, one for typography, one for key imagery—and you have the raw material for a mood board without ever leaving your desk or worrying about image usage rights (since these are newly generated). Of course, it's wise to also include real-world references for realism and diversity, but AI fills in gaps or produces exactly the kind of filler image you might have spent hours hunting for.

Beyond individual images, specialized AI programs attempt to assemble entire mood boards. One such tool is called Kive AI, which can take a textual mood description and pull together a board of stock images automatically, using AI to interpret the theme. Meanwhile, mainstream design thinking apps are adding AI features: Adobe Express (Adobe's easy design tool) has introduced generative features where you can type something like "summer beach color palette" or "retro collage style template" and it will generate a starting layout or set of assets matching that description. Similarly, Canva's Magic Design is an AI-powered feature that lets you upload any media (like a reference image or your own sketch) and it will generate a refined template out of it, which is essentially making a mini mood board or design concept for you. These tools leverage both generative AI and large libraries of content: they might pull relevant icons, apply complementary color schemes, and suggest font pairings—tasks that usually rely on a designer's trained eye, now done in moments by AI.

The advantages are clear: speed and breadth. A process that might have taken a full day (or several)—collecting dozens of inspiration pieces and trying combinations— can be condensed significantly. A designer or innovator can explore many more directions in the same amount of time. This is great for client work where you want to present a few distinct style directions; AI can help you mockup boards for each style quickly, which you then curate and polish. It also benefits less experienced designers or innovators who might not have a mental archive of design references - the AI can surface ideas from across eras and domains, acting as a visual search engine with creative interpretation.

AI-generated images for mood boards can sometimes be too polished or literal, which might prematurely lock a direction. Also, these models may reflect biases present in their training data (for example, generating stereotypical imagery for certain themes), so a critical eye is needed to select what truly aligns with the intended mood and audience. Additionally, with programs that automatically create mood boards, there's a risk of everyone using the same AI sources and converging on similar styles, potentially reducing originality. To mitigate that, designers and innovators should use AI output as a starting point and then mix in unique or personal sources of inspiration. Think of AI as your mood board intern gathering scraps—you as the lead designer or innovator still decide what goes on the board and what story it tells.

AI Assistant in Prototyping

One of the most jaw-dropping applications of AI for many designers and innovators is the ability to generate interface designs from simple text prompts. Tools like Galileo AI and Uizard are pioneers in this space. With Galileo AI, you just describe your envisioned interface in words—for example, "a mobile app onboarding screen for a travel planner, with an illustration and sign-up form"—and the AI will produce a high-fidelity mockup of that screen, according to the UX Design Institute in 2024. Galileo's output isn't a mere static image; it generates editable designs, often providing them in a format you can directly import into Figma or similar tools. In essence, it's as if you typed requirements to a very fast UI designer who then handed you a Sketch/Figma file with layers and components you can tweak. Uizard works similarly: it can convert hand-drawn sketches into wireframes, or even take screenshots of existing apps and turn them into editable designs. It also allows text prompts to generate new screens using pre-built components. Visily is another program in this family, offering AI-generated wireframes and the ability to go from scribble to mockup, complete with suggested themes and stock images.

The benefit is rapid prototyping. Instead of laboring over a wireframe for an hour, a designer can get a first draft in seconds and then spend their time refining or correcting it. This can be especially useful in early design sprints or hackathons, where speed is essential. It also democratizes UI drafting—innovators and other non-designers could whip up an interface idea using AI and have something tangible to discuss with users or stakeholders, rather than sticking to abstract spec documents. For example, Galileo AI can be used by a UX researcher with no visual design background to mockup an idea that emerged in user interviews, just to validate the concept layout. The researcher might say, "Show a dashboard with a graph of spending and a list of recent transactions below it," and Galileo will generate a plausible dashboard screen with those elements. The researcher can then show this to users, gather feedback on the concept, and hand it off to a UI designer for polishing later. This way, AI-generated UIs serve as a bridge between ideas and tangible prototypes.

Many innovators also use AI coding assistants (like ChatGPT, GitHub Copilot, or Replit's Ghostwriter) to help build interactive prototypes or design integrations. If you know a bit of HTML/CSS or JavaScript but you are not an expert, an AI assistant can fill in the gaps. For instance, you can ask ChatGPT, *"How do I create a responsive grid of images in HTML/CSS that looks like this wireframe?"* and paste a description of your layout. It will output code for you, often with explanations. Even within traditional design software: Figma has plugins (like DesignerBot or Magician) that use GPT-3 to generate code snippets or content. Designers who use Webflow (a no-code web design tool) leverage AI to write custom code for interactions or adapt scripts by just describing what they need (e.g. "make this button jiggle on hover").

What this means is that turning a static design into a working prototype is faster and less daunting. A UI/UX designer can focus on the user experience and visuals, and then in the prototyping phase, delegate some coding tasks to the AI. This is particularly empowering for designers who don't have a front-end developer available—the AI becomes your on-demand developer for simple to moderately complex tasks.

AI-generated designs are impressive, but they often follow conventions closely. That's both a strength and a weakness. On one hand, AI has effectively ingested countless good design examples, so it tends to produce something UI-compliant (common layout patterns, standard spacing, appropriate iconography). This can reinforce best practices and save you from beginner mistakes. On the other hand, AI might not venture into highly creative or novel design territories—it averages out what it has seen. The outputs can look somewhat "generic" or homogeneous if used raw. For example, many Galileo AI samples have a similar style of modern flat design, which is great for a clean start but might lack unique character. Designers should view these generated UIs as scaffolding—a base that they will imbue with brand personality and refined details.

Tied to design is the use of AI for evaluating those designs. We touched on predictive analytics like Attention Insight, which provides AI-generated heatmaps and a "clarity score" for designs. This kind of assistant can take your uploaded screen design and output a heatmap indicating which areas are likely to draw attention in the first few seconds of viewing. It uses algorithms trained on data from many users (or based on models of human vision) to simulate this. The clarity score might tell you how intuitive your layout is compared to industry benchmarks, according to the UX Design Institute in 2024. Essentially, it's an AI doing a heuristic usability evaluation. As the UXDI article wisely noted, this shouldn't replace actual user testing, but it can act as an "additional round of testing and validation" to refine designs before investing in full user studies. For a solo designer or small startup without a UX research team, such AI programs provide some quick feedback that's better than designing in a vacuum.

AI Assistants in Design Thinking Facilitation

Design thinking is often a team sport. Brainstorming workshops, design sprints, and co-creation sessions are commonplace in design thinking teams. AI has found a role here as well, by acting as a kind of facilitator or booster for group activities.

Two popular digital whiteboard tools - Figma's FigJam and Miro - have integrated AI assistants to help with common workshop tasks. FigJam's AI features can generate entire board templates based on a prompt. If you're about to run a collaborative session, you can literally ask FigJam AI, "*Set up a weekly team sync board with an icebreaker section, discussion area, and next steps,*" and it will populate the whiteboard with sticky note sections and guiding text. This saves time in prep and ensures you're following best practices (the built-in prompts are "inspired by common use cases" and "best practices" for meetings). So even an inexperienced facilitator gets a well-structured starting point.

During the workshop, FigJam AI can step in to do the tedious bits: say everyone has thrown up 50 sticky notes of ideas. Instead of manually sorting these, you can select them and hit "Sort with AI", and FigJam will categorize them into groups for you. Similarly, you can ask it to summarize a cluster of stickies into a concise take-away. This is like having a co-facilitator who quickly tidies up the whiteboard while you focus on guiding discussion. The Jambot we mentioned is essentially ChatGPT inside FigJam—you can type questions to it during a session. For example, in a brain-storming session if people get stuck, you might ask Jambot, "What are some wild ideas we haven't considered for improving online checkout?" and it will generate a few suggestions as additional stickies. It can even inject a bit of fun (like icebreaker questions or trivia) on the fly.

Miro's AI has parallel features. It can summarize clusters of text, generate ideas on sticky notes when given a prompt, and auto-organize content. A UX Collective review compared the two: Miro's AI was found to excel at generating a broad list of ideas on a topic, while FigJam's AI excelled at providing a more structured output and deeper follow-up detail, according to Lenglemetz's 2023 article comparing them. For example, given the prompt to suggest team-building activities, Miro spit out 15 diverse ideas (like "volunteer day, escape room, cook-ing class" etc.) which is great for range. FigJam, on the other hand, responded by outlining an entire workshop structure for a specific activity (like how to run an escape room challenge with an intro, the challenge, and a debrief). Each AI has its style: Miro's like a fountain of raw ideas; FigJam's like an organizer that frames the ideas into a plan.

When it came to clustering stickies, the same review noted Miro did it flawlessly, cleanly grouping related items, whereas FigJam struggled a bit—hilariously misclas-sifying a sticky note that said "cat" under a furniture category and "banana" under colors. This shows that AI isn't perfect, but even if it does 90% of the sorting right, it's easier to fix the few oddballs than to sort everything manually from scratch. And these systems will improve rapidly as they get user feedback and better training.

In a fast-paced design sprint, time saved is gold. If AI can shave off minutes every hour by cleaning up boards, generating summaries, or providing prompts, that adds up. It keeps the momentum. Also, not everyone in a workshop is equally comfortable contributing spontaneously; an AI can fill the void if participants are quiet, offering something to react to. It's like having an infinite sticky note generator that you can tap when the room goes silent: "The AI suggests maybe exploring a 'game-ified on-boarding'. What do we think of that?"

AI can also help with documentation. After a workshop, you could ask the AI to compile the key ideas and next steps (based on the board content) into a re-port. Instead of someone spending an hour writing up notes, the AI draft can be the starting point, which the facilitator then edits for accuracy. This means teams can move from ideation to execution faster, because the synthesis step is accelerated.

Extending and Building Your Own AI Design Assistants

After exploring all these tools, you might be wondering: can I create something like this myself? What if you want a very specific AI assistant—say, one that knows your company's brand guidelines and can generate on-brand copy, or a plugin that brings AI into your favorite design software? The good news is that many AI services are accessible via application programming interfaces (APIs) and that there are frameworks and platforms to help build custom AI-powered assistants with relatively little code. In this section, we provide guidance on extending AI assistants or building your own, with an emphasis on approaches that are friendly to designers and innovators who may not have a deep coding background. We'll include a couple of example code snippets (in Python and JavaScript) to illustrate how it works in practice, and discuss platforms like OpenAI, LangChain, Replicate, and how to integrate AI into environments like Figma.

Using AI APIs: Quick Start with an Example

One of the most straightforward ways to build a custom AI assistant is to use an API from a cloud AI provider. OpenAI, for example, offers APIs for their models (GPT-3.5, GPT-4, DALL-E, etc.), and many other providers exist for different modalities (e.g., Stability AI for Stable Diffusion images, or AssemblyAI for speech-to-text). Using an API typically means you send a request over the internet with your input (prompt) and parameters, and the service returns the AI's output (completion, image URL, etc.).

Integrating GPT into Design Tools (Figma Plugin Example)

Maybe you want the power of AI right inside your design software, so you don't have to switch contexts. Many modern design tools have plugin ecosystems that allow developers to add functionality. Figma is a great example—it has a robust plugin API where you can write JavaScript code to create custom panels, manipulate the canvas, etc. Designers have built Figma plugins for tasks like populating dummy data, checking accessibility, and now, integrating AI.

```
// This code would be in the main logic file of a Figma plugin
(e.g., code.ts)
```

```javascript
// --- Plugin UI to Plugin Logic Communication ---
// The UI part of the plugin (HTML/JS) would send a message to
this main logic file.
figma.ui.onmessage = msg =&gt; {
  if (msg.type === 'generate-copy') {
   const selectedNode = figma.currentPage.selection[0];

   if (selectedNode && selectedNode.type === "TEXT") {
      // Show a notification to the user that generation has started
      figma.notify("AI is thinking...", { timeout: 2000 });

      // Call the function to get suggestions from the AI
      generateCopySuggestions(selectedNode.id, msg.description);
   } else {
   figma.notify("Please select a text layer first.", b2
   { error: true });
   }
  }
 };
// --- Function to Call the OpenAI API ---
async function generateCopySuggestions(nodeId, description) {
    const prompt = `You are an expert AI UX writer. Suggest three
    concise and compelling text options for the following ele-
    ment: ${description}. Return the result as a numbered list.`;

try {
  // The API call itself happens in the UI thread of the plugin to
  avoid freezing the main thread
  figma.ui.postMessage({
    type: 'call-openai-api',
    prompt: prompt
  });

  // The response from the API will be sent back from the UI thread

  // and handled by another 'onmessage' event handler that updates
the text node.

  } catch (error) {
  console.error("API Call Error:", error);
  figma.notify("Failed to get suggestions from AI.", { error: true });
  }
}
```

```
// In the UI code (e.g., ui.html with a &lt;script&gt; tag):
/*
&lt;script&gt;
 window.onmessage = async (event) =&gt; {
  const msg = event.data.pluginMessage;
  if (msg.type === 'call-openai-api') {
   const OPENAI_API_KEY = "YOUR_OPENAI_API_KEY"; // Key should be
   securely stored
   const response = await fetch("https://api.openai.com/v1/chat/
   completions", {
   method: "POST",
   headers: {
    "Content-Type": "application/json",
    "Authorization": `Bearer ${OPENAI_API_KEY}`
   },
    body: JSON.stringify({
    model: "gpt-4o",
    messages: [{ role: "user", content: msg.prompt }],
    max_tokens: 100
   })
  });
  const data = await response.json();
  const suggestions = data.choices[0].message.content;
  // Notify the user with the suggestions
  parent.postMessage({ pluginMessage: { type: 'display-
  suggestions', content: suggestions } }, '*');
 }
}
&lt;/script&gt;
*/
```

Prompt Templates and Workflows (Advanced Customization)

As you use AI more, you may find yourself reusing certain prompt patterns or wanting the AI to maintain context across multiple interactions. This is where frameworks like LangChain come in handy. LangChain (in Python and JavaScript) is a library that helps chain together multiple AI calls and manage context, memory, or tool usage. It's slightly more technical, but worth mentioning. For example, you could use LangChain to build an AI agent that, when asked a design question, will also search a design knowledge base before answering (this is retrieval augmented generation). Or a chain that first translates a prompt into a more detailed prompt for an image model, then calls the image API, then describes the image output—effectively creating a loop that yields an image with a caption.

Prompt templates are simpler: they let you define a general prompt with placeholders that you fill in. You might define a template like: "You are a helpful design tutor. The user provided this design scenario: "{scenario}". Give a step-by-step critique focusing on usability and aesthetics." Then every time you want a critique, you just plug in the scenario description. This ensures consistency in how you ask things, which can lead to more reliable outputs. You can implement this without any library—even with basic string formatting in code or using tools like the ChatGPT custom instructions feature. But if you build a tool for others, using LangChain's PromptTemplate ensures you don't accidentally prompt wrong.

```
.import openai
# It is recommended to set your API key as an environment variable
for security
# but you can also set it directly in the code.
# openai.api_key = "YOUR_OPENAI_API_KEY"
# Define the prompt for the AI assistant

prompt = "You are a branding assistant. Generate three unique logo
concept ideas for a cafe named 'Java Haven' that highlight its
cozy atmosphere and coffee theme."

try:
 response = openai.ChatCompletion.create(
  model="gpt-4o", # Using a modern and capable model
  messages=[
    {"role": "system", "content": "You are a helpful design assis-
    tant specialized in branding."},
    {"role": "user", "content": prompt}
  ]
 )
 ideas = response['choices'][0]['message']['content']
 print("AI Suggestions for Logos:\n")
 print(ideas)

except openai.error.OpenAIError as e:
 print(f"An error occurred: {e}")
```

Mentioning Replicate—it's a service that hosts many open-source models behind a simple API. If you wanted to incorporate image generation without relying on, say, Midjourney's closed system, you could use Replicate's API to call Stable Diffusion or other models.

For non-coders, companies are starting to offer no-code AI integration tools. For instance, Zapier (an automation tool) has OpenAI integration that enables a user to set up a workflow like "When I add a new feedback form entry in Google Sheets, send it to OpenAI to summarize, then email me the summary." This doesn't require writing code, just configuring blocks. Designers who are comfortable with automation tools can leverage these to create custom AI-assisted pipelines without writing code, though the flexibility is a bit less than coding from scratch.

Making AI Assistants Designer-Friendly

When building or extending an AI assistant, keep in mind the end-user (which might be yourself or your design colleagues). Aim for interfaces that hide the complexity. For example, you might build a small web app that has a text box "Describe what you need" and a dropdown "Choose AI helper (ideas, critique, image, code)"—behind the scenes it routes to different prompts and APIs, but to the user it's just a helpful form. This could even be done in something like a Google Sheet with macros or a Notion AI integration.

Key platforms/libraries to know:

OpenAI API/Azure AI: for GPT models, very popular and well-documented.

Hugging Face Transformers: open-source models, if you ever want to run something locally (might require more setup).

LangChain: great for making more complex applications (chatbots with memory, using external tools like search or knowledge bases).

Replicate: handy for image and other modality models via API (no need to set up your own GPU server).

Node.js and Browser JS: if integrating into web apps or extensions, you'll likely use JavaScript/TypeScript. Libraries like Axios (for HTTP requests, which allows software to communicate with web services - the universal way to connect to online tools that don't have pre-built integrations.) and the fetch Application Programmer Interface (API) are your friends for calling AI.

Figma Plugin API/Adobe UXP: for integrating into design software specifically. Adobe's UXP is the framework for Photoshop/Illustrator plugins (which now can access their AI features too).

Python scientific stack: If doing data analysis or custom training, Python has libraries like Pandas, or PyTorch/TensorFlow if one day you venture into training your own small models (for instance, training a custom image model on your company's product images to generate on-brand visuals).

If all this sounds overwhelming, remember you can start small. Even copying the earlier Python script and running it (with your own API key) is a big step that might only take a few minutes to try. There are also communities (like the AI x Design community, or forums on GitHub, Stack Overflow) where people share code and help each other build these tools. You don't have to reinvent the wheel—many open-source projects exist that you can fork or modify. For example, someone may have open-sourced a basic Figma GPT plugin; you could modify the prompts it uses to better suit your use case.

Some AI models allow you to fine-tune them on your own data. For instance, OpenAI allows fine-tuning certain models on custom text data. A practical design example: you could fine-tune an AI on your company's past marketing copies and brand tone guidelines. Then you have an API endpoint that produces on-brand copy more reliably than the generic model. This is a bit more advanced (and costs extra), but it's a way to extend AI so it knows your specific needs. Alternatively, techniques like few-shot prompting (giving the model some examples each time) can achieve a similar effect without actual retraining.

Empowering Designers with Extensible AI

Building or extending AI assistants might initially seem like the realm of engineers, but as we've outlined, there are many entry points for designers and innovators. The barrier to experimenting is lower than ever—often just an API key and a few lines of script. By tailoring your own AI programs, you can create assistants that fit your exact workflow, whether that's a Slack bot that critiques your drafts, a plugin that fills your wireframes with realistic content, or a standalone app that generates custom visuals for your design system.

The key is to start with a clear problem or use-case: "I spend too much time doing X—can an AI help me do that faster?" Chances are, if it involves generating or analyzing text or images, the answer is yes. From there, you can prototype a solution using the approaches we discussed. It's okay if the first version is hacky—maybe it's a manual script you run occasionally. Over time, you can refine it into a polished tool.

Remember to consider ethics and quality when building AI assistants. If integrating into professional workflows, test them thoroughly. AI can produce wrong or biased outputs, so build in review steps. For example, if your AI assistant generates accessibility suggestions, have a human verify them before implementation. When extending AI, also ensure you are respecting user data privacy (e.g., don't inadvertently send sensitive data to an API without checking policies).

By embracing a bit of code and customization, designers can not only use AI tools but help shape the next generation of them. We are at an exciting point where design and AI technology intersect—design sensibilities are needed to humanize and direct these powerful algorithms, and who better than designers themselves to craft the experience of AI assistance?

Summary

AI assistants are poised to become an integral part of design thinking work—not as replacements for human designers, but as highly capable partners. They bring speed, breadth, and "remix" abilities that complement our human strengths of judgment, empathy, and creativity. From brainstorming ideas in a chat, to generating visuals and code, to automating tedious tasks and providing smart analyses, they help us focus on what we do best: understanding users and crafting delightful solutions for them. As you continue in your design thinking journey, consider your AI assistant not just as a tool, but as a collaborator of your creative team—one that, with your guidance, can elevate your work to new heights.

References

Designity. (2024). Using AI to create mood boards: A Jacob Cass design workshop. Designity. https://www.designity.com/blog/using-ai-to-create-mood-boards-a-jacob-cass-design-workshop.

Guzman, R. (2023, March 13). How I used ChatGPT to critique my own UX work (and it worked). Bootcamp, Medium. https://medium.com/design-bootcamp/how-i-used-chatgpt-to-critique-my-own-ux-work-and-it-worked-9854b6688de9.

Lenglemetz, A. (2023, December 14). Miro vs. FigJam: How their AI assistants stack up. UX Collective. https://uxdesign.cc/miro-vs-figjam-how-their-ai-assistants-stack-up-a6ac0b9d5385.

Nielsen Norman Group. (2023, December 10). Synthetic users: If, when, and how to use AI-generated "research". Nielsen Norman Group. https://www.nngroup.com/articles/synthetic-users/.

SuperAnnotate. (2023, June 28). Introduction to diffusion models for machine learning. SuperAnnotate. https://www.superannotate.com/blog/diffusion-models.

UX Design Institute. (2024, April 25). The top 8 AI tools for UX design (and how to use them). UX Design Institute. https://www.uxdesigninstitute.com/blog/the-top-8-ai-tools-for-ux/.

Appendix 2

AI Resources for Design

In this section you will find the list of AI programs used in this book. For easy use, we separated them into the activity in which we would use them: Prepare & Train, Empathize & Define, Ideate & Select, Prototype & Test, and Implement & Learn. In total, we have listed 113 unique AI programs which can help designers and innovators in design thinking.

Please note that these programs are changing rapidly. When you are reading this book, some of these tools might not exist anymore, others changed to do something else, and others might not be even included in this list. While we will update AI resources when we can on our book website, **ai-designthinking.com**, you should look at this list as a starting point or foundation for your own AI resources. Please think about updating it for your own needs! (This "AI Resources for Design" list was last updated in December 2025.)

Prepare & Train

1. **AlphaSense** (https://www.alpha-sense.com/): market-intelligence search with gen-AI research/reporting.
2. **ChatGPT (GPT-5)** (https://openai.com/gpt-5/): OpenAI's flagship assistant using GPT-5 for deep reasoning, coding, and writing. GPT-5 has evolved to GPT-5.2 as of Dec 2025 (https://openai.com/index/introducing-gpt-5-2/).
3. **ClickUp Brain** (https://clickup.com/brain): workspace AI that connects your projects/docs/data to answer and act.
4. **Claude** (https://www.anthropic.com/claude): Anthropic's AI assistant for writing, coding, and analysis with long-context.

© The Editor(s) (if applicable) and The Author(s), under exclusive license
to Springer Nature Switzerland AG 2026

D. Graff et al., *Design Thinking with Artificial Intelligence*, Palgrave Executive Essentials,
https://doi.org/10.1007/978-3-032-10543-1

5. **Crayon** (https://www.crayon.co/): competitive-intelligence platform for tracking rivals and enabling sales.
6. **DALL·E** (https://openai.com/index/dall-e-3): OpenAI image generation/editing (DALL·E 3). In March 2025, DALL-E 3 was replaced in ChatGPT by "GPT Image" native image-generation capabilities.
7. **Evolv AI** (https://evolv.ai/): AI-led experimentation and digital journey optimization.
8. **GWI Spark** (https://www.gwi.com/platform/spark): AI market-research assistant over GWI's global survey data.
9. **Google Data Studio (Looker Studio)** (https://lookerstudio.google.com): free BI/dashboards with many connectors (rebranded from Data Studio).
10. **Helio** (https://helio.app/): rapid user-research surveys and insights for designers.
11. **IBM Watson Studio** (https://www.ibm.com/products/watson-studio): IDE to build, run, and manage AI/ML models (IBM Cloud Pak / watsonx ecosystem).
12. **Insight7** (https://insight7.io/): AI call/transcript analytics for customer insights and coaching.
13. **LogicGate** (https://www.logicgate.com/): GRC (Governance, Risk, and Compliance) platform with AI features (Spark AI, AI governance) to manage risk/compliance.
14. **Lucidchart with AI** (https://www.lucidchart.com/pages): diagramming with AI (generate, transform, and summarize diagrams).
15. **Midjourney** (https://www.midjourney.com/): independent AI image-generation platform.
16. **MonkeyLearn** (https://monkeylearn.com/): text analysis/classification SaaS (acquired by Medallia in 2022, https://www.medallia.com/platform/text-analytics/).
17. **N8N** (https://n8n.io/): a workflow automation platform that uniquely combines AI capabilities with business process automation.
18. **Notably AI** (https://www.notably.ai/): AI-powered research synthesis with templates, tagging, and insights.
19. **Palantir Foundry** (https://www.palantir.com/platforms/foundry/): enterprise data/operations platform with AI-driven analytics.
20. **Quantilope** (https://www.quantilope.com/): consumer-insights platform with automated/AI methods (e.g., quinn).
21. **Quid** (https://www.quid.com/): NetBase Quid's AI-powered market/consumer intelligence and modeling.
22. **RiskWatch** (https://www.riskwatch.com/): risk & compliance assessment software with standards libraries.
23. **Simply Stakeholders** (https://simplystakeholders.com/): stakeholder-relationship management with engagement, sentiment, and reporting.
24. **Tableau (AI & Einstein Discovery)** (https://www.tableau.com/products/artificial-intelligence): analytics with generative AI (Tableau AI) and Salesforce Einstein Discovery predictions.

25. **Trend Hunter AI** (https://www.trendhunter.ai/): AI-enhanced trends research and GPT tools for opportunity discovery.
26. **VWO** (https://vwo.com/): digital experience optimization and A/B testing suite.

Empathize & Define

1. **ATLAS.ti** (https://atlasti.com/): qualitative analysis software with built-in AI coding and chat.
2. **Atypica.ai** (https://atypica.ai/): AI research agent that simulates consumer personas and runs interviews.
3. **Browse AI** (https://www.browse.ai/): no-code web scraping & monitoring with robot templates.
4. **Canva Magic Write** (https://www.canva.com/magic-write/): AI writing inside Canva for docs/designs.
5. **ChatGPT (OpenAI)** (https://chatgpt.com/): general-purpose AI assistant for writing, coding, research.
6. **Claude (Anthropic)** (https://www.anthropic.com/claude): AI assistant for reasoning, coding, and analysis.
7. **Creately – AI Empathy Map Generator** (https://creately.com/usage/empathy-map-templates/): templates and AI prompts to draft empathy maps.
8. **Delve AI** (https://www.delve.ai/): generates data-driven customer personas from analytics and CRM.
9. **Dovetail** (https://dovetail.com/): research repository with AI features for insights from interviews & feedback.
10. **Expert.ai** (https://www.expert.ai/): semantic/NLP platform for entity, sentiment, and context analysis.
11. **FounderPal – AI User Persona Generator** (https://founderpal.ai/user-persona-generator): quick persona drafts with editable fields and examples.
12. **Hume AI** (https://www.hume.ai/): multimodal "empathic" voice AI and emotion signals (EVI).
13. **Insight7** (https://insight7.io/): analyzes interviews/surveys to surface themes and opportunities.
14. **Looppanel** (https://www.looppanel.com/): interview/transcription platform with sentiment and auto-tagging.
15. **MAXQDA with AI Assist** (https://www.maxqda.com/products/ai-assist): AI summaries, subcode suggestions, and chat within MAXQDA.
16. **Microsoft Azure AI Language** (https://azure.microsoft.com/en-us/products/ai-services/ai-language): sentiment, key-phrase, entity extraction, and CLU.
17. **Microsoft Power Platform – AI Builder** (https://learn.microsoft.com/en-us/ai-builder/overview): add prebuilt/custom AI to Power Apps & Power Automate.
18. **Midjourney** (https://www.midjourney.com/): text-to-image generator for stylized visuals and storyboards.

19. **Miro AI** (https://miro.com/ai/): sticky-note clustering by sentiment/keywords and other AI actions.
20. **Notion AI** (https://www.notion.so/product/ai): AI assistant for notes, docs, and workspace content.
21. **NVivo (Lumivero)** (https://lumivero.com/products/nvivo/): qualitative analysis with Lumivero AI Assistant options.
22. **Otter.ai** (https://otter.ai/): live meeting transcription with speaker ID and summaries.
23. **Rev.ai** (https://www.rev.ai/): speech-to-text API (async/streaming) with multi-language support.
24. **Runway** (https://runwayml.com/): text-to-video/image creative suite (Gen-2/Gen-3 models).
25. **Squibler – AI Story Generator** (https://www.squibler.io/ai-story-generator): rapid story ideation and drafting.
26. **Stable Diffusion (Stability AI)** (https://stability.ai/stable-image): open text-to-image models and tools (SD 3/3.5 family).
27. **Subtxt (Narrative First)** (https://subtxt.app/): AI-assisted narrative design based on Dramatica theory.
28. **TheyDo – Journey AI** (https://www.theydo.com/ai): journey-mining and AI-assisted mapping/insight discovery.
29. **UserPersona.dev** (https://userpersona.dev/): instant AI personas from a short product description.
30. **UX Pilot** (https://uxpilot.ai/): AI-assisted UX design—wireframes, UI flows, and frameworks.
31. **UXPressia** (https://uxpressia.com/): personas and customer-journey mapping with AI persona/chat features.
32. **Visual Paradigm – 5W1H Tool** (https://www.visual-paradigm.com/features/5w1h-tool/): create 5W1H diagrams with templates for analysis.

Ideate & Select

1. **Adobe Firefly** (https://www.adobe.com/products/firefly.html): text-to-image for fast concept thumbnails.
2. **Boardmix (AI Mind Map)** (https://boardmix.com/ai-mind-map/): AI mind-maps and visual organization.
3. **ChatGPT** (https://chatgpt.com/): LLM for prompts, variants, rationales.
4. **Claude** (https://www.anthropic.com/claude): LLM for long-context ideation and critique.
5. **ClipDrop** (https://clipdrop.co/): quick background removal and image cleanup. ClipDrop was acquired twice: first by Stability AI (March 2023), then by Jasper AI (February 2024).

6. **Felo** (https://felo.ai/search): multilingual AI search with mind-map/slide views.
7. **FigJam Voting** (https://help.figma.com/hc/en-us/articles/9359912208663-Run-voting-sessions-in-FigJam): run anonymous voting on boards.
8. **HyperWrite Brainstorming** (https://hyperwriteai.com/aitools/concept-brainstorming-assistant): rapid idea expansion from short briefs.
9. **Ideamap** (https://ideamap.ai/): visual mind-mapping with AI suggestions.
10. **Ideogram** (https://ideogram.ai/): text-friendly image generation (posters/logos).
11. **Julius AI** (https://julius.ai/): analyze data to surface needs/patterns.
12. **Kimi** (https://www.kimi.com/): long-context AI assistant for summarizing and ideation.
13. **Lucidspark Voting** (https://help.lucid.co/hc/en-us/articles/14995416237460-Use-Voting-sessions-to-collaborate-in-Lucidspark): configure and visualize team votes.
14. **Midjourney** (https://www.midjourney.com/): stylized image generation for concept exploration.
15. **Miro AI** (https://miro.com/ai/): clustering, summaries, and prompts on whiteboards.
16. **MyMap AI** (https://www.mymap.ai/matrix-creator): auto-generate decision/2×2 matrices.
17. **MURAL Voting** (https://support.mural.co/s/article/voting-sessions): guided voting sessions with shared results. Mural (https://www.mural.co/) is the visual AI platform that turns alignment into an ongoing way of working, connecting strategy to execution and driving results in one shared workspace.
18. **Napkin AI** (https://napkin.ai/): instant diagrams and one-page visuals.
19. **Notion AI** (https://www.notion.so/product/ai): generate and organize ideas from project docs.
20. **Parabol** (https://www.parabol.co/): retro workflows with group voting and follow-ups.
21. **Perplexity** (https://www.perplexity.ai/): AI answer engine for cross-domain analogies.
22. **Pixian.ai** (https://pixian.ai/): one-click background removal for boards.
23. **Praxie 2×2 Matrix** (https://praxie.com/2x2-matrix-software-tools-templates/): guided axes, plotting, insights.
24. **Prompt Board** (https://promptboard.app/): curated prompt library and management.
25. **Retrium** (https://www.retrium.com/): agile retros with private dot voting.
26. **Stability AI (Stable Diffusion)** (https://stability.ai/): text-to-image and editing pipelines.
27. **Team-GPT/Juma** (https://team-gpt.com/): shared workspaces for collaborative prompting. New domain address: https://juma.ai/.

Prototype & Test

1. **Adobe Firefly** (https://firefly.adobe.com/generate/image): text-to-image with style/reference controls for visual prototypes.
2. **Airfocus Priority Ratings** (https://help.airfocus.com/en/articles/2788532-priority-ratings-app): weighted scoring for concept evaluation. Airfocus was acquired by Lucid Software in April 2025. The link here will redirect.
3. **BPMSG AHP-OS** (https://bpmsg.com/ahp/): web app for Analytic Hierarchy Process (pairwise weighting).
4. **Boardmix Service Blueprint** (https://boardmix.com/templates/service-blueprint/): blueprint templates with AI helpers for service design.
5. **ChatGPT** (https://chatgpt.com/): general LLM assistant for drafting prompts, tests, analyses, and summaries.
6. **Creately AI** (https://creately.com/usage/service-blueprint-templates-creator/): AI-assisted service blueprints and process maps.
7. **Dovetail** (https://dovetail.com/): research repository with AI summaries, tagging, and evidence search.
8. **Figma / FigJam AI** (https://www.figma.com/figjam/ai/): summarize stickies, cluster ideas, draft workshop artifacts.
9. **Futures Platform** (https://www.futuresplatform.com/scenario-analysis-planning-tool): trend library and AI-assisted scenario planning.
10. **Google Forms** (https://workspace.google.com/products/forms/): quick feedback forms and surveys for prototype tests.
11. **Google NotebookLM** (https://notebooklm.google/): source-grounded summaries and terminology from your own docs.
12. **Google Sheets + Gemini** (https://support.google.com/docs/answer/14218565): in-sheet analysis, formulas, and quick charts on test data.
13. **IBM Watson Discovery** (https://www.ibm.com/products/watson-discovery): enterprise search/Q&A and keyword/entity extraction over large corpora.
14. **Ideogram** (https://ideogram.ai/): text-to-image with strong typography for logos, labels, and packaging comps.
15. **Looppanel** (https://www.looppanel.com/): AI notetaker, transcripts, auto-tagging, and research repository.
16. **Lookback** (https://www.lookback.com/): moderated/unmoderated testing with recordings and observer features.
17. **Maze** (https://maze.co/): unmoderated tests, surveys, and AI-assisted analysis.
18. **Miro AI** (https://miro.com/ai/): AI on a collaborative whiteboard for clustering notes and mapping flows.
19. **Notion AI** (https://www.notion.com/product/ai): summarize notes, create action lists, and synthesize research inside docs.
20. **OpenAI ChatGPT Team** (https://openai.com/chatgpt/team/): shared workspace version of ChatGPT for teams.

21. **Perplexity** (https://www.perplexity.ai/): research assistant with cited answers for quick landscape scans.
22. **Photoshop Generative Fill** (https://www.adobe.com/products/photoshop/generative-fill.html): in-canvas AI edits for comps and variations.
23. **Portage** (https://www.portage.so/): AI-enabled strategy and scenario planning workspace.
24. **Quid** (https://www.quid.com/): market/consumer intelligence maps to support concept and scenario evidence.
25. **Runway** (https://runwayml.com/): text/image-to-video for motion prototypes and concept spots.
26. **Stable Diffusion + ControlNet** (https://github.com/Mikubill/sd-webui-controlnet): structure-guided image generation from your sketches/lines.
27. **Uizard Autodesigner** (https://uizard.io/): generate editable UI mockups and multi-screen prototypes from text/images.

Implement & Learn

1. **Aha! Roadmaps AI Assistant** (https://www.aha.io/roadmaps/ai-assistant): draft strategic narratives and roadmaps.
2. **Airtable AI** (https://www.airtable.com/platform/ai): AI inside tables, interfaces, and apps.
3. **AlphaSense** (https://www.alpha-sense.com/): market intelligence and research search.
4. **Asana Intelligence** (https://asana.com/product/ai): AI insights for timelines, status, and risks.
5. **Beautiful.ai — DesignerBot** (https://www.beautiful.ai/ai-presentations): AI slide creation and layouts.
6. **CB Insights** (https://www.cbinsights.com/): market maps and company intelligence.
7. **Canva — AI Presentation Maker** (https://www.canva.com/create/ai-presentations/): prompt-to-deck with brand kits.
8. **ChatGPT** (https://chatgpt.com/): LLM for outlines, summaries, and prompts.
9. **Claude** (https://www.anthropic.com/claude): LLM for tailored rewrites and briefs.
10. **Confluence + Atlassian Intelligence** (https://support.atlassian.com/organization-administration/docs/atlassian-intelligence-features-in-confluence/): AI summaries and drafting in wiki pages.
11. **Copy.ai** (https://www.copy.ai/): vision statements, executive summaries, FAQs.
12. **Crayon** (https://www.crayon.co/): competitor monitoring and win-loss signals.
13. **Gamma** (https://gamma.app/): quick AI decks with web sharing.

14. **Google Slides + Gemini** (https://gemini.google.com/app): AI help to write/rewrite slides and generate images.
15. **Jira — Advanced Roadmaps** (https://www.atlassian.com/software/jira/guides/advanced-roadmaps/overview): multi-team planning and scenarios.
16. **Jira Align** (https://www.atlassian.com/software/jira-align): link strategy to execution at scale.
17. **Looppanel** (https://www.looppanel.com/): AI research repository and analysis.
18. **Microsoft Copilot for PowerPoint** (https://copilot.microsoft.com/): in-app deck drafting and notes.
19. **Miro AI** (https://miro.com/ai/): cluster stickies and create timelines/diagrams.
20. **Notion AI** (https://www.notion.com/product/ai): AI summaries and structured docs/databases.
21. **Otter.ai** (https://otter.ai/): live transcription with summaries and actions.
22. **Pitch — AI Presentation Maker** (https://pitch.com/use-cases/ai-presentation-maker): prompt-to-deck with collaboration.
23. **Planview Copilot** (https://www.planview.com/ai/): AI assistant for portfolio/roadmap analysis.
24. **Productboard AI** (https://support.productboard.com/hc/en-us/articles/151 13485128467-Productboard-AI): prioritize using customer and ops feedback.
25. **Rev** (https://www.rev.com/): accurate transcription from uploads/recordings.
26. **Similarweb** (https://www.similarweb.com/): digital market and competitor signals.
27. **Smartsheet Resource Management** (https://www.smartsheet.com/platform/resource-management): staffing and capacity planning.
28. **Storydoc** (https://www.storydoc.com/): interactive, analytics-enabled decks.
29. **Venngage AI Pitch Deck** (https://venngage.com/ai-tools/pitch-deck-generator): fast pitch decks with charts.

Glossary

We have attempted to write this book in an accessible manner, minimizing technical jargon, acronyms, and the like. That said, we believe it will help to define some basic terms as we discuss AI and design thinking processes.

AI (Artificial Intelligence)

"AI refers to systems that display intelligent behavior by analyzing their environment and taking actions with some degree of autonomy to achieve specific goals" (European Commission, 2018). We take a broad perspective on AI; however, note that many AID tools in this book will utilize generative AI. AI may be commonly used in design across three broad categories which together form a continuum:

1. AI as a tool: currently, most design thinking practices utilize AI as a tool, such that humans interact with AI like any other software. As we will show, this approach limits AI's impact.
2. AI as a collaborator: this is the view we take in this book. Here, AI is more than a tool but not a full designer yet. This requires designers and innovators to adjust the way they work and interact with AI.
3. AI as designer: This is a more futuristic and less understood view of what AI can be for design in the future.

© The Editor(s) (if applicable) and The Author(s), under exclusive license to Springer Nature Switzerland AG 2026

D. Graff et al., *Design Thinking with Artificial Intelligence*, Palgrave Executive Essentials, https://doi.org/10.1007/978-3-032-10543-1

Design

Broadly, design is the creation of a blueprint of a desired future, following the conceptualization championed by Nobel laureate and business management guru Herbert Simon. More narrowly, building on the work of design scholars, we define design as a set of activities that contribute to the creation of physical artifacts or concepts. Note that this definition does not limit who the designer may be – whether a human, AI agent, or other entity.

Designerly Thinking

Designerly thinking is a term used by design scholars to distinguish the broader perspective on professional designers' approach to work, including design cognition and methods, from the applied and specific set of steps associated with design thinking (please see below). It is often described as open, intuitive, and iterative, and is often associated with artistic backgrounds, in contrast to the design thinking, which is often associated also with engineering and business.

Design Thinking

When we talk about design thinking, we refer to the concept developed by IDEO and the "d.school" (a common term for the Hasso Plattner Institute of Design at Stanford University) in the 1990s. The source of design thinking lies in the original research and publications on design thinking research from the 1960s until 1990s, which IDEO and d.school synthesized to a standardized and simplified pre-described process with specific design thinking tools attached. Now a days, design thinking is often defined as a creative, human-centered problem-solving approach. This framework has been very popular outside of the design discipline and is used by many designers and non-designers as the simplified and pre-described process can be more easily taught and applied to traditional (e.g. development of a new product) and non-traditional (e.g. developing a new strategy for military) design problems. Many organizations have implemented design thinking as organizations can plan and control this simplified and standardized framework.

Our book builds on this simplified design thinking process for several reasons. First, we are able to reach more individuals (e.g. designers and non-designers) and so can have potentially a larger impact. Second, we believe that currently non-professional designers can benefit a bit more from AI compared to design era and, hence, are more open to use AI in design thinking. Third, design thinking is easier to understand as its structure, processes and tools are simpler and, hence, it is easier to introduce AI to it compared to designerly thinking. Fourth, many organizations have incorporated design thinking in one or another way. Given these reasons, we developed tools and processes based on the design thinking framework. We will refer to our adapted design thinking framework as *Design Thinking with AI*. Tools used in design thinking will be referred to as design tools, tools used in design thinking with AI as *AID tools*.

Designers and Innovators (Design Thinkers)

We will refer to individuals working in design thinking as designers and innovators or, alternatively, as design thinkers. Design thinking involves often multi-disciplinary teams with individuals from different functions. Rather than referring to each function, we use the word innovator instead. Design thinking is closely linked to innovation and, hence, the term innovator makes a lot of sense. At the same time, we separate design and innovators because at times we will have to discuss individually either innovators or designers. This does not mean that we see designers as not being innovators. However, not every innovator is a designer.

Designers

We refer to designers who are either working in a traditional design field (e.g., industrial design, UX software design) or who have completed a formal design education program. We assume that this group tends to have more depth of knowledge, skills and experience in design. Their work, depending on the context, proceeds according to design or designerly thinking ways.

Design education can tend to be more technical (design programs and schools that emerged in engineering schools) or art based (design programs and schools that emerged in art institutions). Consequently, their education and knowledge will be somewhat different. Whereas designers educated in an art-based school tend to be better educated within the designerly way of working, designers educated in an engineering school tend to be more focused on design thinking practices. We normally refer to both groups as designers but at times we will single out a group and call them engineering-based designers and art-based designers.

Innovators

We refer to non-designers who participate in design thinking as innovators. This is not to say that everyone is the same, but to make this book easier to read. Innovators can have experience in design thinking, but they do not have received education in design. In addition, many design thinking projects occur outside of traditional design tasks (e.g., in military) with often no designers on the team. These individuals might have limited exposure to design thinking through a set of workshops without deeper understanding of design principles. These innovators are very interested in design and the design process, although mostly in pursuit of their innovation goals.

Index

© The Editor(s) (if applicable) and The Author(s), under exclusive license to Springer Nature Switzerland AG 2026

D. Graff et al., *Design Thinking with Artificial Intelligence*, Palgrave Executive Essentials, https://doi.org/10.1007/978-3-032-10543-1

GPSR Compliance
The European Union's (EU) General Product Safety Regulation (GPSR) is a set
of rules that requires consumer products to be safe and our obligations to
ensure this.

If you have any concerns about our products, you can contact us on

ProductSafety@springernature.com

In case Publisher is established outside the EU, the EU authorized
representative is:

Springer Nature Customer Service Center GmbH
Europaplatz 3
69115 Heidelberg, Germany

www.ingramcontent.com/pod-product-compliance
Lightning Source LLC
LaVergne TN
LVHW011058200726
843510LV00003B/909